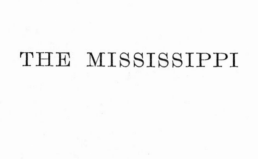

THE MISSISSIPPI

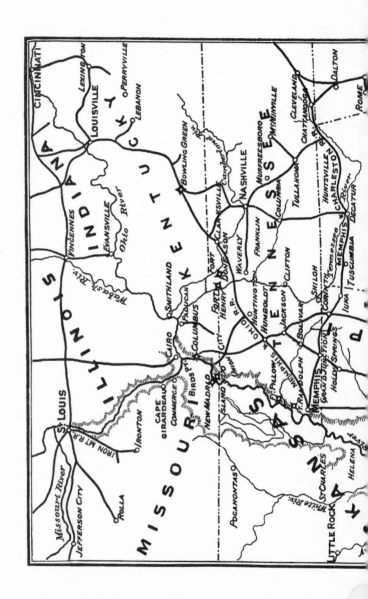

THE THEATRE OF WAR IN THE WEST, 1862–1863.

THE MISSISSIPPI

BY

FRANCIS VINTON GREENE,

LIEUT. OF ENGINEERS, U. S. ARMY; LATE MILITARY ATTACHÉ TO THE
U. S. LEGATION AT ST. PETERSBURG; AUTHOR OF "THE RUSSIAN
ARMY AND ITS CAMPAIGNS IN TURKEY IN 1877-78," AND
OF "ARMY LIFE IN RUSSIA"

CASTLE BOOKS

CAMPAIGNS OF THE CIVIL WAR.—VIII.
THE MISSISSIPPI

This edition published in 2002 by Castle Books,
A division of Book Sales Inc.
114 Northfield Avenue, Edison, NJ 08837

First published in 1882.
Written by Francis Vinton Greene.

ISBN: 0-7858-1580-5

Printed in the United States of America.

PREFACE.

The following pages are founded upon a careful study of the Records of the War of the Rebellion, now in course of publication by the War Department, and not upon the recollection of personal experience, as it was not my fortune to belong to the generation which fought the Great War. I have earnestly endeavored to make them accurate, and believe that they contain no statement of fact which cannot be substantiated by the Records. Such interpretation as has been put upon these facts is, with all deference, submitted to the judgment of the candid reader.

I desire to express my sense of obligation to Colonel R. N. Scott, U. S. Army, in charge of the publication of the Records, for his kindness, not only in affording me unrestricted access to the Archives, but also in giving me information, which his thorough knowledge of the subject alone could give, to assist my search through them.

Washington. August 31, 1882.

CONTENTS.

CONTENTS.

APPENDIX F.

APPENDIX G.

APPENDIX H.

LIST OF MAPS.

THE MISSISSIPPI.

INTRODUCTORY.

THE military operations of the Civil War were practically limited on the west by the irregular line running near the 95th meridian, which forms the western boundary of the States between Louisiana and Minnesota. The territory of the United States east of that line contains about 1,130,000 square miles; and it would be divided into two parts, almost exactly equal in size, by an irregular line from west to east following the course of portions of the Missouri, Mississippi, Ohio, and Potomac Rivers. This was the very line which upon the outbreak of war became the frontier between the two hostile sections.

Singularly enough, in a territory of such vast proportions, the capital cities of both sections were situated on the same slope of a range of mountains not far from the coast, and both were very close to the common frontier, being, in fact, only 115 miles distant from one another. The possession of these capitals was, next to the destruction of armies, the object constantly sought for in the East; for four long years, therefore, excepting the expeditions which gained certain points along the sea-coast, but made no impression on the interior of the Confederacy, the tide of war in the East

VIII.—1

surged back and forth across a small portion of Virginia,
Maryland, and Pennsylvania, until the end finally came at
Appomattox. The site of Lee's surrender was but little
more than one hundred miles distant from the first battle-
field of Bull Run.

In the West the course of the war was entirely different;
beyond the Alleghanies there was no one point which called
for such extraordinary defensive efforts as those which were
expended on Richmond, nor was there any Confederate general who possessed the vigorous defensive skill and resource
of Lee. There the great territorial object was the possession of the Mississippi River; by gaining and holding which
the Union armies would possess a great natural highway
and line of communications for future operations, and would
cut off the Confederacy from the fertile resources of Arkansas, Louisiana, and Texas. For two years and three months
after the fall of Fort Sumter both sides strove incessantly—
the one to gain, the other to hold, the control of the great
river. The contest was finally decided at Vicksburg and
Port Hudson in July, 1863, and then "the Father of Waters
again went unvexed to the sea."

Once fairly possessed of the river, the Western armies
were free to concentrate and move to the interior without
fear of exposing their flank and rear, and they moved on by
Chattanooga, Atlanta, Savannah, and Goldsboro, defeating
hostile armies and eating out the vitals of the country, until
the end saw them almost join hands with their comrades in
Virginia. In these Western operations, which began at St.
Louis in 1861, and ended near Raleigh in 1865, the tide of
conquest was twice met by a counter-current of invasion
under Bragg and Hood, but in neither case was more than
a portion of the Northern armies swept back. The main
force kept steadily onward, and it was the unparalleled

good fortune of the Army of the Tennessee to be constantly advancing, now faster, now slower, against retreating armies during four years of nearly incessant combat, and to accomplish a forward conquering march of well-nigh three thousand miles, the like of which has not been seen in civilized lands during the Christian era.

Of the great chain of events here roughly indicated, those links which cover the movements on the Mississippi are to be described in the following pages.

CHAPTER I.

THE FIRST YEAR'S OPERATIONS.

THE struggle for the control of the Mississippi began at St. Louis, in those exciting events of May, 1861, which have been so well described in the first volume of this series. By the energy and courage of Nathaniel Lyon and Frank P. Blair, Jr., this city was saved to the Union cause, and the secessionists were driven to the western and southwestern portions of Missouri, where the first military operations of the West were initiated by Jackson, Price, and McCullough. At the same time M. Jeff. Thompson, one of the secession leaders of Missouri, was preparing to dispute the possession of the southeastern part of the State along the Mississippi. He first appears in the records at the village of Pocahontas, in Arkansas, a few miles south of the Missouri line, whence, on July 2d, he addressed a letter to Jefferson Davis, offering his services to the Confederacy, and stating that "Missouri has no great leader in whom the people have confidence," and "the only way the fifty to one hundred thousand gallant young soldiers can be made available, and the rich prize of this great State secured, is by a powerful demonstration from this portion of the country." He had previously been commissioned a brigadier-general in the Missouri State Guard, and had raised and brought with him a small force of militia; but the Confederacy does not appear to have highly appreciated his fitness for a great leader, for on July 22d, W. J. Hardee, Brigadier-General, C. S. A., assumed command of the District of Upper Arkansas, and five days later fixed his headquarters at Pocahontas. Thompson, however, was subject only to the orders of Governor Jackson, of Missouri. At the same time Maj.-Gen. L. Polk was in command of "Department No. 2," which embraced West Tennessee and the State of Mississippi,[1] with headquarters at Memphis. On July 27th, he ordered Brig.-Gen. Gideon J. Pillow to proceed from Memphis to New Madrid, with a force of six thousand men, denominated "The Army of Liberation." The total strength of the forces of Pillow, Hardee, and Thompson was from twelve thousand to fifteen thousand men, and it was their intention, so soon as they should be reinforced to a sufficient strength, to advance and take Cape Girardeau, a commanding bluff on the west side of the river, about one hundred miles below St. Louis; thence, in connection with other troops of Polk on the east bank, they hoped to gain possession of Cairo, at the mouth of the Ohio; and thus solidly established on the Mississippi they designed to move northward and westward to the Iron Mountain Railroad and liberate the State.

These expectations were, however, not realized. On August 28th, Brig.-Gen. U. S. Grant, then serving at Jefferson City, Mo., was ordered by Frémont to proceed forthwith to Cape Girardeau and assume command of all troops in the vicinity of the mouth of the Ohio. He was specially directed to fortify Cairo, Bird's Point, and Cape Girardeau, to destroy all fortifications erecting by the Confederates, and to drive their forces away from the river. Grant reached Cape Girardeau on August 30th, and proceeded to

---

[1] Extended on September 2d to include Arkansas "and all military operations in Missouri."

Cairo on September 2d. He arrived none too soon. For a few days before his arrival, Pillow had abandoned his project of liberating Missouri, and had suggested to Polk that the high bluff on the Kentucky bank at Columbus, about fifteen miles below Cairo, should be seized and fortified for defence; and Polk, having made up his mind that the neutrality of Kentucky could not longer be allowed to interfere with military operations, had left Memphis and moved up the river. At New Madrid he took Pillow's troops with him, increasing his strength to about 15,000 men; with these he took possession of Columbus on September 4th, and immediately began fortifying it, while, at the same time, he sent a detachment toward Paducah, at the mouth of the Tennessee River. Grant heard of this on the next day, September 5th, and that night started from Cairo, with two regiments on transports, for Paducah, where he arrived the next morning, just in time to forestall the action of the Confederates. On returning to Cairo, on the 6th, he received an order from Frémont, dated the previous day, to seize and fortify the Kentucky shore opposite Cairo. Grant immediately executed this order.

These early events are related somewhat in detail, because they resulted in giving the Federal forces possession of two points—the junctions of the Tennessee and Ohio, and of the Ohio and Mississippi Rivers—which controlled the water highway from Cincinnati to St. Louis, and were therefore of vital importance to the Union cause.

During the autumn and winter months of 1861, both sides were gathering strength, but their relative positions remained unchanged. On December 31st, Grant's return of "present for duty" aggregated 14,374 men, and they were stationed at Cape Girardeau and Cairo, and on the Missouri and Kentucky shores, opposite the latter point. On the same date, Polk's return of "present for duty" was (after deducting the 1,372 at Fort Henry) 19,661; the greater part of them were stationed at Columbus, and the rest at New Madrid, Fort Pillow, and Memphis. His first point of defence was on the bluff at Columbus, which had been so extensively fortified that it was the habit to speak of it in reports—as later of Vicksburg and other points—as "the Gibraltar of the West." The next was at New Madrid and Island No. 10, opposite the line between Kentucky and Tennessee, where fortifications were begun during the last day of August. Eighty miles farther down the river, and about the same distance above Memphis, was situated Fort Pillow, on a lofty bluff between the Hatchie River and the Mississippi. The fortifications at this point were very extensive, consisting of a water battery at the base of the bluff, and of several small detached works, and a continuous line of strong intrenchments, four to five miles in length, on the ridge. The total length of intrenchments was estimated at ten miles, and their armament was thirty-two guns. Twelve miles below Fort Pillow was a smaller work, called Fort Randolph. In the immediate vicinity of Memphis there were no eligible sites for fortification which would not expose the city to bombardment and destruction, and it was not fortified. Between Memphis and New Orleans there were no fortifications in 1861.

It was not, however, with land defences and armies alone that either side purposed to contest the mastery of the great river. On both sides, and especially on the Union side, the navy was destined to take part in the contest, by means of novel and peculiarly constructed boats, which, carrying large guns for that period, and acting as siege artillery of great power and extraordinary mobility, were to accompany the armies in all their movements, and render invaluable service.

On the Union side, the plans for these vessels were matured early in 1861. After much consultation, in which General Totten, General Meigs, Captain Eads, Naval-Constructor Lenthall, and others presented their views, plans and specifications were drawn up, and the Quartermaster-General was authorized to advertise for proposals. Captain Eads was the lowest bidder, and a contract was made with him on August 5, 1861, for the construction of seven gunboats, to be completed in sixty-five days. These boats were named after river cities, Pittsburg, Cincinnati, St. Louis, Louisville, Cairo, Carondelet, and Mound City, though, from their peculiar appearance, they were commonly known as the "turtles." They were in every way formidable vessels; each was 175 feet in length, 50 feet in breadth, 6 feet in depth of hold, and 512 tons in burthen. The hull was flat-bottomed, with sides inclined at an angle of forty-five degrees, and projecting but one foot above the water. On the hull was constructed a casemate, or box, 150 by 50 feet, with inclined sides 8 feet high, inside of which were the guns and machinery. This casemate was constructed of wood, and plated with $2\frac{1}{2}$ inches of iron on the forward end, and on each side opposite the engine. Each was propelled by a single wheel near the stern, had a speed of nine miles per hour, and carried an armament of 13 guns, principally 6-inch rifles. They were all delivered to the Government at St. Louis, on December 5, 1861. In addition to these, there were two other iron-clads, the Essex and Benton, of 1,000 tons burthen, which were originally snag-boats, and had been purchased by Frémont and rebuilt at St. Louis. They also were ready on December 5, 1861.

Prior to the construction of these boats, Commander John Rodgers, of the Navy, had been sent to the West, and had purchased on the Ohio River three ordinary passenger

boats, the Tyler (afterward called Taylor), Lexington, and
Conestoga, of 400 to 600 tons each, and of great speed; and
had rebuilt them for naval purposes, by tearing off all the
ordinary top-work, and building a wooden rampart to protect
the guns, wheels, and machinery. They were not armored,
but carried a battery of 9 guns each.

In the spring of 1862, Mr. Charles Ellet, a distinguished
engineer, impressed upon the War Department the importance of having a class of vessels which should carry only a
few light howitzers for defence, and should rely for offensive
strength upon their power as rams. He was appointed a
colonel in the army and authorized by Secretary Stanton
to proceed to the West, and purchase and reconstruct on
the Ohio River such vessels as were suitable for his purpose.
The crews of his vessels were supplemented by a force of
volunteers serving in the army, under command of his
brother, Lieut.-Col. Alfred W. Ellet. Colonel Ellet bought
and rebuilt four side-wheel and four stern-wheel vessels,
of sizes varying from 200 to 400 tons, and appeared in the
Mississippi with his fleet in May, 1862.

Still another type of vessel was found in the mortar-boats,
which were scows of sufficient size to carry one 13-inch mortar. They were towed from point to point by tugboats.

A considerable number of vessels of various classes were
also captured from the enemy, so that in the summer of
1862 the fleet in the upper Mississippi contained 45 vessels,
with an aggregate tonnage of 19,464 tons and an armament
of 143 guns, in addition to 38 mortar boats.

On the Confederate side the preparations for naval strength
were hardly less complete. Several boats were bought or
seized on the Mississippi, between Memphis and New Orleans, and converted to military use ; generally by taking off
everything above the hull, and constructing on it a wooden
1*

rampart, plated with railroad iron. Though the plating on
these vessels was heavier than on the Northern ships, yet
their construction was not as strong, their armament was in-
ferior, and their machinery was constantly breaking down.
The Confederates also had several iron-clad rams of a
cigar shape.

The beginning of the year 1862 found both sides fairly well
prepared for active operations. Grant commanded at the
mouth of the Ohio, and had possession of the shores of both
rivers at that point, and of the mouths of the Tennessee and
Cumberland Rivers higher up. Opposed to him was a force
under Polk, a few miles down the Mississippi at Columbus,
and another at Forts Henry and Donelson, a short distance
up the Tennessee and Cumberland rivers. The right of the
Confederate line of defence was at Bowling Green, where
the railroads from Louisville to Nashville and to Memphis diverge. On January 30th, Halleck ordered Grant to attack this
line at its centre, i.e., at Forts Henry and Donelson, and immediately upon receipt of the order Grant started up the Tennessee River with a force of 17,000 men, embarked on transports and escorted by a squadron of four armored and three
unarmored gunboats under Commodore A. H. Foote. Fort
Henry was captured on February 6th, and Fort Donelson on
the 16th. The Confederate line was completely broken, and
the establishment of Grant's force on the railroads in rear of
Columbus rendered the speedy evacuation of that place a
necessity. As soon as authentic information of the fall of
Fort Donelson was received on the 18th, General G. T.
Beauregard, who was then at Jackson, Tennessee, on his way
from Virginia to assume command at Columbus, telegraphed
to the Adjutant-General at Richmond that Columbus was
untenable and advised its abandonment. The Secretary of

War replied on the following day that its evacuation was decided upon, and on February 20th he sent orders to that
effect to Polk.

The destruction of this first line of Confederate defence
in the West carried consternation throughout the South ; it
was seen at once that the future safety of the Confederacy
depended upon holding the Memphis and Charleston Railroad ; it was therefore determined to form a second line of
defence with the left on the Mississippi River at Fort Pillow
or Memphis, the centre at Corinth or near the bend of the
Tennessee River, and the right at Chattanooga ; the position
at Island No. 10 and New Madrid, which had already been
partially fortified, was to be retained as an outpost in advance of the left, but, as the despatches show, with no great
reliance upon its capacity for defence.   Polk was ordered to
send thither from Columbus all his heavy guns, but only a
portion of his troops ; the rest being kept at Humboldt, a
central point on the Mobile and Ohio Railroad.   Beauregard
appears for a moment to have had a visionary idea of assuming the offensive, for on February 21st he addressed a circular letter to the Governors of Tennessee, Louisiana, and
Mississippi, calling upon each of them for 5,000 troops ; and
on the same day he also wrote to Maj.-Gen. Earl Van Dorn,
who commanded in Arkansas, asking for his co-operation.
To the latter he said : "I have just called on the Governors of
Tennessee, Louisiana, and Mississippi for 5,000 men from
each State.   I have 15,000 disposable for the field.   If you
could certainly join me, *via* New Madrid or Columbus, with
10,000 more, we could take the field with 40,000 men ; take
Cairo, Paducah, the mouths of the Tennessee and Cumberland Rivers, and most probably be able to take also St.
Louis by the river.   What say you to this brilliant programme, which I know is fully practicable if we can get the

forces ? At all events we must do something or die in the attempt ; otherwise all will shortly be lost." The Governors of the States promptly responded with promises of troops, but General A. S. Johnston, who was in chief command in the West, does not appear to have attached much importance to the "brilliant programme." His practical mind was engaged in the problem of collecting as strong a force as possible on the Memphis and Charleston Railroad, for the purpose of there fighting a decisive battle, on the issue of which all plans for the future must depend.

Polk meanwhile was removing his stores and guns, 140 in number, from Columbus to Island No. 10 ; on March 2d, everything having been removed except two guns in a remote outwork, he set fire to all his buildings and took his departure, one portion of his command going by transports to New Madrid, and the other by land along the Mobile Railroad. Foote's squadron, accompanied by two regiments under Brig.-Gen. W. T. Sherman, took possession early on the morning of the 4th.

Polk's movements were probably hastened at the last by the advance of Brig.-Gen. John Pope, who had organized a force of about 20,000 men on the west bank of the Mississippi, just above Cairo, and had begun to move south toward New Madrid on February 28th, on which day he had a skirmish with Thompson's Missouri militia. Pope reached New Madrid on March 3d, and after a siege of a month, with the assistance of Foote's squadron, he finally captured the whole of the Confederate forces in that vicinity—about 7,000 men —on April 7th. On the 12th, Pope embarked his army on transports, and, escorted by Foote's squadron, proceeded down the river, arriving near Fort Pillow on the 14th. Plans were made for a combined attack on the 17th, but on that day Pope received orders from Halleck to take his force to Pittsburg Landing without delay, and he started up the river that afternoon. The withdrawal of the army made the attack impossible.

Meanwhile, during the month of March, Grant's army had advanced up the Tennessee River, and Buell's had marched across from Nashville to join it. A. S. Johnston had retreated from Bowling Green, through Nashville and Murfreesborough to the Memphis and Charleston Railroad, and thence to Corinth, bringing with him the troops afterward known as Hardee's Corps; Bragg had come to the same point from Mobile and Pensacola, and Polk from Columbus, with that portion of his troops, which had not gone to New Madrid. Beauregard had collected what few troops there were along the Memphis and Charleston Railroad. Van Dorn had come in person from Arkansas to Corinth, and his troops had received orders to follow him, but had not yet arrived. Both sides being thus concentrated, the first great battle in the West, and the most sanguinary, was fought at Shiloh on April 6th and 7th. Immediately after that battle Halleck assumed command in person at Shiloh, and ordered Pope to join him with his force. Van Dorn's troops also joined Beauregard, who had succeeded Johnston in command on the death of the latter. Beauregard fell back slowly, and Halleck advanced with great caution to Corinth, which was evacuated by the Confederates on May 30th, Beauregard retreating southward on the Mobile and Ohio Railroad. The Union troops being thus in possession of the Memphis and Charleston Railroad at Corinth, the Confederate position at and above Memphis was turned and rendered untenable, in the same manner that Columbus had been turned by the capture of Forts Henry and Donelson. Fort Pillow was therefore abandoned by its garrison on the night of the 4th of June, and Fort Randolph on the follow-

ing day, the greater part of their garrisons being taken down
the river in transports to Vicksburg.

The results of the campaign up the Tennessee River had
been not only the capture of the hostile army at Fort Donelson, and the defeat and loss inflicted upon that at Shiloh,
but also the outflanking of all the Confederate positions on
the Mississippi from Cairo to Memphis and their consequent
abandonment. The Confederates had, however, a strong
fleet at Memphis, under Commodore Montgomery, and before giving up that city they determined to try conclusions
with Foote's fleet, not with any intention to save Memphis,
for there was nothing to prevent Halleck's army from marching into it, but with the hope of destroying or crippling the
fleet.

Foote had remained in the vicinity of Fort Pillow after
the departure of Pope's army on April 17th, but no active
operations had been undertaken further than to bombard
the fort with the mortar boats. On the 9th of May, he
was finally obliged to relinquish the command of his squadron, on account of the wound he had received at Fort Donelson, from which he had been suffering constantly for three
months. He was succeeded by Commodore C. H. Davis.
On the following day, May 10th, about 7 A.M., the Confederate flotilla of eight vessels came out from under the guns
of Fort Pillow, and attacked the Union flotilla, which consisted of seven armored gunboats. A severe battle took
place, in which the Confederates used their vessels as rams
with great effect, completely disabling the Cincinnati and
Mound City, which were both sunk in shoal water, though
they were soon afterward raised and repaired. The Union
ordnance was, however, far superior to that of the Confederates, and its projectiles penetrated four of the latter's
vessels, disabling their machinery, and rendering them help-

less. At the end of an hour, the Confederates withdrew to
the fort, towing their disabled vessels, which were subsequently repaired at Memphis.

Upon the abandonment of Fort Pillow, on June 4th, Davis
proceeded down the river, arriving at dark on the 5th within two miles of Memphis, where he anchored for the night.
At daylight the next morning, June 6th, the Confederate
flotilla was discovered lying at the levee at Memphis. It
consisted of the same vessels which had taken part in the
action off Port Pillow a month previous.

The two flotillas were composed of the following vessels:

UNION.		CONFEDERATE.	
	GUNS.		GUNS.
Benton......................	16	Little Rebel...............	2
Louisville	13	Bragg......................	3
Carondelet	13	Beauregard	4
Cairo	13	Price	4
St. Louis....................	13	Sumpter	3
Queen of the West..........	ram	Lovell	4
Switzerland	"	Thompson	4
Monarch	"	Van Dorn..................	4
Lancaster	"		
	68		28

At 4.20 A.M., the Union flotilla got under way and began
to drop down the river; the Confederates immediately
opened fire, and advanced slowly to meet them, though
maintaining such a position in front of the city that it was
difficult for the Union boats to return the fire without danger of firing into the city. The fire was nevertheless returned, and after it had continued for about twenty minutes,
Colonel Ellet, in the ram Queen of the West, followed by
the Monarch, dashed out from under the Arkansas shore,
passed in front of Davis's flotilla, and steamed at full speed
against the enemy's vessels. Ellet designed to strike the
Beauregard, which was in advance, but he missed this ves-

sel, and crashed into the Lovell, cutting her almost in two, and sinking her in deep water, with the greater part of her crew. While the Queen was still entangled with the Lovell, the Beauregard turned and rammed her, and, in turn, received a blow from the Monarch. The Price, by this time, had joined in the fight, and the Monarch made a pass at her, but missed her, and the Beauregard, endeavoring to strike the Monarch, missed her, and cut away the port-wheel of her own consort, the Price. The Benton, which was in advance of the gunboat fleet, now arrived, and sent a well-directed shot through the boiler of the Beauregard, completing her disablement. The result of this general *mêlée* was as follows: on the Confederate side, the Lovell had been sunk, and the Beauregard and Price were completely disabled. On the Union side, the ram Queen had been disabled, and had run to the Arkansas shore, and the Monarch had followed her, taking the Beauregard in tow, which sunk as soon as she reached shoal water. As the rams Lancaster and Switzerland had turned up the river through some misunderstanding of orders, the rams took no further part in the action.

By this time, however, the gunboats had all closed with the Confederate flotilla, and a running fight ensued, which lasted for about an hour, in the presence of thousands of spectators on the Tennessee shore, and which ended ten miles below the city. In this fight, the Little Rebel received a shot through the steam-chest, and was immediately run on the Arkansas shore; the Thompson was set on fire, and grounded some distance below Memphis, where the fire reached the magazine and blew her up; the Sumpter and Bragg were disabled by shells, and one was captured while the other was run ashore and deserted by her crew. The Van Dorn alone escaped, the Monarch and Switzerland being sent in pursuit, but failing to overtake her.

The result of this engagement was most decisive; three of the Confederate vessels—Lovell, Beauregard, and Thompson—were wholly destroyed, four of them—Little Rebel, Price, Sumpter, and Bragg—were captured, and saved in such condition that with extensive repairs they were subsequently incorporated with the Union flotilla. In addition to this annihilation of the Confederate flotilla, five large transports and a considerable amount of cotton were captured, and a large ram and two tugs on the stocks were destroyed. The Confederate loss in men was not accurately known, but was estimated at one hundred killed and wounded, and one hundred and fifty captured. On the Union side, Colonel Ellet received a wound in the leg, from which he subsequently died, and three men on the Carondelet were slightly injured. No other gunboat but the Carondelet was struck. The city of Memphis was surrendered to Commodore Davis by the mayor immediataty after the fight, and the two regiments which accompanied the flotilla marched in and took possession at 11 A.M.

For the next three weeks Davis remained at Memphis with the greater part of his flotilla; but on June 12th he organized an expedition consisting of the Mound City, St. Louis, Lexington, and Conestoga, accompanied by three of the captured transports, carrying the Forty-sixth Indiana, under Colonel Fitch. This force proceeded down the Mississippi to the mouth of White River, and thence up that stream to the village of St. Charles, where the Confederates had erected some batteries at the crossing of the main road from Memphis to Little Rock. The object of this expedition was to destroy these batteries, clear the river of hostile boats, and open communication with Maj.-Gen. S. R. Curtis, who, after the battle of Pea Ridge, had begun a march eastward to open communications on the Mississippi. The ex-

pedition reached St. Charles on June 16th, and attacked
and captured the batteries on the same day. The loss would
have been trifling but for one well-aimed shot, which penetrated the casemate of the Mound City, and exploded the
steam-drum. Many of the crew were killed outright, others
were frightfully scalded, and some jumped overboard, and
were drowned. Out of 175 people on board, only 35 escaped
uninjured. Having destroyed the batteries, the expedition
returned to Memphis. Curtis did not arrive in time to communicate with the gunboats, but, continuing his march, he
reached the Mississippi at Helena, about eighty miles below
Memphis, on July 13th.

On June 29th, Davis left Memphis, and proceeded down
the Mississippi, with the Benton, Carondelet, Louisville,
and St. Louis, and six mortar boats in tow of transports.
On July 1st he arrived at Young's Point, a few miles above
Vicksburg, and there joined hands with Admiral D. G. Farragut's fleet from New Orleans. The entire river from Cairo
to the Gulf had now been navigated by Union vessels, but
another long year and many weary efforts were required before it was free from Confederate control.

It is now necessary to refer briefly to the early movements
up the Mississippi from its mouth. The ever-memorable
passage of the forts below New Orleans by Farragut's fleet
took place on April 24th, and on the 25th Farragut arrived
off New Orleans. General Lovell, who commanded the Confederate troops in the city, immediately evacuated the place,
retreating up the line of the Jackson Railroad, and on May
1st, Maj.-Gen. B. F. Butler arrived with his troops and took
possession of the city, relieving a few marines who had been
landed.

A portion of Farragut's fleet immediately proceeded up
the river, meeting no resistance more serious than the wordy

protests of mayors of undefended cities. Baton Rouge was taken on May 8th, and Natchez on the 12th. No fortifications were encountered south of Vicksburg, at which place the advanced division, under Commander S. P. Lee, of the Oneida, arrived on May 18th. He immediately summoned the Mayor, as well as the officer commanding the defences, to surrender, but the demand was defiantly refused. A day or two later Farragut himself arrived with additional vessels, and with him came two transports, carrying two regiments and a battery—about fifteen hundred men in all —under command of Brig.-Gen. Thomas Williams, who had been detached by Butler for this service. A reconnoissance of the place was made, and then a council of war was held by Farragut and his commanders, at which Williams was present. Williams was of opinion that his force was altogether too small to accomplish anything against such defences, and a large majority of the naval commanders advised against Farragut's proposition to run by the batteries. Nothing, therefore, was done, and Farragut returned to New Orleans with part of his fleet, and Williams took his troops back to Baton Rouge. These events took place in the latter part of May, 1862.

It appears, from the records, that, on December 18, 1861, Colonel Edward Fontaine, Chief of Ordnance of the Mississippi Army, wrote to Governor Moore, of Louisiana, proposing to go to Vicksburg, make surveys, and begin the erection of fortifications. Moore forwarded the letter to Lovell, who replied that he had no objection to the journey, but he was unable to assist in constructing the fortifications, because he had "no competent officer, no guns, no powder."

Almost immediately after the battle of Fort Donelson, in February, 1862, Bragg, who was then in command at Pensa-

cola, directed Col. J. L. Autry to proceed to Vicksburg with
his regiment, the 27th Mississippi. In the month of March
guns and ammunition were sent from Pensacola to Vicksburg; and, after the battle of Shiloh and the capture of
Island No. 10, in April, 1862, Beauregard drew up a project
of fortification for batteries, containing about forty guns and
a garrison of three thousand men, and sent it to Capt. D. B.
Harris, of the Confederate Engineers, then serving at Fort
Pillow, with a letter of instructions, dated at Corinth, April
21st, directing him to proceed to Vicksburg, collect a force
of 1,000 negroes, and begin the construction of the works at
once. Special directions were given in this letter to locate
batteries so as to prevent the construction of a canal across
the peninsula opposite the city.

The fortifications of Vicksburg were therefore begun in
the latter part of April, 1862. At this time, it will be remembered, Halleck, with all the available Union troops in
the West, was about to begin his advance from Shiloh,
Beauregard, reinforced by Van Dorn, was preparing to defend Corinth, and Farragut was passing the forts below
New Orleans.

When Lovell retreated northward from New Orleans at
the time of its capture, he fully appreciated the importance
of defending Vicksburg, and, therefore, while retaining the
bulk of his force on the Jackson Railroad, he at once des-
patched Brig.-Gen. Martin L. Smith, who had been an officer
of Topographical Engineers before the war, with five regiments to Vicksburg, with orders to assume command and
complete the fortifications with the utmost despatch. Smith
arrived at Vicksburg on May 12th, and served there until
its surrender more than a year afterward. He found three
batteries completed, and a fourth in progress. Continuing work night and day on the others, he had six bat-

teries finished and armed when the advance division of Farragut's fleet arrived on May 18th. For the next ten days he
was in extreme anxiety, fearing that he would be unable to
meet a vigorous attack, but his anxiety was finally relieved
by Farragut's departure. In spite of a desultory bombardment by that portion of the fleet which remained, the ten
batteries originally projected were completed and armed by
the middle of June. Reinforcements then began to arrive.
Breckenridge's corps of Bragg's army, and Ruggles's command from Grenada—in all about 15,000 men—were ordered
to Vicksburg on June 22d ; and Van Dorn, who had superseded Lovell, arrived in person and took command on June
28th.

On reaching New Orleans about June 1st, on his return
from his first trip to Vicksburg, Farragut found most urgent
letters from the Navy Department, impressing upon him the
importance of clearing the Mississippi, only one point of
which, Vicksburg, then remained in Confederate control.
Although Farragut was anxious to attack Mobile, and had
no faith in his ability to take Vicksburg without the aid of
a large land force, yet he prepared as quickly as possible to
make the attempt, in compliance with the wishes of the Department. The mortar-flotilla, consisting of sixteen vessels
under Commander D. D. Porter, was sent up in advance of
him and reached Vicksburg on June 20th. On the same day
Farragut left Baton Rouge with the large vessels of his fleet,
accompanied by transports carrying Williams and his brigade of four regiments and two batteries, numbering about
three thousand men. They reached Vicksburg on June 25th,
having stopped on the way near Natchez and Grand Gulf
to attack batteries which had been erected since their first
expedition, but which were now abandoned on their approach.
Upon arriving at Vicksburg Williams landed his troops on

the Louisiana shore, and collecting a force of about 1,200 negroes from the neighboring plantations he began digging the canal across the peninsula. The line adopted for this was the same as had been laid out several years before, at a time when the States of Louisiana and Mississippi were in dispute as to their boundaries, and the former State had determined to dig a canal which should cut off Vicksburg from the river.

Meanwhile Farragut's fleet was all assembled at Vicksburg by June 25th. It consisted of three ships and seven gunboats, carrying in all 106 guns, and of sixteen mortar-boats carrying each one 13-inch mortar. Williams also placed his ten field guns on the Louisiana shore to assist the fleet. The armament of the Confederate batteries cannot be accurately stated; it probably did not exceed 40 guns, but they had the advantage of being on a bluff about 200 feet high, from which they obtained a plunging fire on the vessels.

The mortar-boats having been anchored in position, Farragut's fleet passed the batteries early on the morning of June 28th. It was simply an artillery duel, lasting about two hours, at the end of which time Farragut came to anchor above the peninsula with two ships and five gunboats; one ship and two gunboats, as well as the mortar-fleet, had remained below the town. His total losses were 15 killed and 42 wounded, and the damage to his fleet, in spite of the heavy firing, was not very serious. Farragut states in his report that "the rebels were soon silenced by the combined efforts of the fleet and flotilla, and at times did not reply at all for several minutes," and the same statement is made by his commanders; Smith, however, states that "not a single gun was silenced, none disabled, and the serious bombardment of the preceding seven days had thrown nothing out of fighting trim." It is probable that some of the guns ceased firing for a time but that none of them were permanently silenced or disabled. In any event, it was perfectly evident that the navy could do no serious damage to the batteries. Farragut clearly stated the case in his report by saying, "The forts can be passed, and we have done it and can do it again as often as may be required of us;" but "I am satisfied that it is not possible to take Vicksburg without an army of 12,000 to 15,000 men."

The combined fleets of Farragut and Davis therefore remained in the vicinity of Vicksburg, part of them above and part below the town; Williams with his little force continued digging the canal, and the Confederates worked away at their batteries, not only increasing the number of those at Vicksburg but erecting new ones at Grand Gulf, about fifteen miles down the river.

The line for the canal was not well located, for it was perpendicular to the direction of the current, and at each end the current impinged upon the shore opposite to that on which they were digging. It would have been of no service if completed, but before its completion the river suddenly rose one night and inundated and destroyed all that had been accomplished. Williams's troops were much prostrated with sickness, and as he could accomplish nothing where he was he prepared to return to Baton Rouge.

Farragut was also expecting an order to return down the river, when, on July 15th, an event occurred which caused him deep mortification. Early on the morning of that day some of the light-draft gunboats of Davis's flotilla had been sent up the Yazoo River on a reconnoissance to obtain information concerning the large iron-plated ram, Arkansas, which was known to be building up that stream, and of whose strength extraordinary reports had been circulated. The vessels had not been long gone before firing was heard, and soon after they appeared at the mouth of the Yazoo, coming down with all speed and closely followed by the Arkansas. It so happened that not one of Farragut's vessels had steam up, and in broad daylight in the morning the ram passed directly through his fleet, receiving its broadsides almost without injury, and proceeded to the shelter of the batteries at Vicksburg. Farragut was much chagrined, and determined at once to run past the batteries again that night and endeavor to destroy the ram in the passage. He succeeded in passing the batteries with a loss of 5 killed and 16 wounded, but in the darkness and confusion no damage was done to the Arkansas. The river was now rapidly falling and Farragut became anxious lest his large vessels should be unable to return to deep water. It was, therefore, with great relief that he received, on July 20th, the expected order from the Navy Department to return. He waited a few days for Williams to embark his men, and then on the 27th started down the river. On the same day Davis's flotilla started up the river, and Vicksburg was left entirely free. Williams's troops returned to Baton Rouge, where two gunboats remained with him, the rest of Farragut's fleet going on to New Orleans, where it arrived July 29th.

All immediate danger at Vicksburg was therefore over, and in the various artillery engagements which had taken place during the two months since the fleet first arrived, the Confederates had lost only 22 men in killed and wounded. They were very properly jubilant at their successful defence, yet with commendable promptitude they determined to renew the offensive. For this purpose Van Dorn issued orders on the same day, July 27th, that the fleets moved off, directing Breckenridge to select 5,000 men from his corps and proceed by rail, via Jackson, to Camp Moore, on the New Orleans Railroad, just south of the Louisiana line; here he was to be reinforced by the command of Ruggles and then proceed to attack Baton Rouge. The object of this movement was to regain possession of a point on the Mississippi south of the mouth of Red River, and thus retain control of the navigation of that river, by which supplies could be brought from Western Louisiana and Texas. Breckenridge reached Camp Moore on July 28th, and organizing his force into two divisions began his march against Baton Rouge on the 30th. His force consisted of eighteen regiments and four batteries and he states that its strength was 6,000 when he began his march, but owing to sickness it was so reduced that the morning report of August 4th showed only 3,000 effectives, and he "did not carry into the action more than 2,600 men." This would give only about 130 men per regiment, and it is doubtless an under-estimate.

Williams's force consisted of six regiments and three batteries; it is said that one-half of the men were on the sick list, suffering from fevers contracted at Vicksburg, and the estimate of 2,500 "present for duty," which was made at the time, is probably quite accurate. He was anticipating an attack, and had placed his men in readiness for battle on the north and east of the town. The Confederates opened the battle at daylight, and it lasted with considerable energy for the space of six hours. A portion of the Union line was at first forced back, and their camps, which were in advance of the line, were occupied and plundered by the Confederates. About 10 A.M., however, their advance was completely checked; one division and three brigade commanders had been killed or wounded, the men had lost very heavily, and were suffering for water, and the ram Arkansas, which had descended the river with the purpose of driving off the Union gunboats and assisting in the battle, had not made its appearance. Breckenridge, there-fore, gave up the contest, and retired to a creek about two miles in rear, where he remained during the afternoon, in-tending, as he claims, to renew the fight as soon as the Arkansas should come in sight. Late in the afternoon, however, he received word that the Arkansas was dis-abled about five miles up the river, and he therefore con-tinued his retreat during the night about twelve miles to the north, halting on a small stream known as the Comité River. During the battle, Commander W. D. Porter, with the Essex and four other gunboats, was stationed in the river opposite the right flank of Williams's troops, and, when the Con-federates began to retreat, these vessels fired on them with considerable effect. The next morning three of the vessels proceeded up the river, and a few miles above the town they came in sight of the Arkansas, and immediately opened fire upon her. One of the engines of this vessel had broken down on the previous day, and, in stopping to repair it, she had been prevented from taking part in the battle. On the morning of the 6th, she got up steam, but had proceeded only a short distance when the other engine gave way. Be-fore it could be repaired, the Essex and other Union vessels came in sight, and the commander of the Arkansas, deeming his vessel in no condition to fight, ran her ashore, landed his crew, set fire to the vessel, and turned her adrift. She floated down the river, and blew up as soon as the fire reached the magazine.

The Union loss in this engagement at Baton Rouge was reported at 90 killed, and 250 wounded. The Confederate returns make their loss 84 killed, 307 wounded, and 56 miss-ing; total, 447. In addition to two colonels of regiments, the Union troops lost their commander, General Williams, a valuable and experienced officer, who had served on General Scott's staff throughout the Mexican War. He was killed at the head of his men just before the close of the action. Among the Confederate killed and wounded were Generals Clark and Helm, and two colonels commanding brigades.

Breckenridge's attack had thus been unsuccessful, but the object of his expedition, which was to gain possession of a point below the mouth of Red River, was fully achieved. Two days after the battle, instead of returning to Camp Moore, and thence back into Mississippi, he marched his men to Port Hudson, thirty miles above Baton Rouge, and began the construction of heavy batteries, for which the site was admirably adapted. On August 19th, the batteries being well advanced, he left a portion of his command, under Ruggles, to garrison them, and with the rest rejoined Van Dorn at Jackson, Miss. Port Hudson remained in the possession of the Confederates from this time until after the fall of Vicksburg in the following summer. On the other hand, the troops which had composed Williams's command abandoned Baton Rouge and returned to New Orleans.

It was now within a few days of one year since Grant had arrived at Cairo, and Polk at Columbus, and active operations for the control of the great river had begun. During that year the river had been cleared and held from Cairo down to Vicksburg; New Orleans had been taken, and the fleet had ascended to Vicksburg. That point alone remained to the Confederates, and, for a while, they held it by the frailest possible tenure. One more effort, with a land force of 10,000 men, at any time during the months of May or June, 1862, and the entire river would have been securely in possession of the Union forces. That effort was not made; whether it could, or could not have been, it is

difficult to say. Perhaps Halleck might have marched his
whole army to Vicksburg by a rapid movement after the
evacuation of Corinth, trusting to success to establish his
base on the Mississippi; possibly he might have sent 10,000
men via Memphis, or back via the Tennessee River, and
thence down the Mississippi. But Halleck himself did not
think so. When Farragut reported, after passing the batteries on June 28th, that an army was necessary to take
Vicksburg, Halleck answered that "the scattered and weak-
ened condition of my forces renders it impossible, at the
present, to detach any troops to co-operate with you at
Vicksburg." At all events, the effort was not made, and the
opportunity rapidly slipped away. The Confederates were
reinforced at Vicksburg, the navy could do nothing unaided,
and on their departure, the Confederates immediately resumed the offensive, and regained control of the river, from
Baton Rouge to Helena, Ark., a distance of 300 miles in a
straight line, and twice as far by the windings of the river.
Within this distance, batteries were erected or strengthened
wherever the river touches the eastern bluffs—at Port Hudson, at Natchez, at Grand Gulf, at Vicksburg; and a fort
was also erected a short distance up the Arkansas River,
from the cover of which gunboats could issue forth and destroy all unarmed vessels. The Confederacy thus gained a
lease of life for another year on the Mississippi.

CHAPTER II.

IUKA AND CORINTH.

In the second volume of this series General Force has traced the events of the first military operations in the West, from Fort Henry to Corinth. Although conducted along the line of the Tennessee River, their object, as already stated, was to aid in the great problem of gaining control of the Mississippi, and their result was the repossession of that river from Cairo to Memphis. They were concluded on May 30, 1862, by the evacuation of Corinth by the Confederate army, under Beauregard, and its occupation by the Union army, under Halleck. The first great step in the problem having thus been accomplished by the Union army, the question arose as to what should be the next step. On June 1st, the situation was as follows: Halleck had under his command at, or near Corinth, the largest army ever assembled west of the Alleghanies; its return is given in full in Appendix B., but it may be summarized by saying that, after deducting the detachments under Mitchell and others, its strength present and absent was 173,019, of which 128,315 were present, and of these latter 108,538 were fit for duty on the morning of that day. In addition to these troops, near Corinth, Mitchell's division of Buell's army, numbering about 6,500 effectives, was at Huntsville, Ala., moving along the Memphis and Charleston Railroad toward Chattanooga; another division of the same army, under

Morgan, numbering nearly 9,000 effectives, was at Cumberland Gap in East Tennessee; and a brigade of 3,000 men remained in Nashville. Finally, Curtis, with an army of about 10,000 men, was in Northwestern Arkansas, preparing to march toward the Mississippi. The Union armies, therefore, had a total effective strength, in round numbers, of 137,000 men, about two-thirds of which were concentrated at Corinth, and the rest scattered in Arkansas, along the Tennessee River, and in Eastern Tennessee.

Opposed to them the Confederates had an army under Beauregard, which was retreating from Corinth along the Mobile and Ohio Railroad toward Tupelo. Its return of May 28th, which is given in full in Appendix C, shows a total, present and absent, of 112,692, of which 75,429 were present, and of these latter 57,147 were considered effective or fit for duty on the day of the return—over 18,000 being sick. Opposed to Mitchell was a brigade of 2,000 men in Chattanooga, under General Leadbetter, who had been detached from the army of Kirby Smith; the rest of which army, numbering 12,000 men, was near Knoxville, confronting Morgan's division at Cumberland Gap. The Confederates had also a detachment under Lovell at Jackson, and another under M. L. Smith, at Vicksburg, the two numbering about 8,000 men. In Arkansas their total strength was about 26,000, although the troops were considerably scattered and were poorly armed.

The total effective force of the Confederates in the West was therefore about 105,000 men, against 137,000 in the Union armies opposed to them, although the paper strength of the two armies was about 175,000 and 220,000. The Confederate armies were greatly discouraged and demoralized by the almost unbroken series of reverses which they had sustained during the last four months. The Union troops were correspondingly elated at their success. What was to be their next move?

This question was the most vital in character and its solution the most far-reaching in consequences, that ever arose in the West, and it should therefore be examined in all its bearings. It has generally been held that Halleck's action at this juncture was the worst possible under the circumstances, but the case was not free from embarrassment and complication, and these should be carefully considered. A glance at the map will show that there were two great highways leading into the heart of the Confederacy; one was down the Mississippi Valley to Vicksburg and thence to Mobile, and the other was along the railroad from Chattanooga to Atlanta and thence to the sea-coast. The starting-points for both were along the railroad from Memphis to Chattanooga, which, though much injured, was now in Halleck's possession. This railroad extended northeastward from Chattanooga to Richmond, and was the only through route at that time leading eastward from the Mississippi River within the limits of the Confederacy. South of this the only railroad connection between Memphis or Vicksburg and Atlanta or Chattanooga was via Mobile. Halleck had therefore an interior line of communications for operations in both directions. The distances, however, were very great —from Chattanooga to Corinth over 200 miles, and from Corinth to Vicksburg over 300 miles. If, then, Halleck took the whole of his force to Chattanooga, he left the Mississippi River and its parallel railroads open for an advance of the Confederates to the mouth of the Ohio, and if he marched his whole army toward Vicksburg he left the road open from Chattanooga via Nashville to Louisville and Cincinnati. It was of far more importance to hold these cities than to overrun the whole Confederacy. Moreover, it seemed very doubtful if so large an army as 100,000 men could be supplied any longer in the vicinity of Corinth. Up to this time Halleck had drawn his supplies by the Tennessee River, but this river was now rapidly falling, and there was reason to believe that the navigation would soon become so difficult that supplies in large quantities could not be forwarded by that route. Halleck must then resort to the railroads, but these had been destroyed by the Confederates in their retreat, all the way from Columbus. Until they could be repaired the army must disperse to subsist.

There was still another reason in the fact that McClellan imagined that Beauregard's troops had been sent to Richmond, and he therefore urged that a portion of Halleck's army should be brought to the Peninsula, and the Government seemed disposed to accede to his representations. It was evident that if any considerable part of the army was detached to so distant a point as Virginia, all that had been gained in the West would be lost ; and of course the larger Halleck's army in one body the more urgent would be the demand from McClellan.[1] On purely military grounds, therefore, the propriety of keeping his army together was at least open to question. If we consider the political grounds, the question was still more difficult. Mr. Lincoln's heart ached for the suffering Unionists in East Tennessee, To be a Union man in the vicinity of Knoxville in 1862 meant something more than the mere expression of opinion, it meant the constant facing of death. "Treason" to the Confederacy was then indeed made odious, and its punishment was hanging without trial. The sufferings which these brave men had endured for their devotion to the Union had induced Mr. Lincoln to write constant despatches

---

[1] See appendix D, at the end of the volume.

during the preceding winter to Halleck and Buell urging an advance into East Tennessee ; he had yielded his judgment on the representation that this was not a judicious military move ; but now that the Mississippi had been opened to Memphis he again urged the relief of East Tennessee, and his appeals were not without effect. On June 5th he telegraphed Halleck, enclosing a despatch from McClellan, recommending the occupation of Chattanooga, and later (June 30th) he telegraphed that the expedition to East Tennessee must not be abandoned under any circumstances. To the first telegram Halleck replied that preparations for Chattanooga had already been made, and in fact on June 2d he had notified Buell that he might expect an order to move his whole army eastward.

That an energetic commander might have done more than Halleck did seems incontestable ; he might have sent a portion of Buell's army—not to slowly repair the railroad—but to march with all haste to reinforce Mitchell, seize, fortify, and hold Chattanooga against all comers, and draw its supplies directly from Nashville. With the balance of his force, enough to largely outnumber Beauregard, he might have pursued the latter with vigor, bringing him to battle without fortifications or else continuing his pursuit to Vicksburg, Halleck meanwhile drawing his own supplies by boat or rail from Memphis. But it is universally admitted that energy in the field was not one of Halleck's characteristics. His orders were cautious to the extent of feebleness, and while his troops were scattered about trying to hold and repair 300 miles of railroad—from Memphis to near Chattanooga— running parallel to the enemy's front, the enemy under Bragg (who had superseded Beauregard) seized the initiative, divided his forces, and by a movement which was pre-eminently remarkable for its boldness, its skill, and its suc-

2*

cess, transferred a part of his army to Chattanooga, whence he led Buell a stern chase straight to Louisville. The Union opportunity was thus lost, and Bragg was allowed to control the course of events in the West; the Union armies were not again united until Vicksburg had been taken, and the whole force put under Grant's direction in order to drive Bragg out of Chattanooga in November, 1863.

Halleck's orders for the dispersion of his army were as follows : on June 3d, McClernand was sent with his own and Wallace's divisions of the Army of the Tennessee to Bolivar, on the Mississippi Central Railroad. On June 4th, Pope, who was pursuing Beauregard south of Corinth, was notified not to bring on a battle, Halleck adding, " I think the enemy will continue his retreat, which is all I desire." Pope's army went into camp near Rienzi. On June 9th Sherman was ordered with his own and Hurlbut's division to move along the railroad to Memphis, and on the same day Buell received his definite orders to march his whole army eastward along the railroad to Chattanooga. On the 10th, the order of April 30th, by which the army had been divided into right wing, center, left wing, and reserve, was revoked, and Grant, Buell, and Pope, were ordered to resume command of their Armies of the Tennessee, Ohio, and Mississippi respectively. Halleck remained at Corinth for five weeks longer, but nothing was done but slowly to repair the railroads, against which the Confederates occasionally made a dash. On July 16th he left for Washington, to assume his new duties as General-in-Chief. Grant was left in command of all troops in the vicinity of Memphis and Corinth and as far back as Columbus, Ky., but as Halleck expected to return in a few weeks and keep his headquarters in the West, no successor was appointed to his late command nor did he give any definite instructions as to the

movements of troops in that region.   His first telegram
to Grant, dated July 31st, is in these words: "You must
judge for yourself the best use to be made of your troops.
Be careful not to scatter them too much; also to hold them
in readiness to reinforce Buell at Chattanooga if necessary."

This dispersion of Halleck's army, combined with Bragg's
bold offensive—and possibly also the disastrous course of

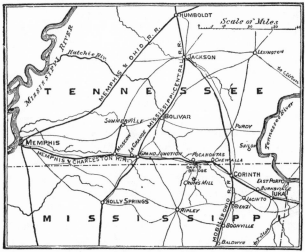

Memphis to Iuka.   1862.

events at this time in Virginia—reduced all the Union armies
in the West to the defensive.   Grant was left with about
60,000 men, composed of Pope's "Army of the Mississippi" (now commanded by Rosecrans, Pope having been
ordered to Virginia) and the "Army of the Tennessee," except Wallace's division, which had been sent to Curtis at
Helena.   But Bragg's invasion of Tennessee soon caused
such alarm that two divisions, and subsequently a third

division, of Rosecrans's army were sent to reinforce Buell, reducing Grant's force to about 42,000. With these he was required to guard the line of road—two hundred miles long—from Memphis to Decatur, and he was specially directed to keep open his communications with Buell. Under these requirements no concentration of his force nor offensive measures were to be thought of. He therefore occupied three important points of his road—Memphis, Corinth, and Tuscumbia—with considerable bodies, and posted the rest of his men at Jackson and Bolivar, central points in rear, from which they could readily be moved in any required direction. In this position he awaited the movements of the enemy into whose hands the power of initiative had passed.

On the Confederate side Bragg remained in camp at Tupelo, Miss., until July 22d, when he issued orders sending the Army of the Mississippi, numbering about 35,000 men, under Hardee, to Chattanooga by rail, via Mobile; he went with this column in person. At Chattanooga his army was augmented by recruits, and by calling in detachments, and, on August 16th, he moved northward toward Kentucky, in conjunction with Kirby Smith's army from Knoxville. No successor was appointed to Bragg in Mississippi, and, by his departure, the Confederate forces in that region were reduced to two independent bodies, each about 16,000 in strength; one, under Van Dorn, was charged with the defence of the river, and the other, under Price, was to guard the Mobile and Ohio Railroad south of Corinth. Van Dorn's troops were scattered from Holly Springs to Vicksburg, and a few days after Bragg's departure Van Dorn ordered the expedition against Baton Rouge, as already narrated. Price's troops were less scattered, most of them being in the vicinity of Tupelo.

Nothing of any consequence took place for a month. In the latter part of August a cavalry raid was undertaken by Generals Armstrong and Jackson, who moved from Holly Springs to the vicinity of Bolivar, with a force of 3,700 men, and did some damage to the railroad between Jackson and Bolivar.

On September 2d, Price received a despatch from Bragg, saying that Buell was "in full retreat upon Nashville," and directing him to "watch Rosecrans and prevent a junction, or, if he escapes, follow him closely." Price immediately communicated this to Van Dorn, and proposed a junction of their forces, but Van Dorn replied that he could not get all his men together at Holly Springs until the 12th. Price thereupon determined to move forward alone. His advance reached Iuka on the 13th, and had a skirmish with the small garrison stationed there; on the following day his main force came up and entered the place. Three days later he received a despatch from Bragg, stating that documents captured at Nashville proved that part of Rosecrans's army had been there (which was true, as two divisions of that army had been sent to Buell in August), and asking Price to hasten his advance into Tennessee. Price, however, knew very well that Rosecrans was between Iuka and Corinth, and felt certain that Bragg had been misled in his information. As the spirit of his orders was to attack Rosecrans, he had no hesitation in abandoning his expedition to Tennessee. He therefore sent despatches on the 17th to Van Dorn, again proposing the union of their forces, and an attack on Corinth. On the 19th he received Van Dorn's answer, acceding to his proposition, but asking him to move to Rienzi in order to effect a junction. Van Dorn, having secured Port Hudson, and the gunboats having retreated up and down the river, had left small garrisons at Vicksburg

and Port Hudson, and collected all the rest of his force at
Holly Springs, and was now ready for the offensive. Price
made preparations to march toward Rienzi the next morning, when, late on the afternoon of the 19th, his pickets
were driven in by Rosecrans at Iuka.

This battle was brought about in the following manner :
Grant was watching Price's and Van Dorn's movements as
carefully as possible, in daily expectation of an attack ; but
on September 10th he confessed that he was unable to " de-
termine the objects of the enemy." On the following day
he telegraped that everything indicated an attack on Corinth within the next forty-eight hours. He therefore made
some changes in the position of his troops, moving Hurlbut's division from Memphis to Bolivar, Ord's from Bolivar
to Corinth, and drawing in Rosecrans's troops from Iuka
and Tuscumbia to the vicinity of Corinth. His army was
then at three central points, Memphis, Bolivar, and Corinth,
ready to move promptly as soon as the enemy's movements
were developed. Price's advanced guard, as already stated,
entered Iuka on September 13th, and on the 15th a reconnoissance by Rosecrans's cavalry developed the fact that
Price occupied Iuka in force. Grant immediately prepared
to attack him. In the absence of positive knowledge as to
the enemy's plans, three suppositions were possible. First,
that Price intended to cross the Tennessee for the purpose
of joining Bragg, or attacking Buell's rear. Halleck telegraphed to Grant on the 17th, to do everything in his power
to prevent this, as a junction of Bragg and Price " would be
most disastrous." Second, that Corinth was to be attacked
simultaneously, by Van Dorn from the southwest, and by
Price from the east or northeast. Third, that Price would
endeavor to draw Grant away from Corinth in pursuit, while
Van Dorn should attack that place from the southwest.

Whatever the enemy's plans might be, Grant satisfied himself that Van Dorn could not reach Corinth with any considerable force in less than four days, and he determined to attack Price at once, and, if possible, overwhelm him, and return to Corinth before Van Dorn could arrive. Grant, therefore, ordered Rosecrans to move south about twelve miles to Rienzi and Jacinto, leave small detachments in those places to prevent a surprise on Corinth from the south, thence move rapidly eastward with the bulk of his force—about 9,000 men—till he was opposite Iuka, then turn northward and attack on the roads coming from Jacinto and Fulton. Ord, with about six thousand men, was to move along the railroad to Burnsville, then take roads north of the railroad, and attack on the north and west of Iuka. The whole plan of attack was based on occupying the Jacinto and Fulton roads, thus cutting off Price from all retreat to the west or south. If the attack were successful, he would be driven against the Tennessee River, where it was hoped to crush him.

Grant went in person with Ord's column, which reached Burnsville on the 18th, and encamped within six miles of Iuka, its advance moving forward to within a few miles of the town, and skirmishing with Price's cavalry. Preparations were made to attack at 4.30 A.M., the following day. After midnight, however, word was received from Rosecrans that, through the fault of a guide, his march had been slightly delayed, and one of his divisions was still at Jacinto, twenty miles from Iuka; he would, therefore, not be able to reach Iuka before one or two o'clock on the following afternoon. Grant thereupon ordered Ord not to attack until he heard firing from the other side of Iuka. During the 19th, the direction of the wind was such that the firing was not heard. Rosecrans sent word, at 12.40 P.M., that he was within eight miles of Iuka, but this was not received by Grant until after night. Hearing nothing from Rosecrans during the day, and no sounds of firing, Grant and Ord concluded that Rosecrans could not reach the field that day, and Ord was therefore instructed to skirmish with the enemy, but not to bring on a general engagement.

Rosecrans, however, had moved at daylight, and pushing his men with great energy, his leading division, under Hamilton, reached a point about two miles southwest of Iuka,

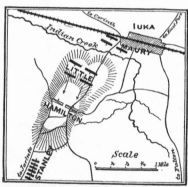

Iuka, September 19, 1862.

on the Jacinto road, about 4 P.M. Here they encountered strong opposition from the enemy, and the battle was at once opened. Hamilton formed his division across the forks of the road, on the wooded knoll shown on the accompanying map. Stanley's division, as it came up, was halted on the road in rear, and only one regiment of it was hotly engaged. Hamilton posted a battery at the forks of the road, and the battle was mainly a contest for this point. Price had two divisions, commanded by Generals Little and Maury. Little's division was in the outskirts of the village on the south, and Maury's on the north. As soon as his skirmishers were driven in on the Jacinto road, Price ordered Little's division to advance on that road, and Maury to move into the village, and be in readiness to assist, if necessary. He was not called upon, however, the battle being fought on the Confederate side by Little's division, and mainly by two brigades of it, numbering between three and four thousand men. These two brigades attacked Hamilton's position at the forks of the road with great vehemence, and after some unsuccessful efforts, finally carried that point, capturing the battery, and forcing Hamilton's line back a few hundred yards, but again losing both the battery and the position under a determined advance of Hamilton's men, assisted by one regiment of Stanley's. Darkness then put an end to the fighting, and Hamilton's division was withdrawn to the field in rear, its place being taken by Stanley's division, which had been but slightly engaged. Price at once began his preparations for retreat, and during the night, Rosecrans heard the rumbling of his wagons moving off to the southeast. At daylight, Stanley's men moved cautiously forward, and found that the enemy's position was abandoned; they then pressed on to the village, but found nothing but a few stragglers in it. Price's whole command had escaped by the Fulton road. Stanley's division was pushed forward in pursuit on the Fulton road, and Hamilton was countermarched on the Jacinto road, but at night, both found themselves distanced by the enemy, and gave up the pursuit. It will be seen from the map that Rosecrans, in his eagerness to reach the field on the appointed day, and in accordance with the report he had sent to Grant (but which was not received until night), had pushed forward on the Jacinto road, and on arriving near the town had been immediately attacked by the enemy, and forced into action. He therefore had no opportunity to move Hamilton's division over to the Fulton road, as had been arranged in the orders for the battle. This road was thus left open, and Price availed himself of it to escape with great promptness. Rosecrans sent word to Grant at

10.30 P.M. of the 19th, informing him of the engagement of the afternoon, and asking him to attack in the morning in force, adding, "We will try to get a position on our right, which will take Iuka." Grant, therefore, pushed forward with Ord's troops early on the 20th, but on arriving at Iuka found that Price had escaped. The opportunity to destroy Price was lost by the unfortunate, but unavoidable, lack of concert on the 19th, and by the precipitation with which Rosecrans came to the field, and was forced to fight without occupying the Fulton road. Price, as we have seen, had, at that time, no intention of going to Tennessee, but he succeeded in returning southward, and subsequently in joining Van Dorn, in accordance with the agreement which had been made between them.

Rosecrans reported his losses in the battle of Iuka at 144 killed, 598 wounded, and 40 missing—total 782, nearly 700 of which were in Hamilton's division, which brought only 2,800 men into action. There is a great discrepancy in the reports of the Confederate losses. Price, in his report dated September 26th, puts them at 86 killed and 408 wounded—total 496 ; but Rosecrans's Provost-Marshal certifies that he buried 265 who were found dead on the field, that 120 more died in hospital, that 342 wounded were found in Iuka, 361 were taken prisoners, and it was estimated that 350 wounded were carried off—making a total of 1,438. General Little was killed just as his division was coming into action.

Price retreated southward and reached Baldwyn, on the Mobile and Ohio Railroad, on September 23d, and immediately notified Van Dorn at Holly Springs of his arrival. Rosecrans and Ord returned to Corinth.

Previous to this time Grant had found that it was impossible to maintain the railroad from Memphis to Corinth, which ran parallel to the enemy's front and was subject to

frequent raids by the enemy's cavalry. This line had therefore been practically abandoned from Chewalla to the vicinity of Memphis, and communication was kept up by means
of the railroads in rear, forming two sides of a triangle from
Memphis to Humboldt and Humboldt to Corinth. The railroad east of Corinth was also practically abandoned, as nothing had been heard directly from Buell for several weeks.
In order to put himself in direct communication with both
wings of his army, at Memphis and at Corinth, Grant established his headquarters at Jackson, on October 1st. The returns of his army on that day show that he had 48,000 effective men, as follows: 7,000 under Sherman at Memphis,
12,000 under Ord at Bolivar, 23,000 under Rosecrans at
Corinth, a small reserve of 6,000 at Jackson, ready to be
used whenever needed. On September 30th, movements of
the Confederates were apparent in the vicinity of Grand
Junction, on the Memphis and Charleston Railroad. These
movements were of such a character that Grant was left in
doubt whether Bolivar or Corinth was to be the point of
attack. On the following day, however, it was learned that
the Confederates were concentrated at Pocahontas, about
twenty miles northwest of Corinth, and Grant became convinced that Corinth was to be the objective. He immediately notified Rosecrans to be prepared, and directed
Hurlbut at Bolivar to watch the enemy's movements and attack him on the flank if an opportunity offered.

Meanwhile, on September 25th, Van Dorn had received
Price's letter announcing his arrival at Baldwyn, and had
immediately requested him to move to Ripley, and had put
his own forces in motion for the same place. These latter
consisted of a division under Lovell, containing three brigades under Generals Rust, Villepigue, and Bowen. Rust's
brigade was composed of a portion of the troops that Breck-

enridge had led to Baton Rouge (Breckenridge having now
gone in person to join Bragg), Villepigue's of the troops
that had formerly garrisoned Fort Pillow and had since been
stationed on the Mississippi Central Railroad, and Bowen's
of a portion of Lovell's original command at New Orleans
and Jackson. Van Dorn and Price met at Ripley on September 28th, and Van Dorn took command, being the senior
officer. The return of his troops on that day shows that,
after deducting the garrisons left at Vicksburg, Port Hudson, and other places, he had about 22,000 in the field,
Price's troops numbering about 14,000 and Lovell's about
8,000. About 15,000 exchanged prisoners had lately arrived
in the interior of Mississippi, but they had not yet been
armed. On the other hand, new regiments had been formed
at the North, and several of them were destined to Grant's
command, but they had not yet arrived.

Van Dorn having got his army together at Ripley on
September 28th, moved northward on the following day,
and reached Pocahontas on October 1st. Here he carefully
surveyed the field in front of him and matured his plans for
the offensive. The reasons governing his action are stated
with great clearness in his admirable report of these operations, dated October 20, 1862. Three points in front of him,
Memphis, Bolivar, and Corinth, were strongly fortified,
forming the arc of a circle of which the chord was about
one hundred miles long. He judged that to take Memphis
would give no military advantage, and it was doubtful if it
could be held without heavy guns against the Union gunboats. To attack Bolivar was to penetrate into the re-entrant of the three fortified places and to render himself liable
to disastrous attacks on both flanks. But " if a successful
attack could be made upon Corinth from the west and northwest, the forces there driven back on the Tennessee and cut

off, Bolivar and Jackson would easily fall, and then, upon
the arrival of the exchanged prisoners of war, West Tennessee would soon be in our possession, and communication
with General Bragg effected through Middle Tennessee.
The attack on Corinth was a military necessity requiring
prompt and vigorous action." There can be no doubt that
this reasoning was perfectly sound ; a successful attack
upon Corinth would in all probability have forced Grant
back to Kentucky in the same manner that Bragg had carried Buell back to Louisville, and all the results of the campaign from Fort Henry to Corinth would then have been lost.

Van Dorn, therefore, started to attack Corinth with the
utmost energy. Having reached Pocahontas on October 1st,
he turned sharply to the east, crossed the Hatchie, and bivouacked at Chewalla on the night of the 2d. The march
was resumed at daylight on the 3d, Lovell's division in advance, marching on the right of the Memphis and Charleston Railroad. Arriving near Corinth, about 10 A.M., his line
of battle was formed with Lovell's three brigades in line,
each supported by a reserve, on the right or south of the
Memphis and Charleston Railroad ; Price's corps was on the
left, in the angle between the two railroads, Maury's division, with two brigades in line and one in reserve, connecting with Lovell, and Hébert's (formerly Little's) division,
similarly formed, on Maury's left. Jackson's cavalry brigade was on the right of the whole line, and Armstrong's on
the left. Van Dorn's intention was to open the attack with
Lovell's division, in the hope that Rosecrans would strength-
en his left by withdrawing from his right, and then his main
force, under Price, was to make the principal attack on
Rosecrans's right.

In the meantime, Rosecrans had been fully informed of
the enemy's approach, and had drawn into Corinth all the

detachments posted in observation on the exterior. His force consisted of the two divisions of his own army, under Stanley and Hamilton, and the 2d and 6th divisions of the Army of the Tennessee, commanded by Davies and Mc-Kean. His position was well defended by a line of re-

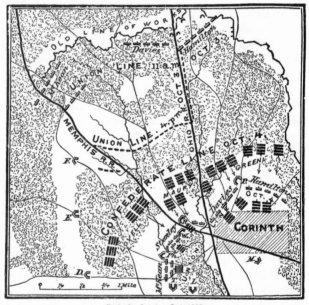

Corinth, October 3-4, 1862.

doubts, constructed within a short distance of the town, and by an outer line of intrenchments, about two miles in advance, which had been built by the Confederates prior to their evacuation in May. During the night of October 2d to 3d, Rosecrans issued orders, directing his divisions to move at 3 A.M., and take post in advance of his line of

redoubts, and about half-way to the outer line; Hamilton's division was on the right, facing north, Davies in the
centre, and McKean's division on the left, on the Chewalla
road, with three regiments advanced to the outer line of
works. Stanley's division was just south of the town, in
reserve. These positions were assumed about 9 A.M.

Van Dorn, meanwhile, had been advancing from Chewalla,
skirmishing all the way with the outposts of McKean's division, and about 10 A.M., he deployed into the formation previously given. Lovell, on the right, at once came in contact
with the three regiments of McKean's division, posted in an
advantageous position on a hill at the intersection of the
Memphis Railroad with the outer line of works. Deeming
it important to hold this hill, Brig. Gen. J. McArthur, commanding the first brigade of McKean's division, moved
forward with four regiments to the support of the three
already posted there. At the same time, Davies asked, and
obtained, permission to move his division forward to the
outer line of works. These two advances were eccentric,
and the result was a considerable gap between Davies and
McKean's divisions. A severe contest took place on this
outer line, Lovell's division being opposed to McArthur,
and Maury's division attacking the left of Davies's. The
Confederates finally penetrated between Davies and Mc-
Arthur, and the whole Union line was forced back, and took
up a second position about half a mile in advance of the
inner redoubts, Davies refusing his left flank, and McArthur
his right. Lovell's division was now moved past the left of
McKean's division, and came in front of the redoubts on the
southwest of the town. This caused McArthur, as well as
Crocker's brigade of McKean's division, to fall back to these
redoubts, and, at the same time, Price's entire corps made
another violent attack upon Davies's division, and forced it

back upon Battery Robinett, where it re-formed and held its position until night. One brigade of Stanley's division was sent to Davies's assistance during his retreat, and the rest of this division was preparing to assist, when, about 5.30 P.M., the enemy's attack ceased. Meanwhile, Hamilton's division, on the extreme right, had taken but little active part in the action. In the morning it was formed on the east of the Mobile and Ohio Railroad, facing north, and from there advanced to the outer line of intrenchments. The enemy's attack, however, was entirely beyond Hamilton's left, and upon Davies's division. Hamilton changed front to the left, so as to face the railroad. He then intended to attack the enemy's left flank, as he was advancing against Davies, but one of his brigades diverged too far to the right, and the other was considered too weak to attack alone. Before this error could be corrected, the enemy had ceased his attack, possibly alarmed, as Hamilton claims, by the presence of the latter on his left flank.

The battle closed for this day at sunset, a little before six o'clock. It had been most encouraging for the Confederate arms. Rosecrans had been driven back for a distance of about two miles and had taken refuge in the redoubts just outside of the town; the Confederates passed the night within a few hundred yards of these redoubts, and they hoped on the morrow to complete the destruction of the Union army. This army, however, was by no means demoralized or disheartened. During the night its position was rearranged so as to make a strong defence in the morning. McKean's division was placed on the extreme left in the vicinity of Battery Phillips, south of the Memphis Railroad; Stanley's division took post across that road in Batteries Williams and Robinett, relieving Davies's division which retired to Battery Powell on the north of the town, and there formed facing northwest; Hamilton's division formed the extreme right, beyond Davies's division and facing north. Rosecrans's force of 23,000 men was therefore concentrated on the arc of a circle around Corinth less than two miles in length, and the prominent points of this line were defended by strong redoubts.

Van Dorn also rearranged his troops during the night. Lovell's division was placed on the south of the Memphis railroad, facing east toward the town. Maury's division was in front of Battery Robinett with three batteries established so as to cover the whole ground on the west of the town; and Hébert's division was formed on his left. His orders were that at daylight Hébert should open a vigorous attack on the left, pivoting on his own right and swinging his left down along the Ohio Railroad against Battery Powell and the town; at the same time Maury's batteries were to open on the west against Battery Robinett and his infantry were to move straight on Corinth between the two railroads. When Hébert's and Maury's divisions were well engaged Lovell was to attack vigorously from the southwest.

This whole plan miscarried, in Van Dorn's opinion, owing to the delay in Hébert's division, which was to open the engagement. This division did not attack at daylight, and at 7 A.M. Hébert reported in person to Van Dorn, saying that he was sick. His senior brigade commander was ordered to take command of the division and carry out the movement ordered. But it was nearly nine o'clock before the division got started, and meanwhile Maury's men were already engaged, so that the attack was somewhat disjointed. It was, however, conducted with great gallantry and determination. Hébert's division, under Brig. Gen. Martin E. Green, advanced with four brigades in echelon, the left thrown forward; the whole division pivoted on the right and swung around until

VIII.—3

it occupied a position facing south in the woods north of
Corinth. It then rushed forward from these woods, the two
brigades on the right, composed of Missouri troops, directing their attack against Battery Powell, and the other two
against Hamilton's line to the east of that battery. These
latter brigades were warmly received by Hamilton and were
driven off after a severe contest without reaching his works ;
but the Missouri troops captured Battery Powell with all
its guns, forcing back the infantry in and near it, and spread-
ing confusion among the artillery posted for its support. A
portion of Davies's division subsequently rallied, however,
and assisted by a brigade of Hamilton's division, recaptured
Battery Powell with its guns, driving out the Missouri
troops with great loss.

As soon as Maury heard heavy firing on his left he gave
the order for his division to move forward straight toward
Corinth. Two regiments of Moore's brigade on his right
at once came against Battery Robinett, which they entered and there engaged in a desperate hand-to-hand encounter with the men of Stanley's division defending it. In
this they were worsted, Colonel Rogers, commanding the
2d Texas, being killed in the midst of the work ; they
were then driven out. The rest of this brigade, and Phifer's brigade on its left, moved straight forward against the
left flank of Davies' division, swept it away, and penetrated
into the heart of the town. Here they were met by some reserve regiments of Sullivan's brigade, which formed the left
of Hamilton's division, and being in disorder in the streets
and subjected to cross fire of artillery from both flanks
of the Union army, they lost heavily and were forced to retreat. The remaining brigade (Cabell's) of Maury's division,
was sent to reinforce the Missouri troops that had captured
Battery Powell, but before they arrived the latter troops

had already been routed; Cabell charged up against Battery
Powell but was met by a terrible fire and was unable to
reach the parapet; he was at once forced to join in the retreat, although a portion of one of his regiments on the right
was able to reach the town in company with the rest of
Maury's men, and retreated with them.

The duration of this fighting in and around Corinth did
not exceed an hour, but its character was most sanguinary.
While it had been in progress, Lovell was preparing to
make an attack on the southwest, and had entered into some
skirmishing in front of Battery Phillips. But before his
preparations for assault were complete, he received an order
to send one brigade to check the onslaught upon Maury's
troops at they came out of town; and this order was quickly
followed by another to employ his whole division as a rear-
guard for the army, which was now in full retreat.

The fighting was over, and the Confederates were all
moving off by noon. Rosecrans rode over the field, and
satisfied himself of the enemy's retreat, but decided not to
begin pursuit until the following day. General Grant
blamed him for this delay, but Rosecrans justified it on the
ground that his men were worn out by "two days of fighting, and two almost sleepless nights of preparation, movement, and march." He notified his troops to rest themselves, replenish their ammunition, and be ready to start
after the enemy in the morning.

While the battle was going on during the 3d, Brig.-Gen.
J. B. McPherson, who had been charged with the reconstruc-
tion of the railroads, but had held no command, arrived at
Jackson from Columbus, and was ordered by Grant to take
command of two unassigned brigades stationed along the
railroad between Jackson and Corinth, organize them into
a division, and push on to Corinth. He picked up his four

regiments during the 4th, carried them by train to within
twelve miles of Corinth, then disembarked, and marched
the rest of the way, reaching Corinth, and reporting to
Rosecrans at 4 P.M. He was ordered to move his division
at daylight in pursuit of the enemy on the road to Chewalla.
On the morning of the 4th, also, Hurlbut, in obedience to
orders from Grant, moved with his division from Bolivar to
Pocahontas, with orders to intercept the Confederate retreat. He bivouacked for the night on the west bank of
the Hatchie River, just south of the railroad. On the following morning Ord arrived and took command of this
column. Van Dorn's army passed the night at Chewalla.

Early on the morning of the 5th, Van Dorn continued
his retreat, and Rosecrans's troops moved out from Corinth
in pursuit, McPherson in the lead, followed by Stanley,
and McKean's and Hamilton's divisions on parallel roads.
Through some mistake in taking the roads, all four divisions
ran against each other about seven miles from Corinth; the
columns were delayed, and had gone no farther than Chewalla by nightfall. Van Dorn reached the Hatchie, opposite Ord's command at Davis's Mills, early in the morning,
and his advance guard seized the bridge, but it was immediately attacked by Ord and driven back across the bridge.

A very considerable affair ensued between Ord's little
command and the whole of Van Dorn's army, in which Ord
was severely wounded. Van Dorn was not pressed in his
rear by Rosecrans, whose troops were over twelve miles
away, and he managed to defend himself against Ord, and
to continue his retreat on the east bank of the Hatchie for
six miles to Crum's Mill. Here there was a bridge on which
he crossed his whole army during the night. The following
day he continued his retreat to Ripley, and thence to Holly
Springs. Rosecrans and Hurlbut pursued as far as Ripley,

when, owing to their lack of preparation for an extended movement, Grant ordered them to return to Corinth and Bolivar.

For the numbers engaged, this was one of the most hotly contested battles of the war. Rosecrans reported his losses at 315 killed, 1,812 wounded, and 232 missing; total, 2,359. Concerning the Confederate losses there is the usual discrepancy. Their official returns give 505 killed, 2,150 wounded, and 2,183 missing; total, 4,838. On the other hand, Rosecrans states that he took 2,268 prisoners, and his Medical Director says that 1,423 Confederates were buried on the field. The usual proportion of wounded to killed being about five to one, this would make Van Dorn's total loss, including prisoners, over nine thousand. On the Union side General Hackleman was killed; General Oglesby and a number of colonels commanding brigades or regiments were also wounded.

Upon hearing of Van Dorn's defeat at Corinth, Jefferson Davis nominated J. C. Pemberton to be Lieutenant-General, and directed him to proceed forthwith to Mississippi. He arrived at Jackson, Miss., and assumed command on October 14th. Van Dorn was severely blamed for the loss of the battle of Corinth, and one of his brigade commanders prepared charges against him for "undertaking an important expedition . . . without due consideration," and for general failure and neglect of duty. He applied for a court of inquiry, and one was ordered, consisting of Generals Price, Tilghman, and Maury. This court completely exonerated Van Dorn, and unanimously reported that every allegation made against him was fully disproved, and that no further proceedings were necessary. Van Dorn continued in command of a division, under Pemberton, and subsequently under Bragg, until his death in May, 1863.

Rosecrans, on the other hand, received full credit for his two victories. Immediately after Iuka he was made a Major-General, his commission dating back to March, 1862; and three weeks after the battle of Corinth he was ordered to Louisville, and appointed to the command of the Army of the Cumberland, in place of Buell.

As the battle of Antietam (September 17th) brought Lee's invasion of Maryland to a close, and the battle of Perryville (October 8th) was the culmination of Bragg's advance into Kentucky, so this battle of Corinth (October 5th) marks the farthest point reached in the Confederate wave of reaction along the Mississippi, which had followed the unsuccessful naval operations at Vicksburg, and the dispersion of Halleck's army. From this time forward, the Confederates were thrown on the defensive; the Union army resumed the offensive and steadily advanced, slowly at first, but none the less surely.

CHAPTER III.

THE FIRST MOVE AGAINST VICKSBURG.

On October 24th the order was issued from the War Department ordering Rosecrans to supersede Buell, and denominating the troops under Grant, as the Thirteenth Army Corps. The "Army of the Mississippi" thus lost its distinctive designation. The troops in the whole of Grant's department numbered about 48,500 at the middle of the month, and were thus distributed :

District of Memphis, Major-General Sherman 7,000
District of Jackson, Major-General Hurlbut................... 19,200
District of Corinth, Brigadier-General Hamilton 17,500
District of Columbus, Brigadier-General Dodge............... 4,800

Total... 48,500

The reverses sustained by the Union armies in the East during the summer, had necessitated a further call, on July 2d, for 300,000 volunteers, to serve for three years or the war, and in October a large number of these were already raised and organized. As early as October 8th, Halleck had notified Grant that he might expect "a large body of new levies." In view of the favorable turn of affairs in Virginia and Kentucky, the defeat of Van Dorn, and the prospect of reinforcements, Grant now felt at liberty, for the first time since Halleck's departure in July, to make preparations for the offensive, and he immediately turned his thoughts in that direction. On October 26th, he addressed —somewhat hesitatingly—a letter to Halleck, suggesting "the destruction of the railroads to all points of the compass from Corinth," and the concentration of his forces near Grand Junction. He then thought that he "would be able to move down the Mississippi Central Road, and cause the evacuation of Vicksburg, and capture or destroy all the boats on the Yazoo River." Grant hastened to add, "I am ready, however, to do with all my might whatever you may direct, without criticism."

It does not appear that any answer was returned to this letter, or any notice taken of it. Grant was therefore forced either to lie idle, or to do what he could on his own responsibility in the absence of instructions. He was not authorized to abandon Corinth or any other of the many positions held by his scattered force, but he thought that by taking two divisions from Bolivar, under McPherson, and three from Corinth, under Hamilton, he might assemble a force of about 30,000 men in the vicinity of Grand Junction, and from there move southward, while Sherman made a slight demonstration out from Memphis. Orders to this effect were issued on November 1st, and on the 4th the troops arrived at Grand Junction and La Grange, where Grant joined them in person on the same day. Halleck was informed of this movement on November 2d by a telegram, in which Grant stated his intention to move on to Holly Springs, and possibly to Grenada, repairing the railroad and telegraph as he advanced. Halleck telegraphed his approval of the advance, "as soon as you are strong enough for that purpose." He also added that orders had been sent to the troops at Helena (in the department commanded by Curtis, at St. Louis) to cross the river and threaten Grenada.

On the receipt of this despatch, Grant ordered Hamilton
to push out reconnoissances with his cavalry toward Holly

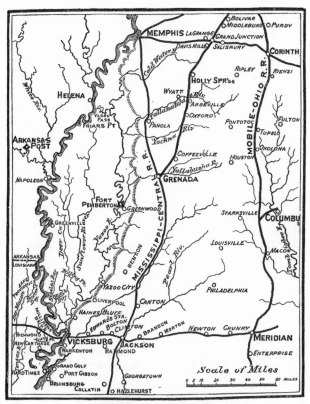

Memphis to Vicksburg. 1862–1863.

Springs and Ripley, and develop the position of the enemy.
But on November 6th he received a telegram from Halleck,
promising a reinforcement of 20,000 men in a few days.

3*

The prospect of so large a reinforcement induced Grant to suspend his operations until they should arrive, and he immediately sent a despatch to Sherman, countermanding the order for his advance. McPherson, however, was directed to send two divisions of infantry to reconnoitre toward Holly Springs. He came upon a force of the enemy, estimated at 10,000 men, behind the Coldwater, in advance of Holly Springs, and learned that there were two other bodies of 10,000 and 13,000 men respectively, at Holly Springs and Abbeville. He then returned to the vicinity of Grand Junction, reaching there on the evening of the 9th.

On the same evening Grant telegraphed to Halleck that the reinforcements were arriving very slowly, and if they did not come on more rapidly, he should attack as he was. Halleck replied that several regiments had already left Illinois for Memphis, and more were to leave in a few days. He added, "Memphis will be made the depot of a joint military and naval expedition on Vicksburg." This was very vague, and, as rumors had been floating about for several days that an independent expedition was fitting out to descend the Mississippi, under McClernand, it became necessary for Grant to learn definitely what his status was, and whether these rumors were true. As he said in his letter to Sherman, of November 6th, it was impossible for him to make any plans until he learned where and how the other Union armies were to advance, so that all might co-operate. He therefore telegraphed to Halleck in these words: "Am I to understand that I lie still here while an expedition is fitted out from Memphis; or do you want me to push south as far as possible? Am I to have Sherman move subject to my order, or is he and his forces reserved for some special service? Will not more forces be sent here?" Halleck replied: "You have command of all troops sent to your Department, and have permission to fight the enemy where you please." On the 13th, Grant telegraphed that his cavalry had entered Holly Springs, the enemy having retreated behind the Tallahatchie, but stated that he did not deem it advisable to move forward until he was prepared to follow up any success. He also asked for additional locomotives to be sent to Memphis. To which Halleck replied that it was not advisable to repair the railroad south of Memphis; that operations in Mississippi "must be limited to rapid marches upon any collected forces of the enemy," and that "the enemy must be turned by a rapid movement down the river from Memphis as soon as sufficient force can be collected." This was the first intimation of any definite plan, and was an outline of the movement executed by Grant and Sherman during the month of December.

The explanation of the contradictory despatches above quoted, and the lack of instructions from Halleck to Grant, is found in the fact that the authorities in Washington were at this time acting at cross purposes. In the month of August, Maj.-Gen. John A. McClernand, then commanding a division under Grant, had obtained leave of absence, and had gone to Washington. His correspondence with the President and the War Department is not on record, but it is known that he had frequent interviews with the President, with whom he had long been acquainted, both personally and politically, in Illinois. In these interviews McClernand endeavored to impress upon the President the great importance, in a political, military, and commercial view, of opening the Mississippi River to New Orleans. He suggested an independent expedition as the best means to accomplish this purpose. Both the President and the Secretary of War were convinced by his arguments, and, on October 21st, the latter issued a secret order, directing McClernand to proceed to Indiana, Illinois, and Iowa, raise and organize volunteers, and send them to Memphis or Cairo, "to the end that, when a sufficient force, not required by the operations of General Grant's command shall be raised, an expedition may be organized, under General McClernand's command, against Vicksburg, and to clear the Mississippi River, and open navigation to New Orleans." Mr. Lincoln endorsed on the back of this order, that, though confidential, it might be shown to the Governors of States and other persons, in General McClernand's discretion, and that he took a deep interest in the success of the expedition.

No intimation of this order was given to Grant, but it was necessarily communicated to Halleck. As an educated soldier, Halleck could not but see that McClernand's course was in violation of all military discipline, that the expedition must necessarily have a demoralizing and disorganizing effect on Grant's army, and that two commanders on the Mississippi, having the same object in view, were not only unnecessary, but liable to bring about disaster. McClernand had also served under his command, and he probably did not entertain so high an opinion of his abilities as did the President and Secretary. It is believed—though written evidence of this is not extant—that Halleck protested against the entire proposition, but without avail. McClernand undoubtedly left Washington with the impression that he was to have sole command of the expedition; and he proceeded to Illinois, whence he reported, on November 10th, that twenty regiments had been raised and forwarded, and twelve more were nearly ready. These were the very troops to which Halleck referred in his despatches to Grant as coming to reinforce *him*. McClernand seems to have gained some inkling of this, for, on the 13th, he telegraphed Stanton : "I infer that General Grant claims the right

. . . . to control all troops sent to Columbus and Memphis;" to which Stanton replied that the troops were not withdrawn from his orders, but sent temporarily to Memphis and Helena for organization.

Thus, while Stanton and McClernand were making their plans for an independent movement down the river, Halleck and Grant were arranging an advance with the whole force along the Mississippi Central Railroad, Grant being in ignorance of McClernand's propositions and Halleck not feeling at liberty to communicate them, because McClernand's status was not publicly announced, and, possibly, not fully determined. Meanwhile Grant resolved to push forward on his own responsibility, and on November 15th he notified Sherman to meet him at Columbus, where he explained his intentions in detail. With the troops near Grand Junction he would move direct to Holly Springs, while Sherman was to move out with part of his force from Memphis and join him on the Tallahatchie. Curtis was to be asked to send a force across the river from Helena to threaten the enemy's rear at Grenada. The orders for this movement had already been given, when, on November 23d, Grant received a despatch from Halleck, inquiring how many men could be spared to go down the river to Vicksburg, " reserving merely enough to hold Corinth and West Tennessee." Grant replied that 16,000 men could be spared from Memphis (where reinforcements had arrived), but none from the rest of the Department, as orders had already been given for an advance against Pemberton, an outline of which was given. He asked if these orders should be countermanded. Halleck replied, "Proposed movement approved. Do not go too far."

Accordingly Sherman moved out from Memphis on the 24th, McPherson and Hamilton from Grand Junction on the

27th, and a portion of the troops from Helena, under Brig.-
Gen. A. P. Hovey, on the 27th.   Grant reached Holly Springs
with the main body on the 29th; his cavalry crossed the
Tallahatchie December 1st, his infantry occupied Abbeville on the 2d, and Sherman reached the Tallahatchie at
Wyatt on the 2d.   Washburn's cavalry, forming the advance of Hovey's column, pushed to within seven miles of
Grenada on the 29th and on the following day destroyed a
small portion of both railroads about ten miles north of
Grenada.   He then moved up the Memphis road to Panola,
and thence back to the Mississippi, the entire force reaching
Helena on the 8th.   There was constant skirmishing between all of these advancing columns and the retreating
Confederates, during the six days beginning with November
28th, but at no point did it rise to the importance of an engagement.

On the Confederate side the operations during the month
of November had been limited to observation of the enemy's
movements, every detail of which, including the reports of
McClernand's projected river expedition, seems to have been
promptly and accurately reported to them.   Pemberton kept
his headquarters at Jackson, and Van Dorn commanded the
troops near Holly Springs and Oxford; which were formed
into two corps, under Lovell and Price, each of two divisions.   The losses at Corinth had been more than made up
by returned prisoners, and Van Dorn's effective strength was
about 24,000.   M. L. Smith still commanded at Vicksburg,
with about 6,000 men, and Brig.-Gen. W. N. R. Beale at Port
Hudson with 5,500.   There was also a small force at Jackson, so that in all Pemberton had something less than 40,000
men.   He constantly reported to the authorities at Richmond that his force was entirely inadequate to hold his positions, and asked for reinforcements from Bragg, and from the

Trans-Mississippi Department under Holmes, stating that unless these were sent he must withdraw his whole force to Vicksburg for its defence. When Grant first advanced from Grand Junction, Pemberton ordered Van Dorn (November 8th) to retire from Holly Springs to behind the Tallahatchie, and again urged upon the authorities his desperate situation. When Grant renewed his advance at the close of the month, and the troops from Helena moved against his rear, Pemberton promptly abandoned his fortifications on the Tallahatchie, and fell back behind the Yallabusha at Grenada. He established his troops in the latter position on December 5th, and on the same day Grant entered Oxford and Sherman arrived at College Hill, a few miles northwest of that place.

Grant had now advanced about sixty miles from Grand Junction, but his supplies were still drawn from Columbus, Ky., over a single-track road, 180 miles long, to Holly Springs, where he established a depot. His request for additional locomotives and cars had been disapproved, and he had been instructed not to repair the railroad south from Memphis. A good deal of rain had lately fallen, making the roads very difficult for hauling, and it was impossible for him to advance farther without some more permanent arrangements for his supplies. He had received no definite instructions as to the movements required of him, or the general plans of the War Department. His advance had been conducted without any hearty support from Washington and apparently somewhat in opposition to the plans of the authorities, for three times within a month it had been arrested by telegrams from Halleck. If his advance was to be continued the railroad from Memphis must be repaired and the other roads abandoned or destroyed. In order to learn, if possible, what it was intended that he should do, he telegraphed Halleck on December 4th, " How far south would you like me to go ? " and he stated that it would be impossible for him to advance beyond Grenada and hold his present line of communications. He suggested, therefore, that he might cut the Mobile and Ohio Railroad at Tupelo, and hold the enemy on the Yallabusha, while a force from Memphis and Helena descended the river to Vicksburg. This was in accordance with Halleck's despatches of November 10th and 15th.

Halleck replied on the following day, approving of the plan of cutting the railroad at Tupelo, but doubting the propriety of attempting to hold the country south of the Tallahatchie. He preferred simply to hold the line from Memphis to Corinth with a small force, while the main body descended the river. The troops for Vicksburg were ordered to be back in Memphis on the 20th. On the 5th, Grant telegraphed that the roads were becoming bad, and again expressed his confidence in the result of an expedition down the river against Vicksburg, provided the troops from Helena took part. On the 7th, Halleck replied, giving Grant authority to move his troops as he thought best, and also to retain all troops from Curtis's command which had crossed the Mississippi. Upon receipt of this discretionary authority Grant immediately sent for Sherman to discuss the matter. He had two plans in view, *first*, to send Sherman back to Memphis with two divisions, there to be reinforced by troops lately arrived and the troops at Helena, and then to move down the river in transports to the mouth of the Yazoo, land there and attack Vicksburg in rear, while he himself pressed forward from Oxford in co-operation ; or *second*, to bring his entire force to Grenada, establish a depot there, repair the railroad back to Memphis, and then move rapidly against Jackson and the rear of Vicksburg. There were very grave objections to the first plan, because the enemy had a short interior line of railroad from Grenada to Vicksburg, enabling him to concentrate rapidly at either point, while the two parts of the Union army would be practically cut off from direct communication with each other, and if any accident should happen to delay either column co-operation between them would be impossible. Neither column would be in any danger of disaster, for Sherman could return to his transports and Grant could easily defend himself in retreat, if necessary, against Pemberton; but there were many chances against complete success. On the other hand, the direct movement by land would necessitate the repair of the railroad to Memphis, which would require considerable time; beyond Grenada, there would be no railroad, and the common roads were in a very bad condition for hauling. The advance would necessarily be very slow, and meanwhile the Confederates might be reinforced. By going down the Mississippi it was thought that much time might be saved, and that possibly Sherman might arrive on the Yazoo without the knowledge of the Confederates and surprise them before troops could be brought from Grenada.

After a full discussion of the matter Grant decided in favor of the first plan, and on December 8th, gave Sherman his orders to return to Memphis with one division, take command of all troops in Memphis and on the east of the Mississippi opposite Helena, organize them into brigades and divisions, and proceed down the river in co-operation with the gunboat fleet under Admiral Porter, to reduce Vicksburg in such manner as his judgment should dictate. These orders were reported the same day to Halleck, who telegraphed his approval, but added that "the President may insist upon designating a separate commander; if not,

assign such officers as you deem best. Sherman would be
my choice as the chief under you."

Sherman left College Hill the next morning, sending a
detachment of cavalry across the country to Helena to no-
tify General Steele of his part in the expedition, and taking
Morgan L. Smith's division with him to Memphis, where he
arrived December 12th. There he fitted out his expedition
and descended the river, as will be subsequently described.

It had been his intention to leave Memphis on the 18th,
but the transports did not arrive in time, and the embarkation took place on the 19th, and the expedition started on
the 20th. On the 18th, Halleck telegraphed to Grant that
the President directed that McClernand should command
the river expedition. Grant forwarded this order by telegraph the same day to McClernand at Springfield, and to
Sherman at Memphis. Both telegrams had to go by way of
Columbus, Ky., and as Forrest cut the line on the morning
of the 19th, neither reached its destination. Sherman thus
proceeded in accordance with the original programme, in
complete ignorance of McClernand's assignment; and he
had already arrived in the vicinity of Vicksburg before Mc-
Clernand left Illinois.

Meanwhile the Confederate authorities had become thoroughly alarmed for the safety of the Mississippi, and on November 24th General J. E. Johnston had been assigned to
the command of all Confederate troops between the Alleghanies and the Mississippi; the principal part of which
were in Bragg's and Pemberton's armies. He reached Chattanooga on December 4th, and had barely time to communicate with Bragg before Jefferson Davis arrived to give his
personal attention to affairs in Mississippi. After consultation with Bragg, Davis ordered Stevenson's division and
Vaughn's brigade of McCown's division—about 9,000 men

in all—to be detached from Bragg's army and sent to Pemberton's relief. He then started in person for Jackson and Vicksburg, requesting Johnston to accompany him. They arrived at Jackson on December 19th, the day that Sherman was embarking at Memphis. After visiting Vicksburg and Grenada, Davis returned to Richmond, leaving Johnston in general charge of all operations in the West. His position was anomalous and unsatisfactory, for the two armies of Bragg and Pemberton were so widely separated that they could not act in concert, and communication between them was so precarious and uncertain that it was impossible for one man to efficiently direct both. On the other hand, two commanders with either one of the armies were unnecessary. Johnston appreciated this and asked Davis to assign him to some other duty, but his request was refused.

Upon arriving at Chattanooga and learning the condition of Pemberton's army, Johnston had at once telegraphed to Bragg, asking him to send a force of cavalry from Tennessee to fall upon Grant's communications with Columbus. Bragg did not receive the despatch, but he had already made the dispositions requested, on the strength of information received direct from Pemberton. Brig.-Gen. N. B. Forrest was detailed for the duty with a force of about 2,500 cavalry. He left Columbia, Tenn., on December 11th; and on the same day Rosecrans, at Nashville, telegraphed Grant as follows: "Tell the authorities along the road to look out for Forrest." No point was indicated, but Grant at once instructed the commanding officers at Corinth and Jackson to be on their guard against a movement by Forrest. Forrest reached the Tennessee at Clifton, about fifty miles east of Jackson, on the 13th, crossed it on an old flat-boat—his animals swimming—on the 14th and 15th, and advanced toward Jackson; on the 16th he reached Lexington, where he met

a force of 700 cavalry and two guns under Col. Robert G.
Ingersoll, who had been sent from Jackson by General
Sullivan to reconnoitre.   (See map on page 35.)

This force was entirely routed, and nearly one-fourth of it,
including Col. Ingersoll, was captured. On the 19th, Forrest pushed on toward Jackson. Meanwhile, Brig.-Gen.
Sullivan, commanding the District of Jackson, had received
information, on the 15th, of Forrest's arrival at Clifton, and
on the 17th, of his having crossed the river and being in
motion toward Jackson. He communicated these facts to
Grant on the same days. Grant immediately telegraphed
to Sullivan to attack Forrest in front, and to Dodge, at
Corinth, to move out and attack him in flank; also to
Brig.-Gen. Lowe, at Fort Henry, to move south and prevent
any more Confederates from crossing. These orders were
repeated in vigorous terms on the 18th. Dodge moved
promptly with two brigades, leaving Corinth at midnight of
the 18th, and marching toward Jackson; but Sullivan's
troops were scattered, and he had been able to send out
only two regiments when Forrest arrived in the vicinity of
Jackson, and attacked them on the 19th. Forrest drove
this force back into Jackson, but not deeming it prudent to
attack that place, which was well fortified, he hastily withdrew during the night, and turning northward on the line of
the Mobile and Ohio Road, he attacked and captured in succession all the small posts, and destroyed the railroad as far
as the Kentucky line, where he rested on the 25th. Thence
he began to retrace his steps toward the southeast, along
the branch railroad running from Union City through
Dresden. (See map, *Frontispiece.*) Meanwhile, Sullivan
had been reinforced at Jackson by troops sent back by
Grant from Oxford, and had collected a force of about
4,000 men. He sent this force forward to Humboldt

and Trenton, and then, hearing that Forrest was at Dresden, marched across to Huntington to intercept his retreat. Forrest, however, passed around his rear, between Huntington and Humboldt, and would have escaped easily, but for delay in crossing his wagons through a muddy stream, where the bridges had been destroyed. As soon as this was passed he continued his march toward Lexington, and Sullivan pushed after him with all haste, moving south on the direct road from Huntington to Lexington. On December 31st, at a point known as Parker's Cross Roads, a few miles north of Lexington, the leading brigade of Sullivan's command, and Forrest's troops came in sight of each other on converging roads, and a fight was inevitable. This brigade numbered about 1,500 men, and Forrest was more than a match for it; he gradually drove it eastward and southward from the cross-roads, but the fighting lasted several hours, and during this time Sullivan was advancing with his other brigade, and, about 3 P.M., came upon Forrest's rear. Forrest was then obliged to extricate himself as best he could, and he succeeded in escaping with a loss of about 300 men, six guns, and several caissons and ammunition wagons. Continuing his retreat through Lexington that night and the following day, he was approaching Clifton, on the morning of January 1st, when he discovered a regiment of Union cavalry, sent by Dodge from Corinth, across the road. This was quickly driven off, and he reached the river bank at noon. Raising the same old flatboat which had served him two weeks before, but which had since sunk, he ferried his men and wagons over, and swam his animals, and by eight o'clock in the evening he was safe on the eastern bank of the Tennessee. An additional force of cavalry sent from Corinth did not reach Clifton until January 3d, and was then merely able to exchange shots across the river.

In this raid Forrest had destroyed the railroad from point to point throughout the distance of sixty miles from Jackson to Columbus; and with a loss of less than 400 men, he claims to have killed, wounded, and captured nearly 2,500 of his enemy. Grant's communications with Columbus and Washington were cut off from the 19th to the 30th of December, and the transportation of supplies was interrupted for a longer period.

While Forrest was thus striking against the upper part of Grant's communications, another move was made against that portion of them between Holly Springs and Grand Junction. Just prior to that time, viz., on December 13th, Grant had sent the greater part of his own cavalry on a raid against the Mobile and Ohio Road in the vicinity of Tupelo. They were engaged on this expedition, when, on the 19th, word was received that a considerable body of Confederate cavalry had left Grenada the day previous, and was moving northward past Grant's left flank, with the evident intention of striking his rear. Van Dorn had, in fact, taken personal command of all the cavalry in his army—about 3,500 men— and moved northward for this purpose. Grant immediately collected what cavalry he had left and sent them back as rapidly as possible to defend the railroad, and at the same time telegraphed to the commanding officers of Holly Springs, Grand Junction, and other points in rear, notifying them of the movement of the enemy's cavalry, and directing them to be prepared, and to defend their posts at all hazards. These orders were received and acknowledged on the afternoon of the 19th, yet, nevertheless, at daylight on the 20th, Col. Murphy, commanding at Holly Springs, was completely surprised by Van Dorn, and surrendered his whole command of 1,500 men almost without firing a shot. Van Dorn stopped for a day to burn up the supplies forming Grant's depot, estimated at $1,500,000 in value, and then pushed on northward to Davis's Mills, just south of Grand Junction, where he was beaten off on the 21st. He then advanced to Bolivar, where he was unsuccessful in a skirmish on the 24th, which induced him to retrace his steps. He attacked the little post of Middleburg, just south of Bolivar, where he was met by a most gallant defence, and was driven off. He then passed to the east of Grand Junction, and reached Ripley on the 25th. Grant had sent all his available cavalry in pursuit, under Col. Mizner, but the pursuit was feeble, and Van Dorn was not overtaken. Mizner gave up the chase beyond Ripley, and Van Dorn returned in safety to Grenada, passing again beyond Grant's left flank.

These two simultaneous raids of Forrest and Van Dorn had a most decisive effect upon the issue of the campaign. Van Dorn destroyed the depot of accumulated supplies, and Forrest destroyed the only road by which fresh supplies could be brought up. The country had been exhausted by the support of two armies subsisting on it in part for several months. There was no alternative for Grant but to fall back and open direct communications with Memphis. He immediately put his army on three-quarter rations, made preparations to gather up whatever food was still left in the country, and issued orders to fall back behind the Tallahatchie on December 21st. On the 23d Grant wrote from Holly Springs to "The Commanding Officer, Expedition down the Mississippi," saying that the Confederate raids had broken up his communications, that he had fallen back behind the Tallahatchie, and that any farther advance on his part was impracticable. He would therefore be unable to hold the enemy on the Yallabusha, except by a mere demonstration. This was six days before Sherman attacked at Chickasaw Bluffs, and, had the letter reached him, it would

doubtless have modified Sherman's operations. But it had
to go by courier to Memphis, and there await a boat going
down the river. McClernand arrived at Memphis before
any boat left, and the letter was delivered to him. Sherman, therefore, did not hear of its contents until communicated to him by McClernand on January 3d, several days
after his assault had been made. There was no communication of any kind between Grant and Sherman from the time
the latter left the vicinity of Oxford, on December 8th, until
the arrival of the steamer which brought McClernand.

During the last week in December, Grant gradually withdrew a portion of his troops from the Tallahatchie, sending
them to the vicinity of Grand Junction, with orders to re-
open and guard the railroad from Memphis to Corinth. He
remained in person at Holly Springs, and the greater part
of McPherson's command was posted in advance on the Tallahatchie. Telegraphic communication had meantime been
re-established with Washington, via Columbus, and on
January 8th Grant received a telegram from Halleck, dated
the night before, saying that Richmond papers had been
received, giving full accounts of Sherman's repulse at Chickasaw Bluffs, and urging him in the strongest language to
take all disposable force in Mississippi and West Tennessee,
and reinforce Sherman at once. Grant immediately gave
orders to abandon Holly Springs and move back to the
vicinity of Grand Junction. He then repaired to Memphis,
arriving there on January 10th, sent letters of inquiry to
McClernand and Porter, and telegraphed to St. Louis for
transportation to take 16,000 men to Vicksburg.

It is now necessary to follow the course of Sherman's movements down the Mississippi. He reached Memphis on his
return from Oxford, as already stated, on December 12th; and
immediately sent dispatches of Grant's and his own to Por-

ter, at Cairo, asking for the co-operation of his fleet, and to
the Chief Quartermaster at St. Louis, requiring transports
for 30,000 men to be at Memphis in time to start on the
18th.   It was short notice, but by the energy of Col. Robert
Allen and Capt. L. B. Parsons, sixty-seven boats arrived at
Memphis on the morning of the 19th, and the embarkation
began on the same day.   Porter's fleet had arrived the previous day.   Sherman had brought back with him the division of M. L. Smith, and at Memphis he found the new regiments sent forward by McClernand; these he organized
into two divisions, under A. J. Smith and G. W. Morgan.
The troops at Helena were organized into a fourth division
under Brig.-Gen. F. Steele.   The whole force amounted to 50
regiments and 10 batteries, and numbered in all about 32,000
men with 60 guns.   The expedition left Memphis on December 20th, stopped at Helena on the 21st to pick up
Steele's division, resumed its journey on the 22d, and reached
Milliken's Bend, twenty miles above Vicksburg, before daylight on the 25th.   Here A. J. Smith's division was landed
on the Louisiana shore, to advance against and break up the
railroad coming into Vicksburg from the west, over which
great quantities of supplies were transported to the Confederates.   On the 26th, the remaining three divisions continued on to the mouth of the Yazoo River, and moved up that
river thirteen miles, where they disembarked on the bottom
lands between the Yazoo River and the Walnut Hills.   A. J.
Smith's division rejoined them the next day.

These hills are simply a portion of the great bluff bound-
ing the valley of the Mississippi River on the east.   The
waters of the Mississippi run sharp against this bluff at
Vicksburg, but just above that city the river and bluff
diverge, the latter trending off to the northeast, and not
being met again by the Mississippi short of Memphis, a dis-

tance of over two hundred miles in a straight line. The
space between the river and the bluff, which is sixty miles
wide at its widest part, is low bottom land filled with innum-
erable creeks and bayous and lakes marking former beds of
the river. All of these waters are drained southeastwardly
into the Yazoo River, which runs along the base of the
bluff for over one hundred miles, and is formed at its head
by the Yallabusha and Tallahatchie Rivers, draining the
high land north and east of Grenada.

It was Sherman's intention to descend the Mississippi
as rapidly as possible, and, while Grant held the bulk of
Pemberton's force on the Yallabusha, near Grenada, to
surprise, if possible, the Confederates at Vicksburg, and
gain possession of a point of the Walnut Hills, near
Haines' bluff, twelve miles northeast of Vicksburg, from
which his force could be supplied by the Mississippi
and Yazoo Rivers. Then, if he was strong enough, he
would take Vicksburg himself; if not, he hoped to cut
the railroad between Vicksburg and Jackson, and then
defend himself on the banks of the Yazoo until Grant's
force, pushing Pemberton south from Grenada, could join
him. The whole plan was based on the idea of a surprise
on Sherman's part, and a co-operation between the two
armies. It entirely miscarried. The co-operation of Grant's
force was rendered impossible, as we have seen, by the destruction of his supplies and communications by Van Dorn
and Forrest; and the anticipation of a surprise was not realized. The Confederates not only had spies in Memphis,
and in every plantation along the river bank, but they had
small detachments of cavalry, partisans, and guerillas concealed along the river. Sherman's progress was reported by
them with great accuracy twice a day from the hour of leaving Memphis. These reports reached Pemberton on De-

cember 23d and 24th from so many different sources as to
leave no doubt of their accuracy. The whole plan was
thus revealed to Johnston and Pemberton, who immediately
took steps to frustrate it.

On the 23d, Vaughn's brigade was ordered from Grenada
to Vicksburg, followed on the 25th by one brigade, and
on the 26th by the other brigade of Maury's division.
These movements were quickly made by rail. On the 26th
word was received that Sherman's troops were landing up
the Yazoo, and Pemberton immediately went in person to
Vicksburg, ordering Price's corps, at Grenada, and Stevenson's division, lately arrived at Jackson from Chattanooga,
to follow him. Instead, then, of having to contend with
the 6,000 men forming the garrison of Vicksburg, Sherman had not less than 12,000 men in front of him in fortified positions along the bluff. The bluff was fully two
hundred feet high, and had an unbroken view of the
whole bottom land as far as the Yazoo. A thousand men
posted in trenches on this bluff ought easily to keep
off, and slaughter ten thousand moving to attack, and the
enterprise was doomed to failure. Sherman, however,
knew nothing of the arrival of Confederate reinforcements,
and having proceeded thus far, it was out of the question for him to withdraw without making a vigorous assault.

Sherman landed his troops at Johnson's plantation, opposite the mouth of Steele's bayou, on December 26th. The
triangular space between Vicksburg, Haines' Bluff, and
Johnson's plantation is bounded by the Yazoo River on one
side, and the Walnut Hills on the other. It is low, alluvial land, overflowed in the highest stages of the river,
and filled at all times with a number of bayous and swamps.
In the whole twelve miles between Haines' Bluff and Vicks-

burg there were but five points where it was practicable
to pass from the Yazoo through the network of bayous to

Chickasaw Bluffs. December 29, 1862.

the bluffs. All of these points were commanded by Confederate batteries. At the point where Sherman landed he
had Chickasaw Bayou on his left and a former bed of the

Yazoo, commonly known as "the Lake," in his front. Still
farther to his left was another stagnant bayou called Thompson's Lake. Chickasaw Bayou, Thompson's Lake, and "the
Lake" all unite at a point about two miles from the Yazoo
and half a mile from the bluffs, and at this point a small
brook running out from the hills empties into them.

In landing, Steele's division formed the extreme left, on
the left of Chickasaw Bayou, Morgan's division came next
on the right of that bayou, M. L. Smith's division next, and
A. J. Smith's on the right, following the road leading from
Johnson's plantation direct to Vicksburg. These positions
were taken on the 27th, and during that day the four columns moved forward skirmishing slightly with the enemy.
On the 28th a general advance was made, in the nature of
a reconnoissance, as far as the lake in front of the bluff; in
this reconnoissance M. L. Smith was seriously wounded
in the hip and obliged to leave the field, a loss greatly
regretted by Sherman in his report. On the left, Steele
found his way blocked by Thompson's Lake, which could
only be crossed on a narrow corduroy causeway, completely
enfiladed by one of the enemy's batteries, which would mow
down the narrow head of column as fast as the men could
show themselves; he was therefore ordered to return to
the Yazoo River, cross back in the transports to the other
side of Chickasaw Bayou, and come up in support of Morgan's division; this he did during the afternoon and night
of the 28th. In the centre, Morgan, who had the only pontoon train in the command, laid it across a small bayou sup-
posing it to be the old lake near the bluff; on reaching the
latter he found that there was a natural crossing over it.
On the right A. J. Smith advanced along the main road on a
line with the other columns. There was considerable skirmishing throughout the day with the advanced pickets of

the Confederates, but the losses were slight, the Confederates retiring to the bluff. The troops passed the night of the 28th in position along the lake parallel to the bluff and about five hundred yards from it. The next morning (29th) further reconnoissances were made and orders were then given for the assault. The main attack was to be made against the centre of the enemy's line by Morgan's division, supported by Steele's; A. J. Smith, with the division of M. L. Smith and one brigade of his own, was to cross a narrow sand bar across the lake about a mile below the point of Morgan's attack, and then advance against the levee, on the other side of which the Confederates were strongly intrenched; this attack was to be a demonstration in the nature of a diversion in favor of Morgan, or a real attack, according to the amount of success achieved. On the extreme right the rest of A. J. Smith's division was to make a demonstration on the road to Vicksburg.

At twelve o'clock the signal for the assault was given and immediately De Courcy's brigade of Morgan's division crossed the lake and advanced through a terrible fire over the half mile of gently sloping ground in the nature of a glacis, which led up to the Confederate works on the bluff. On his left, Blair's brigade of Steele's division crossed the lake near its junction with Chickasaw Bayou, and made a similar advance through an equally hot fire. These two brigades reached the enemy's works, but they were entirely unsupported; Thayer's brigade of Steele's division took a wrong direction and only one regiment was brought into action; Lindsey's brigade attempted to build a bridge across the lake on De Courcy's right, but did not succeed and did not cross the lake at all; Sheldon's brigade of the same division was not brought into action further than to come up in rear of Lindsey where it lost a dozen men by stray shots.

The attack of M. L. Smith's division was not successful; one
regiment in the lead, the Sixth Missouri, crossed the sand-
bar but found that the only way to climb the levee was by a
narrow path barely wide enough for two men abreast; the
Confederates were almost over their heads, and but forty feet
from them, and it was impossible to advance against their
fire on this narrow path; this regiment therefore sheltered
itself by digging out part of the bank of the levee with their
hands and remained there until darkness enabled them to
retreat. The whole brunt of the assault was made by the
two brigades of De Courcy and Blair, and one regiment
(Fourth Iowa) of Thayer's brigade, numbering not more
than 6,000 men in all; they advanced with the utmost gallantry right up to the Confederate works, but arrived there
they looked around and saw that nothing was coming to
their support. The other two brigades of Morgan's division did practically nothing to assist them. Cut to pieces
by front and cross fire, De Courcy's and Blair's men were
finally forced to yield, and between 3 and 4 P.M. they fell
back and recrossed the levee. De Courcy's brigade lost
about 700, Blair's 743, and the Fourth Iowa 111 men; the
losses in the rest of the force amounted to less than 400,
the exact total being 1,929, viz.: 191 killed, 982 wounded,
and 756 missing. The batteries against which the attack
was made were defended by only six regiments of S. D.
Lee's brigade, which formed a part of the original garrison
of Vicksburg under Martin L. Smith. Their loss was less
than 100 men, and the entire losses of the Confederates during the skirmishing of the 27th and 28th and the assault of
the 29th was only 57 killed, 120 wounded, and 10 missing;
total 187.

Sherman's troops remained in their positions close to the
lake during the night of the 29th. He at first thought of

renewing the assault in the morning, but concluded that the
position was too strong, especially as the enemy would now
concentrate all his force upon the point where the attack
had been made.   He therefore determined to hold his present ground, but send 10,000 men to try an assault higher
up the river at Haines' Bluff.   Porter agreed to escort the
transports and cover the landing, and the movement was
fixed for the night of December 31st.   The troops were
selected and embarked during the night, and Sherman
then returned to his original position, intending to engage
the enemy there as soon as cannonading should be heard
above.   At daylight, however, he received word that the fog
was so dense that the boats could not move, and the affair
must be postponed until the next night.   During the day
he received further word from Porter that, on the next
night, the moon would not set until 5.25 A.M., so that the
landing could not be made in darkness.   Porter considered
the affair too hazardous under these circumstances, and it
was therefore abandoned.

The position in which Sherman's troops were now situated
was extremely disagreeable and dangerous; they were bivouacked in the low, marshy, bottom land, where a slight
rise in the river any night might swamp and drown the
whole command; the water-marks on the trees ten feet
above the ground had an ominous look, and all were of
opinion that any further assaults were impracticable.   Sherman therefore determined to re-embark his men, and return
to the mouth of the Yazoo River, which was done without
opposition from the enemy on January 2d.   Here he met
McClernand, who had reached Memphis on December 28th,
left on the 30th, and arrived at Milliken's Bend on January 1st.   He exhibited his orders placing him in command of the river expedition, and Sherman immediately re-

linquished the command, and, in his own words, "subsided quietly into the more agreeable office of a corps commander," with the intention to "endeavor to make it a good one."

The project of a combined movement on Vicksburg, partly by land and partly by the river, thus ended in complete failure. The failure was due to the destruction of Grant's supplies through the cowardice or incapacity of the officer in command at Holly Springs, and to the formidable character of the Confederate position for defence, both of which were contingencies which could not have been foreseen. Yet it cannot be forgotten that the Mississippi was opened from Cairo to Memphis in the most brilliant and successful manner by the campaign from Fort Henry to Corinth, conducted in rear of the river by a united army; that all attempts against Vicksburg by the river failed, and, after months of unsuccessful efforts through creeks and bayous, it was finally taken by a campaign against its rear, starting from the south of Vicksburg. It is therefore a question for discussion whether it would not have been better to have established a base at Memphis, repaired the railroad south of that point, and advanced with every available man united in a single force, along the Mississippi Central Railroad, for the purpose of bringing Pemberton to battle and crushing him. If he declined battle, he must either have retreated on Mobile, leaving Vicksburg free, or else have retreated into Vicksburg, whence he could have been followed as far as Haines' Bluff, and a base established there, as was done in the spring of 1863. The risks of such a movement were far less than in the final campaign from Bruinsburg through Jackson to Haines' Bluff. It will be remembered that a direct movement from Memphis against the rear of Vicksburg was the one suggested by Grant in his letter to Halleck, of Oc-

4*

tober 26th, before he had any intimation of the plans of Halleck or the President. Grant, however, had only a limited discretion in the matter, and the responsibility for the movements in December, 1862, whether wise or unwise, must rest with the authorities in Washington. While Grant approved, and even urged, the movement down the river, yet all other movements were rendered impossible by his orders.

There is one other feature which must be stated in order to complete the discussion of this first movement against Vicksburg, and that is the co-operation expected from New Orleans. No allusion has hitherto been made to it, because there was no such co-operation, but it was fully intended that there shonld be, and in nearly all of Halleck's telegrams to Grant in November and December, 1862, reference was made to the co-operation of General Banks. That officer had been directed to supersede Butler in command of the Department of the Gulf by orders issued on November 9, 1862 ; and his instructions laid special stress on the importance of moving up at once to open the Mississippi. Owing, however, to the delay in collecting the reinforcements which were to accompany him, Banks did not sail from New York till December 4th, nor reach New Orleans till December 14th. A large part of his force was immediately sent up the river, without disembarking at New Orleans, to Baton Rouge, of which they took possession without resistance. But they did not feel strong enough to advance against Port Hudson until three months later. The troops on the lower Mississippi had, therefore, no influence upon the movements of December, 1862, against Vicksburg.

The question of what was now to be done with the troops forming the river expedition cannot be more clearly stated than in the following words, taken from a letter written to

Halleck by Sherman, dated "On board Forest Queen, January 5, 1863 : "

"I reached Vicksburg at the time appointed, landed, assaulted, and failed. Re-embarked my command unopposed and turned it over to my successor, General McClernand. At first I proposed to remain near Vicksburg to await the approach of General Grant or General Banks to co-operate, but as General McClernand had brought intelligence, the first that had reached me, that General Grant had fallen back of the Tallahatchie, and as we could hear not a word of General Banks below, instead of remaining idle I proposed we should move our entire force in concert with the gunboats to the Arkansas, which is now in boating condition, and reduce the Post of Arkansas, where seven thousand of the enemy are intrenched and threaten this river. One boat, the Blue Wing, towing coal barges for the navy and carrying dispatches, has been captured by the enemy, and with that enemy on our rear and flank our communications would at all times be endangered. General McClernand agreed, and Admiral Porter also cheerfully assented, and we are at this moment *en route* for the Post of Arkansas, fifty miles up the Arkansas River."

McClernand had assumed formal command on January 4th, styling his troops the "Army of the Mississippi" and dividing them into two corps, the first under Morgan consisting of Morgan's and A. J. Smith's divisions, and the second under Sherman, consisting of Steele's and Stuart's (formerly M. L. Smith's) divisions. The entire force left Milliken's Bend on the 5th, and proceeded up the Mississippi to the mouth of White River, arriving there on the 8th ; ascending that stream a few miles they passed through a cut-off into the Arkansas, and on the evening of the 9th, they came in sight of the Arkansas Post, called by the Confederates Fort Hindman.

A portion of the Mississippi squadron accompanied the transports as an escort. During the six months which had elapsed since it left Vicksburg in July, 1862, this squadron had been largely augmented, and it now numbered 11 iron-clads, 38 unarmored gunboats, 6 rams, and 15 tugs and des-patch boats, in all 70 vessels with a capacity of 16,905 tons, a force of 5,500 men, and an armament of 304 guns.

Porter had with him on this expedition the following de-tachment from his squadron, viz. :

DeKalb (formerly St. Louis), Lieutenant-Commander Walker.	13 guns.
Cincinnati, Lieutenant Bache	13 "
Louisville, Lieutenant-Commander Owen	13 "
Monarch, Colonel A. W. Ellet	Ram.
Black Hawk, Lieutenant-Commander Breese	8 guns.
Lexington, Lieutenant-Commander Shirk	7 "
Rattler, Lieutenant-Commander Smith	6 "
Glide, Lieutenant Woodworth	6 "
	66 guns.

Fort Hindman was a four-sided bastioned work, about one hundred yards on a side, built on a bluff about twenty-five feet above the river level, at a bend of the river where it had an unobstructed view for over a mile in either direction ; it was supplemented by a line of trench running from one angle of the fort in a direction perpendicular to the river for about a mile, where it terminated in an impassable bayou. About a mile and a half lower down the river were some other trenches built on the levee. The entire armament consisted of two 9-inch columbiads, one 8-inch columbiad, and 14 field guns ; the garrison numbered about 5,000 men under command of Brig.-Gen. T. J. Churchill.

McClernand's expedition proceeded up the Arkansas on January 9th, the gunboats in the lead, followed by Sher-man's corps, and then Morgan's, in transports. Late in the afternoon they halted about three miles below the fort, and began landing during the night. At noon of the 10th, Sher-

man's corps began the march, Steele's division in the lead.
This division took a wrong direction, owing to ignorance of
the roads, and was recalled during the afternoon, but did not
rejoin its corps until the next morning.   The other division,
under Stuart, moved along the river bank, and found the
outer defences on the levee abandoned, they being completely

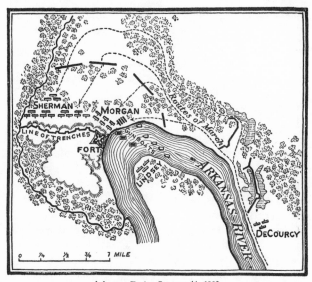

Arkansas Post.   January 11, 1863.

enfiladed by the fire of the gunboats.   Continuing its march,
and arriving in the vicinity of the fort, Stuart's division
left the river, and moved off to the right.   Morgan's corps,
which was following, came in on its left next to the river
bank.   During the night, Sherman's corps took position
about one thousand yards in front of the trenches, with
his right resting on the bayou ; Morgan, with three bri-

gades, being on his left, and extending to the river. One brigade (De Courcy's) of Morgan's corps was left in reserve to
guard the transports at the point of landing, and another
(Lindsay's), with four guns, had been landed on the other
bank on the river, marched across the neck of the bend, and
taken position above the fort, so as to cut off all retreat up
the river, and prevent the arrival of reinforcements from that
direction. During the evening, the gunboats moved up
toward the fort, and opened a vigorous fire, which did great
damage. Their superiority in artillery was so great that
the Confederates were entirely unable to answer the fire.
The troops passed the night in the position above mentioned.

On the morning of the 11th further reconnoissances were
made of the ground in front of the enemy's trenches, and
the troops were slightly moved so as to take the most advantageous places for the assault. About noon, McClernand
sent word to Porter that everything was ready, and asked
him to begin the bombardment of the fort, as previously
arranged. The gunboats then moved up the river to within
a few hundred yards of the fort, and, at 1 P.M., opened
fire with their 66 pieces. The artillery of the fort was
soon silenced, the larger guns being all destroyed, and the
bombproofs being knocked to pieces. As soon as the sound
of the navy guns was heard, the field artillery, numbering
about 45 pieces, which was disposed in the intervals of
Sherman's and Morgan's line, immediately opened fire, and
kept it up for the space of about half an hour. The artillery then ceased, and the infantry rushed forward to the
assault along the whole line. They had a distance of about
four hundred yards to cross in order to reach the trenches,
part of it open and part cut up by gullies and depres-
sions, which afforded a certain amount of shelter. Their

progress was at first rapid, but they soon encountered a
withering fire from behind the intrenchments, which stag-
gered and sobered them, and retarded their progress.   About
3 P.M., Sherman sent word to Morgan that his left was very
heavily pressed, and Morgan directed A. J. Smith to send
three regiments to Sherman's assistance, and sent back word
for De Courcy's brigade to come up and join him.   The
firing, meantime, was kept up without any relaxation, and
the Union troops gradually worked their way forward until
they were within less than one hundred yards of the intrenchments, and were preparing for a final assault, when
the cry ran along the Confederate line, "Raise the white
flag, by order of General Churchill.   Pass the order up the
line."   Churchill and his brigade commanders all deny having given any authority for such an order, and the origin of
it cannot be traced.   But the flags appeared at several
places at the same moment, and both Sherman and Morgan
gave orders to cease firing, and sent aides-de-camp into the
work.   At the same time they moved their troops close up to
the parapet in order to be prepared for any emergency, and
Sherman directed Steele to move along the bayou around the
left of the enemy's line, and prevent any escape in that direction.   Sherman now entered the trenches in his front, and
Morgan rode into the fort, and both demanded a surrender.
An awkward moment ensued, as one of the brigade commanders opposed to Sherman refused to surrender, claiming
that the white flag had been raised without authority.   A
single shot might have produced great loss of life, but, fortunately, before any accident happened, General Churchill
arrived, and told this officer there was nothing to do but
surrender, and he sullenly ordered his men to stack arms.
Churchill himself surrendered the fort to McClernand about
4.30 P.M.

The Confederates lost about 200 men in killed and wounded, and the number of their prisoners counted and sent North on the following day was 4,791. The Union loss was, 129 killed, 831 wounded, and 17 missing; total, 977, exclusive of 31 killed and wounded on the gunboats. Their trophies were the fort and everything in it, including 17 pieces of artillery, large and small, and a very considerable amount of ammunition and subsistence stores.

McClernand remained at Arkansas Post for the next three days, occupied in gathering up captured property, sending off prisoners, and destroying the fortifications. During this time he was in some doubt as to his future movements. On the 14th he had consultations with Porter and Sherman, and addressed letters to them stating his fixed intention to ascend the Arkansas to Little Rock, and thence march against a force stationed at Brownsville, about midway between the Arkansas and White Rivers. He was also in correspondence with the commanding officer at Helena for the purpose of securing his co-operation in a movement to the interior of Arkansas, the two expeditions to act as a diversion for the Union troops operating in Missouri. But McClernand hesitated to ascend the Arkansas with his transports, as the river was falling and he might not be able to return. In the midst of his doubts a peremptory order from Grant arrived on the evening of the 14th, directing him to return forthwith to the Mississippi. It appears that on January 8th, while entering the White River on his way to Arkansas Post, McClernand had written to Grant stating his movements and the reasons for them. Besides giving the perfectly valid reason that the Post of Arkansas was a constant menace to the navigation of the Mississippi he hinted vaguely at the possibility of co-operating with Curtis's force in Arkansas and creating a diversion for the troops in Missouri. Grant

received this on the 11th; he at once feared that McClernand might become involved in a campaign in Arkansas
which it might require weeks to complete, and meanwhile
his troops would be detached from the all-important object
of capturing Vicksburg.   He therefore wrote on the 11th to
McClernand, disapproving of his project, which might answer for some of the purposes suggested but would have no
bearing on Vicksburg, and directed him to return at once to
the Mississippi unless he was acting under orders from superior authority.   At the same time he telegraphed Halleck
that "McClernand has gone on a wild-goose chase to the
Post of Arkansas," to which Halleck replied on the following day, "You are hereby authorized to relieve General
McClernand from command of the expedition against Vicksburg, giving it to the next in rank or taking it yourself."
On the 13th Grant received a report from McClernand announcing the capture of Arkansas Post, to which Grant replied directing him to return to Milliken's Bend unless he
had some object not visible from a distance.   McClernand
received this on the 15th, and thereupon issued orders to return.   Sherman embarked on the 16th and Morgan on the
17th, and all united at Napoleon, at the mouth of the Arkansas, on the 17th.   Here they were joined by General
Grant, who had come down from Memphis to gain a personal
knowledge of the course of affairs.   After remaining two days
he returned to Memphis to complete his preparations for reinforcing McClernand, and the latter descended the river to
Milliken's Bend.

   Before leaving Arkansas Post on the 16th, McClernand addressed a private letter to the President, enclosing his correspondence with Grant, complaining in bitter language
that "my success here is gall and wormwood to the clique
of West Pointers who have been persecuting me for months,"

and urging that his army "should be made an independent command, as both you and the Secretary of War, as I believe, originally intended." It is doubtless an ungracious act to disapprove a man's projects at the very moment of success; nor can there be any doubt that the utilization of McClernand's force by a prompt move on Arkansas Post and an immediate return was a judicious project, and it was well executed. But the correspondence of January 14th, above quoted, shows conclusively that Grant's perceptions were perfectly correct, and that McClernand did not intend to stop at Arkansas Post but to initiate an independent campaign in Arkansas by going to Little Rock and beyond; which would have been indeed a "wild-goose chase," leading to various complications and deranging all plans against Vicksburg by the abstraction of 30,000 men. It was fortunate that such a scheme was nipped in the bud.

CHAPTER IV.

THE course of events, as narrated in the last chapter, no less than his instructions from Washington, now compelled Grant to direct his operations against Vicksburg by the river route, and to reduce everything east of Memphis to the defensive. He determined to take command of the river expedition in person, as authorized by Halleck, and to reinforce it with all available troops, as directed by the latter's telegram of January 7th. Orders of the War Department, dated December 18, 1862, had directed the troops in General Grant's command to be organized into four army corps, to be known as the 13th, 15th, 16th, and 17th, and to be commanded respectively by Major-Generals McClernand, Sherman, Hurlbut, and McPherson. This organization was now effected. McClernand's and Sherman's corps were already down the river. McPherson's corps was formed of the divisions of McArthur, Logan, and Quinby, the first of which was sent forthwith down the river, the other two being directed to march to Memphis and hold themselves in readiness to embark on transports whenever ordered. The remaining troops on the line of the Memphis and Charleston Railroad, and in rear of it as far back as Columbus, composed Hurlbut's corps. They were to remain in observation and defend the points where they were stationed. The troops in Helena and at other points in

Arkansas were also placed under Grant's orders, and were
assigned to McClernand's corps. A brigade under Ewing,
just arrived from the north, was sent forward to Sherman.

McClernand's and Sherman's corps meantime moved from
the mouth of the Arkansas to Young's Point, opposite Vicksburg, with instructions to cut a canal across the peninsula.
Grant had visited these troops at Napoleon on January 17th,
and then returned to Memphis to hasten the movements of
McPherson's corps, and to give orders for the guidance of
the troops along the Memphis and Charleston Railroad.
From Memphis on January 20th he reported to Halleck concerning the condition of affairs in his department and his
plans for the future. From his conversation at Napoleon
with Porter, McClernand, and Sherman, he had formed the
opinion that the work of reducing Vicksburg was one of time
and would require a large force in the final struggle. His
first inclination would have been to strike across the low
lands of the Yazoo Delta from Milliken's Bend, and come to
the Yazoo above Haines's Bluffs, thus turning the right flank
of the Confederate position ; but this plan was out of the
question at the present time, for the low lands in the Delta
were all under water. He therefore considered it necessary
to get below the city in order to use his troops effectively,
and as the best means of accomplishing this he proposed to
cut a canal across the peninsula opposite Vicksburg, but instead of following the line of Williams's canal, he intended to
start the head of it higher up stream at a point where the
current impinged with more velocity, and to have the lower
end of it debouch below the bluffs at Vicksburg, so that the
canal should not be enfiladed by the batteries. By the aid
of this canal he expected to go past Vicksburg and land on
the east bank of the Mississippi.

All this was written by Grant before he had ever been at

Vicksburg. The canal scheme seemed feasible from what he had heard, and the authorities in Washington approved highly of it. Halleck telegraphed back to pay particular attention to the canal, for the President attached much importance to it. Grant's views of the value of the canal, however, changed very quickly after his arrival on the ground.

In this same report of January 20th he announced his intention to command in person the troops on the river, unless otherwise directed. After remaining a week longer at Memphis, and receiving no orders to the contrary, he left for Vicksburg and arrived there on the 29th, assuming command on the 30th. McClernand protested vigorously against this, but Grant had ample warrant for his action and merely forwarded his protest to Washington, whence nothing more was heard of it. On his arrival at Young's Point, Grant found the 15th Corps stretched across the peninsula, working hard at the canal, and its right flank resting on the river below Vicksburg; the 13th Corps and one division of the 17th were on the left of the 15th. Porter was present with a fleet of gun-boats. Upon examining the line of the canal Grant " lost all faith in its ever leading to any practical results." It was on the same line that had been previously excavated, except that its upper end had been slightly deflected in the hope of catching the current. It was " at right angles with the thread of the current at both ends, and both ends were in an eddy, the lower one coming out on the bluffs completely commanding it. Warrenton, a few miles below, was capable of as strong defence as Vicksburg," and the enemy had turned his attention to that point. He therefore ordered other routes to be prospected, although the troops were still kept employed on the canal, as it was not yet considered advisable to abandon it entirely. The

other routes were,[1] first by way of Yazoo Pass (nearly opposite Helena) into the Coldwater, Tallahatchie, and Yazoo
Rivers, so as to get at the enemy's rear beyond his right
flank at Haines' Bluff; and second by way of Lake Providence, on the Louisiana shore sixty miles above Vicksburg,
into Bayou Macon, the Tensas, Washita, Red, and Mississippi
Rivers, by which the enemy's rear might be reached beyond
his left flank at Warrenton.

It will be seen that Grant's army was in the low bottom
lands of the Mississippi, the roads of which were submerged
in places to such an extent as to prevent all movements over
them. Vicksburg, in his front, was unassailable, and the
problem was to turn its flanks by means of canals, creeks,
and bayous. By the Vicksburg Canal and the Lake Providence route it was intended to turn the enemy's left flank;
by the Yazoo Pass route and a route subsequently attempted
through Steele's Bayou it was intended to turn his right
flank. The efforts of the army throughout the months of
February and March were directed with unremitting and as-
siduous labor to these flanking projects. They will be described in turn.

The work on the canal was prosecuted, mainly by Sherman's corps, from January 22d to March 7th. Dredge-boats
were brought to assist the labors of the troops, and it was
planned to excavate a canal sixty feet wide and nine feet
deep. The excavation was nearly completed when, on
March 7th, the river rose suddenly, broke down the barrier
at the upper end, and flooded the whole peninsula, driving
the troops on to the levee to escape drowning. The direction of the canal was such, however, that this body of water
simply flooded its banks, but produced no scour through

---

[1] See map on page 57.

it. After this, work was continued for about two weeks by the dredge-boats, but the Warrenton batteries soon got the range of the latter so accurately, that they were driven off, and work on the canal was then abandoned. The canal scheme was a failure.

It is a most singular fact that the project upon which such a vast amount of labor was unavailingly expended in the midst of the war, has since been substantially accomplished by nature, at a time when it was not desired, and in a manner which has caused great disaster, and threatens absolute destruction to the town of Vicksburg. " Grant's Canal" can still be traced in the low ground opposite Vicksburg, in a narrow ditch, with two or three feet of stagnant water; while the Mississippi flows through the peninsula, just south of the former railway terminus called De Soto, in a channel a mile wide, and at times one hundred feet deep, leaving Vicksburg confronted at low water by a bar of mud, completely cutting off all access to the river. For several years after the war, the current gradually cut away the shore of the peninsula near De Soto, until it was finally less than one hundred yards in width on either side of the railroad embankment. On the afternoon of April 27, 1876, this embankment gave way, and the water broke through the peninsula; the next morning a steamboat passed through the break, and the next year the break was the main channel. The result has indicated the point " where the current impinged most strongly," and where the canal should have been located to insure success; but it was a point where the Confederate batteries had such complete control in 1863 that no working party could have lived under them for a moment, nor could any transport have passed through had the canal been completed.

The Lake Providence project seemed at first to be more

promising. It would have been a long and tedious route, had it ever been used, as the distance from Lake Providence to the mouth of Red River is over 200 miles, and from there back to Vicksburg by the Mississippi, 150 miles more ; but it might have been useful in sending reinforcements to Banks, had such a movement proved feasible or advisable. With the navigation of the Red, Washita, and Tensas Rivers there was no difficulty, nor did Bayou Macon offer any serious obstacle to the passage of boats. But between Bayou Macon and Lake Providence—a distance of about six miles —the only connection was by a small stream known as Bayou Baxter, which, about midway of its course, spread out into a broad cypress swamp in which the stream was lost. The operations necessary to make this route navigable were to clear a channel through this swamp, to dig up the stumps of trees with which it was filled, and to cut a hole in the levee opposite Lake Providence.

Upon his arrival at Young's Point, Grant had immediately sent an officer to reconnoitre this route, a brigade of McArthur's division of McPherson's corps accompanying him. His report being favorable to the success of the undertaking, Grant went to Lake Providence in person on February 5th, and from there sent orders to McPherson at Memphis to bring his entire corps to the same point and prosecute this work vigorously. Lack of transports, however, delayed McPherson for nearly three weeks, and on his arrival he found the work of clearing a channel through the swamp much more serious than had been anticipated, the cutting of stumps below the surface of the water being very difficult in the absence of proper tools. McPherson continued to work at it throughout the month of March. The levee was cut on March 18th, and the water rushed through Bayou Baxter, giving a very good channel with two exceptions, viz.: there

were twelve or fifteen stumps under water which could only
be cut by a sawing machine, and there was a shoal at the
point where Bayou Baxter entered Bayou Macon, which
could be removed in a few days by dredging.   With these
obstacles removed the route would be navigable for boats
having a draught of six feet.   McPherson so reported at the
end of March, but by this time Grant had formed plans for
moving south from Milliken's Bend by land.   The Lake
Providence scheme was thus of no avail.

The Yazoo Pass project was the most favorable of all, and
for a time gave promise of definite results.   Nearly opposite
Helena the distance from the Mississippi to the Coldwater
is only ten miles in a straight line, and along this line runs
a winding bayou called the Yazoo Pass.   The Coldwater,
Tallahatchie, and Yazoo Rivers are all navigable for light-
draught boats, and through this Pass in former times was
the direct route from Memphis to Yazoo City.   The bottom
lands being, however, lower than the surface of the Mississippi in high water, some years prior to the war a substan-
tial levee, nearly 100 feet thick and 18 feet high, had
been built across the Yazoo Pass in order to reclaim the
overflowed land.   This destroyed the use of this Pass as
a navigable route; it was now desired to restore it, and
the problem was simply to cut the levee and allow the
water to resume its former course.   Col. Wilson of Grant's
staff had been sent from Young's Point on February 1st to
cut the levee, and Gen. Gorman, commanding at Helena,
was instructed to lend him any assistance required.   The
levee was cut by exploding a mine in it on February 3d, and
the water immediately rushed through in a torrent.

On the 7th the current had so far subsided that a gunboat was able to enter the Pass, when it was discovered that
although the channel was deep enough it was greatly ob-
VIII.—5

structed by overhanging trees, large numbers of which had
been felled by the Confederates within the last few days.
The Pass as well as the Coldwater ran through a dense forest, and it required but a few minutes' labor to cut down
trees, forming obstructions which could not be removed in
several days. Additional troops were at once brought over
from Helena and set to work removing these obstructions,
but it was not until the 21st that they were sufficiently
removed to allow vessels to reach the Coldwater. Meanwhile, on receiving favorable reports from Col. Wilson, Grant
had issued orders on February 15th, to the commanding
officer at Helena to send Ross' division through the Pass
into the Coldwater, Tallahatchie, and Yazoo Rivers, to test
its availability for the movement of a large body, and to
destroy the railroad bridges on the Yallabusha at Grenada. Porter had sent four light-draught gunboats, two
iron-clads, and one ram to accompany the troops, protect
the transports, and destroy any Confederate boats on the
rivers. For lack of proper boats Ross did not leave Helena
until the 23d. It required six days for his men to force
their way through the Pass, but they entered the Coldwater,
with boats more or less damaged, on March 2d. By this
time Grant had received a further report from Wilson,
dated February 24th, announcing the Pass as open, and
navigable for vessels under 180 feet in length and of pro-
portionate beam. Grant thereupon determined to attempt
to utilize this route for a large force, possibly his entire
army, in order to effect a landing above Haines' Bluff;
and on March 5th he sent orders to McPherson, who was
nearest to the Pass, to move his whole corps in that direction as soon as transports could be obtained. Quinby's division, just arrived at Lake Providence from Memphis but
not yet disembarked, was to return at once to Yazoo Pass;

the large transports were then to be sent back to bring
Logan's division and subsequently McArthur's; and J. E.
Smith's division, then ready to embark at Memphis, was to
be stopped at Yazoo Pass. This would give McPherson five
divisions, or about 30,000 men, with which he was to make
his way down the Yazoo and effect a lodgment at Yazoo
City. Simultaneously a cavalry division was to move east
from Helena, and another, from Hurlbut's command, south
from La Grange, to break up the enemy's communications
east and south of Grenada.

While these preparations had been making by the Union
army and navy, the Confederates had been by no means idle.
Their pickets and spies along the river gave them prompt
and accurate information of each departure of troops from
Memphis, and of the movements of transports from point to
point. When McClernand returned to Young's Point, on
January 22d, they feared an attack upon Warrenton, and
made preparations to meet it. But they were equally vigi-
lant in regard to the Yazoo. As early as January 23d, troops
were sent from Grenada to obstruct the Yazoo Pass; this
was a week before Grant had even thought of this route.
At Haines' Bluff, a raft, which had already been constructed, was considerably enlarged and strengthened; detachments were also sent to cut the levees above Young's
Point, and flood the country where McClernand's troops
were bivouacked. Nothing was left undone to obstruct and
hinder the enemy's approach. Not only Jefferson Davis,
but several of Pemberton's subordinate commanders were
native Mississippians, personally familiar with the country
they were defending, and their knowledge enabled them to
anticipate any possible plans of the Union commander.

At the same time considerable changes were made in the
position of the Confederate troops, which about this time

were disposed as follows, viz., at or near Vicksburg, about 25,000 men (of whom 20,856 were reported fit for duty), under Stevenson, guarding the defences from Haines' Bluff on the right to Warrenton on the left; at Grenada, about 20,000 men (15,590 for duty), under Loring, charged with guarding the Yazoo; at Jackson and other points were detachments not brigaded, amounting in all to perhaps 4,000 men, making a total effective force of about 40,000 men. Johnston had returned to Chattanooga during the latter part of January, but still exercised a general supervision over affairs on the Mississippi. Pemberton kept his headquarters at Jackson, whence he could go to Vicksburg or Grenada, as required, in a few hours by train. Van Dorn, with all the effective cavalry, amounting to about 6,000 men, had been ordered to report to Bragg in Tennessee, and during the month of February he marched past the Union left at Corinth to Columbia, Tenn.

Constant reports were received by Pemberton of the progress of the Federal troops and boats in cutting the levee at Yazoo Pass, and removing the obstructions in the Pass. As soon as he heard that boats had entered the Coldwater, he sent orders to Loring, at Grenada, to proceed at once to the mouth of the Yallabusha, taking enough troops with him to defend that point. A few heavy guns were sent by boat up the Yazoo to assist him in the defence. Loring reached Greenwood with two regiments on February 21st, and immediately approved the selection, just made by an engineer officer, of a site for a fortification at a point about five miles below the mouth of the Yallabusha. At this point, the Tallahatchie and Yazoo Rivers are only 500 yards apart, and by holding the narrow neck of land between them, all passage down the Tallahatchie would be prevented, while the Yazoo and Yallabusha Rivers remained open for the

Confederate boats carrying supplies to Grenada. The construction of a line of works, called Fort Pemberton, was at once begun, and a raft was prepared to block the navigation of the Tallahatchie. Reinforcements and artillery also arrived, and on March 10th the earth-and-cotton parapets were in a good state of defence, mounting eight guns, and defended by about 2,000 men.

The Union gunboats and transports arrived in front of this position on the 11th. The troops consisted only of Ross' division, numbering about 4,000 men, it having been impossible to obtain transports of a proper size to convey any of McPherson's corps. The journey through the Pass and down the Coldwater and Tallahatchie had been one of extraordinary difficulty, in consequence of the overhanging trees and other obstructions in the narrow channel, and the fleet moved very slowly—only a few miles a day. All opportunity for surprise was thus lost. The ground in front of Fort Pemberton was overflowed so that the troops could not approach the fort. It could only be attacked by the navy, and the gunboats moved forward and opened fire on the 11th. A few casualties were sustained on either side. On the following day a battery was constructed on a piece of dry land, about 800 yards from the fort, and, on the 13th, the bombardment was renewed. The fleet suffered considerable injury, and inflicted almost none upon the fort; it thus became evident that further progress on the Yazoo expedition was at an end, and in a few days it started back up the Tallahatchie. On the 21st, about midway between Fort Pemberton and the mouth of the Coldwater, it was met by Quinby with one brigade of his division. This officer had arrived at Yazoo Pass from Lake Providence on the 8th, and had disembarked his division on the shore near Helena, nearly all his transports

being too large to enter the pass. After waiting here six
days and despairing of receiving a sufficient number of
small boats for his whole division, he had finally taken the
few boats he had with him which were suitable for navigating
the Pass, and had started forward on the 14th with one brigade. He encountered the same difficulties that had delayed
Ross, and his boats were equally injured in this extraordinary
navigation. On meeting Ross, Quinby assumed command,
being the senior officer, and at once turned the whole expedition back again to Fort Pemberton, arriving there on the
23d. A feeble fire was opened by the gunboats on the same
afternoon, but nothing was accomplished by it. Quinby
had hoped to find a landing-place for his troops while his
transports were sent back for the rest of his division, but in
this he was disappointed. There was no ground suitable
for camping or moving any large body of men. He then
formed a plan to move around the east side of Fort Pemberton, crossing the Yallabusha on a pontoon bridge, and thus
cutting the communications of the fort and compelling its
surrender. He sent a boat back to Helena on the 27th to
bring the bridge materials, but it was met on the way, about
April 1st, by another boat bringing an order to abandon
the whole expedition and return to the Mississippi as
quickly as possible. Grant had found that it would be
impossible to procure the necessary number of light-draught
boats to carry a large force into the Yazoo by this route,
and had notified McPherson, about the middle of March,
to send no more troops after Quinby. On the 28th, the
Steele's Bayou expedition having returned without success, Grant had determined to bring his entire force to Milliken's Bend, and had sent orders to McPherson to recall
Quinby at once. Quinby's entire force withdrew from
Fort Pemberton on April 5th, and the Yazoo Pass project

thus followed the fate of those at the canal and at Lake Providence.

While it had been in progress, Grant had received information that the Confederate troops at Grenada had been sent to Yazoo City and Greenwood, and that these troops were being reinforced by others from Vicksburg. It looked for the moment as if Ross might be surrounded by superior forces, his precarious line of water communication barricaded, and his entire command captured before assistance could reach him over the same route that he had travelled. It therefore became necessary to take prompt measures to relieve him, and, in reconnoitring for this purpose, in company with Porter, Grant discovered a route by which he thought he could not only relieve Ross, but perhaps also effect a landing for a large body on the Yazoo. This led to the fourth, and last, of these abortive projects, which was known as the Steele's Bayou Expedition.

The route proposed was up the Yazoo to Steele's Bayou, up that bayou, about forty miles, to a small cross creek, known as Black Bayou, through that into Deer Creek, and up Deer Creek, about thirty miles, to another cross creek, called Rolling Fork, through that to a comparatively large stream, called the Sunflower, and thence, down that stream, about fifty miles, coming into the Yazoo about midway between Haines' Bluff and Yazoo City. The entire distance from Young's Point to Haines' Bluff by this route would have been nearly 200 miles. Porter and Grant reconnoitred the route as far as Black Bayou, and were convinced that with some slight cutting of trees, it would be navigable for any class of river steamers. There was a depth of five fathoms of water in Steele's Bayou. But the difficulties of the route were in the two cross bayous, Black and Rolling Fork, where the channel was not wide enough

for a boat to turn, and where axemen could quickly barri-
cade the channel by felling trees across it. It was hoped,
however, to get into the Sunflower before the Confederates
were aware of their approach. Once in that stream nothing
could prevent the descent of the gunboats.

On his return from the reconnoissance, March 16th, Grant
ordered Sherman to take a part of his corps and thoroughly
reconnoitre this route, with reference to its adaptability for
moving a large force. Porter was to accompany him with a
fleet of five iron-clads, four mortar-boats, and two tugs.
Sherman immediately put one regiment, the 8th Missouri, many of whose men were boatmen, on board of two
boats, which were placed at his disposition, and sent them
into Steele's Bayou to remove trees, etc., while he ordered
three regiments of Stuart's division to go up the Mississippi, and disembark at a point above Milliken's Bend,
where the Mississippi and Steele's Bayou are only a mile
apart. The next day, 17th, Sherman started after Porter on a
tug, and overtook him just after he had passed through Black
Bayou. The gunboats had been greatly delayed at this
point by trees, drift-wood, etc., and had made but four miles
in twenty-four hours. Porter continued his movement, and
Sherman returned to hasten forward his troops; which were
brought up in relays by the two boats as far as Black Bayou,
and then disembarked to move forward by land. Porter
proceeded at the rate of about half a mile an hour during
the 17th and 18th, and at evening of the latter day was
within a few miles of the Rolling Fork. No enemy had yet
been seen, but on resuming work on the 19th, smoke was
seen through the woods in the direction of the Sunflower,
and soon afterward shells began falling from the same direction. Porter landed a force of seamen to prevent any advance against him, but they were not strong enough for the

purpose, and were obliged to re-embark that evening. During that day and the next sharpshooters swarmed through the woods, picking off any men who showed themselves on the boats or attempted to remove obstructions, cutting down trees in front and in rear of the ships, and sinking a coal-barge to obstruct the channel. Porter's situation now became most critical. The Confederates had heard of the expedition the day after its departure, and had immediately dispatched a brigade of infantry, and several pieces of artillery from Haines' Bluff up the Sunflower. These had arrived at the junction of the Sunflower and Rolling Fork, erected a battery there, and were preparing to pass in rear of Porter, completely obstruct the channel, and capture his entire force. Porter realized his situation, and was even meditating the destruction of his vessels, and the escape of his men through the swamps to the Mississippi; but before doing this he sent a negro back through the swamp to inform Sherman of his critical condition, and to ask the assistance of his troops at the earliest possible moment. Sherman received the message during the night, and immediately sent forward the men with him, about 800 in number, and then went back alone in a canoe to meet the remainder and hurry them forward. He met the latter on boats during the same night, and the boats immediately increased their speed, and came crashing forward through the trees, regardless of damages, until finally their progress was arrested in Black Bayou. Here Sherman disembarked his men and pushed forward by land, picking his way through the cane-brake by lighting candles. Porter was already in retreat on the 21st, when the advance column came to his relief; Sherman, with the second column, was but a few miles in rear, when at noon of that day he came in contact with a force of Confederates, who retreated after a short skirmish. The

5*

latter had passed around Porter's boats, and between Sherman's columns, and were preparing to permanently block the channel, in accordance with the plan already mentioned, when Sherman arrived just in time to prevent it. Sherman now went forward to meet Porter, from whom he learned the state of affairs, and the hopelessness of any further efforts. They then turned back; but the gunboats had to back out, stern foremost, all the way to Steele's Bayou—thirty miles—and they were three days in passing over this distance. Sherman's troops finally regained their camps opposite Vicksburg on the 27th.

Grant was greatly disappointed at the failure of this his fourth effort to find some way to reach solid ground on the flanks of the Vicksburg position. Every possible route by bayous and creeks in the whole bottom land between Vicksburg and Memphis had now been tried, and all without success. He therefore issued orders to McClernand on March 29th to move toward the little hamlets of Richmond and New Carthage, with a view to making his way to the Mississippi at some point below the batteries at Warrenton and Grand Gulf, which formed the left flank of the enemy's position at Vicksburg. At the same time he addressed a letter to Porter, stating the nature of this movement, and suggesting that the gunboats be sent past the batteries at Vicksburg to act against those at Grand Gulf, and cover a landing in that vicinity. Porter replied at once, expressing his entire willingness to co-operate in any possible manner, but stating that once the gunboats were below Vicksburg it would be impossible for them to return. In that case there would not be enough vessels left to protect a landing on the Yazoo near Haines' Bluff, should such a movement become desirable. Before abandoning all efforts, therefore, to reach hard ground by way of the Yazoo, Grant determined to make a reconnoissance of the position at Haines' Bluff, which he did on a gunboat in company with Porter and Sherman on April 1st. The result of this reconnoissance was thus stated by Grant, in a letter to Porter dated April 2d : " I am satisfied that an attack upon Haines' Bluff would be attended with immense sacrifice of life, if not defeat. This, then, closes out the last hope of turning the enemy by the right. . . . Having, then, fully determined upon operating from New Carthage, either by the way of Grand Gulf or Warrenton . . I renew my request to prepare for running the blockade at as early a day as possible."

Grant was now at the turning-point, not only of this campaign but of his whole career. He had not then the world-renowned fame with which we have so long been accustomed to associate his name ; at that time he occupied a position in popular estimation similar to that held by Hooker, Rosecrans, and Banks, who then commanded the other principal armies, and like them he was on trial. He had gained a great victory at Fort Donelson, and he had fought a most desperate battle, which was not a defeat yet hardly a victory, at Shiloh in the previous year. But for twelve months he had apparently done nothing, the defence of the Memphis and Charleston Railroad and its attendant battles of Iuka and Corinth having made but little impression on the public mind. For the last three months his army had been lost to sight in the overflowed swamps of the Mississippi, whence came rumors of abortive expeditions, camp fevers, and dissatisfaction. Many people were beginning to believe that Grant belonged to the same dreary class of failures as McClellan, Burnside, Fremont, and Buell, and they importuned the President to relieve him. It was a gloomy period. The war had been in progress for two full years, and as yet the North had gained no really decisive victory except at Fort

Donelson.   During the preceding summer the Army of the
Potomac had been driven back into Maryland, and the Army
of the Cumberland to the Ohio River.   Both armies had partially regained their ground, and then everything had come
to a standstill for months; in trying to break which the
·Army of the Potomac had only incurred renewed defeat and
slaughter at Fredericksburg and Chancellorsville.   Such
was the general situation, and in Grant's particular operations the prospect was as unpromising as everywhere else.
He was on a wrong trail—that was evident to every one ; and
it would not have been difficult to prove that the responsibility for it did not rest upon Grant.   But Grant's mind did
not run in the direction of arguing responsibility upon other
people's shoulders.   He was accustomed to take things as
they were and to devote his whole energies to making the
best of them.   He had now for two months tried every con-
ceivable plan for crossing the low lands of the Yazoo Delta
and reaching the high ground beyond the enemy's right
flank.   They had all failed.   What should now be done ?
Three plans only were possible.   First, to assault the enemy's
batteries.   Second, to go back to Memphis and recommence
a campaign along the Mississippi Central Railroad.   Third,
to find a way through the swamps opposite Vicksburg, cross
the Mississippi near Grand Gulf, and operate against the
rear of Vicksburg, trusting to victory for supplies.

The first plan would lead to slaughter and almost certain
defeat.   The second was the only plan which could be justified by general military principles.   It was urged by Sherman in a well-known letter, quoted at length in his memoirs,
but it was not accepted by Grant because in this particular
instance those political necessities which always override
purely military reasons demanded an advance and forbade
anything which might have the appearance even of turning

back. The third plan was full of dangers and risks; lack of success in it meant little less than complete destruction. If it did succeed, however, the success would be complete and decisive, and to Grant's mind the emergency seemed to be one which warranted the risk, though he was well aware of its desperate nature, which nothing but success would ever justify. The third plan was adopted; and from it first Vicksburg, and then Chattanooga and Appomattox followed in regular succession.

The final project thus determined upon was to open up a series of circuitous bayous running from Milliken's Bend, and also from the vicinity of Young's Point past Richmond to New Carthage, on the west bank of the Mississippi, about thirty miles below Vicksburg.[1] Water was to be let into this system by cutting a canal from Duckport near Young's Point, and troops and supplies were to be forwarded on flat-boats and barges, urgent requisition for which had been made on the Quartermaster at St. Louis. A force of at least 30,000 men was thus to be assembled at New Carthage, and at the same time the gunboats and a number of transports were to be run past the batteries. All being assembled at New Carthage the troops were to be embarked on the transports and flat-boats, and were to attack Grand Gulf, after its batteries had been silenced by the gunboats. Once in possession of Grand Gulf, the whole army was to be brought over and the campaign prosecuted in rear of Vicksburg along the Big Black.

Orders were accordingly given to begin work on the canal at Duckport, to open the bayous, reconnoitre and repair the roads along them, make the necessary bridges, collect supplies, and bring McPherson's corps and all other avail-

---

[1] See Map facing page 135.

able troops to Milliken's Bend. At the same time Steele's
division of Sherman's corps was sent up the river to Greenville, about one hundred and fifty miles above Vicksburg,
where it disembarked and marched through the country
along Deer Creek as far down as Rolling Fork, collecting
subsistence for its own use, destroying all supplies of any
value to the enemy, and distracting the latter's attention
from the main movement toward New Carthage.

While the work was being prosecuted on the canal, Osterhaus' division of McClernand's corps was gradually feeling
its way toward New Carthage. Richmond was occupied on
March 31st, and New Carthage on April 6th. Osterhaus
skirmished on the way with a small detachment of cavalry,
reinforced on April 4th by three regiments of infantry from
Grand Gulf, which did little or nothing to retard their progress.

Between April 12th and 14th, the feasibility of this route
having been established, the remaining divisions of McClernand's corps took up the march from Milliken's Bend for New
Carthage, but owing to the necessity of making and repairing roads through the soft, black soil, and of constructing a
large number of bridges over various minor bayous, the
march was so much delayed that it was the 20th of April before the corps could be assembled.

On the night of April 16th the gunboats ran past the batteries of Vicksburg. This was not an untried experiment.
On the morning of February 2d, the ram Queen of the West,
commanded by Col. Charles R. Ellet, had run the gauntlet in broad daylight, the intention to run by just before
dawn having been frustrated by some accident to the machinery which caused a slight delay. This vessel was in no
way armor-plated, and her only protection was found in
bales of cotton. She was under fire for fifty minutes and

was struck twelve times, had one gun dismounted and destroyed, and her cabin knocked to pieces, but she sustained no damage impairing her efficiency. On the way she attempted to ram the Confederate vessel Vicksburg, lying at the levee, but in this she was only partially successful. She then proceeded down the Mississippi, in company with the transport De Soto, to the mouth of Red River and up that river for some distance, capturing several transports conveying Confederate supplies.

On the night of February 13th, the gunboat Indianola, under Lieut.-Com. George Brown, also ran the batteries with perfect success, and proceeded down the river to assist the Queen of the West. Just after passing Natchez, on February 16th, she met a small steamboat carrying Col. Ellet and a portion of his crew. Ellet reported that the Queen of the West had engaged a Confederate battery in Red River on the 14th, and in the midst of the engagement had run aground and been abandoned, 21 persons of her crew being captured. With the rest Ellet had at first escaped in the De Soto, but this boat had run into the bank in a fog, and broken off her rudder. He had then set fire to her and abandoned her, transferring his men to the captured boat New Era, and with her making good his escape. In the same boat he proceeded up the river, running past the batteries at Grand Gulf, and finally reaching the vicinity of Vicksburg.

The Indianola remained in the vicinity of Red River for a few days, and then began to retrace her steps up the river. The Confederates had quickly raised and repaired the Queen of the West, and with this vessel, the ram Webb, which had been for some time in Red River, and two smaller boats protected by cotton—making a fleet of four vessels in all—they cautiously followed the Indianola from point to point

up the river, and, on the night of February 24th, just after
passing Grand Gulf, they steamed up rapidly to the attack.
The Indianola was encumbered by coal barges, but immediately turned to meet them, and a very severe engagement
followed, lasting an hour and a half. The Indianola was
superior in armament to all the other vessels combined, but
the night was very dark, and her guns could not be used
effectively. The Confederate vessels relied upon ramming,
and in the course of the engagement the Indianola received
seven severe blows, the last of which left her helpless and
in a sinking condition. Her guns were then thrown overboard, and she was run ashore, where her officers and crew
were surrendered.

This left the Confederates again in command of the river
navigation between Vicksburg and Port Hudson, but on the
night of March 14th, Farragut passed the batteries at Port
Hudson—as will be subsequently described—with the Hartford and a small vessel called the Albatross, with which he
arrived below Vicksburg on March 19th. He considered
these two vessels insufficient to maintain the blockade of
Red River, and he therefore desired that Porter should send
one iron-clad and two rams below Vicksburg, to assist him
in that enterprise, as well as to break up the batteries near
Warrenton, which were increasing in strength at that time
from day to day. Porter was then absent on the Steele's
Bayou Expedition, but Brig.-Gen. A. W. Ellett, commanding
the Marine Brigade, offered to assume the responsibility of
sending two rams. These vessels, the Lancaster and Switzerland, started to run past the Vicksburg batteries before
daylight on March 25th. Owing to delay—as in a previous
case—they went past in broad daylight, and one of them,
the Lancaster, was blown up by the enemy's shells and completely destroyed, while the Switzerland was very seriously

disabled. Farragut was thus obliged to return to the Red River without the assistance of any of Porter's vessels.

The result of these various attempts, successful and unsuccessful, justified the belief that suitable vessels could run the gauntlet of the batteries without very great risk, provided proper precautions were taken as to the time of passage, and the protection of unarmored boats by cotton. Porter, therefore, had no hesitation in determining to run past with his iron-clad fleet, as soon as Grant had decided that it would not be necessary for them to return up stream. Preparations were made to undertake the passage on the night of April 16th. At ten o'clock on that night, the fleet cast loose from its moorings at the mouth of the Yazoo River, and slowly steamed down the Mississippi. Porter led in his flag-ship, the Benton, followed at short distances by the Lafayette, with the captured vessel Price lashed on the starboard side, then by the Louisville, Mound City, Pittsburg, and Carondelet. Three transports, the Forest Queen, Silver Wave, and Henry Clay, protected by cotton bales and loaded with army supplies and ammunition, followed next, and the gunboat Tuscumbia brought up the rear. Each vessel had a barge in tow, carrying ten thousand bushels of coal. The Benton rounded the point at Vicksburg a few minutes after eleven o'clock, and was almost immediately discovered by the Confederate batteries, which opened fire vigorously. At the same time the torch was applied to houses and other inflammable material on both banks of the river, thus lighting up the entire scene of action. Each vessel was under fire for about half an hour at Vicksburg, and a few minutes at Warrenton, the entire duration of the cannonade being about an hour and a half; and in return each one poured its broadside into the streets of Vicksburg as it went by within a few yards of the shore.

About 2 A.M. the fleet pulled up and anchored at New Carthage. It was found that every vessel had been struck a
number of times, but the amount of real damage was sur-
prisingly small; a few coal barges had been sunk or lost in
the mêlée, and the transport Henry Clay had been abandoned by her crew in a panic, after which her cotton had
taken fire from a bursting shell, and she had burned up.
With these exceptions, there was no damage done that
could not be repaired in a very few days. The only casualties were ten or twelve men slightly wounded.

Grant had gone to New Carthage on the 17th, and having
seen that the passage of the fleet was a complete success he
returned to Milliken's Bend to hasten the movements of his
army. It was impossible to move his troops by barges and
flat-boats through the system of bayous, as had been originally intended, partly because only a small number of barges
had been received, and partly because the canal and bayous
were not yet ready for navigation. Water had been let into
the canal, near Duckport, on April 13th, but much work still
remained to be done in dredging out the bottom, trimming
the banks, cutting trees, etc. Grant, therefore, determined
to move on by the roads until the canal should be ready,
but, in fact, it never was of any service. On the 22d, it had
been dredged out so that small steamers passed through it as
far as Richmond, but a day or two later there was a sudden
fall of several feet in the river, and it was rendered totally
useless. The troops were, therefore, forced to make the
movement by land, constructing several miles of corduroy
roads for the artillery and wagons; and the supplies were
sent partly by the roads, and partly by transports running
past the batteries.

On April 20th, the final orders were issued for the movement across the peninsula. McClernand's corps formed

the right wing, McPherson's the centre, and Sherman's the left wing; and the troops were to move across in that order, following each other as rapidly as the narrow road would permit.   At that date, McClernand's corps (four divisions) was assembled along the road near New Carthage; two divisions of McPherson's corps were already at Milliken's Bend, and the third was on the way down the river from Lake Providence; two divisions of Sherman's corps were near Duckport and Young's Point, and the other division (Steele's) was under orders to return from Greenville.

McPherson's leading divisions were immediately put in motion toward Richmond, and six more transports were loaded with supplies, and protected with cotton to pass the batteries.   They took twelve barges in tow, and were manned by volunteers from the army, mainly from Logan's division. They made the passage on the night of April 22d, five of them getting through safely, and one, loaded with hospital stores and appliances for the wounded, being sunk.   Having seen these vessels safely started, Grant moved his headquarters, on the 23d, over to Smith's plantation, near New Carthage, to take personal control of the movements for crossing the river.   When he arrived he found that New Carthage was still surrounded by water, and was entirely unsuitable for concentrating a large force.   McClernand had already been reconnoitring to find a suitable point lower down the river, and had discovered a road leading from Smith's plantation around Bayou Vidal to Perkins' plantation, about eight miles below New Carthage.   By repairing this road, and building about two thousand feet of bridges over cross bayous, it would be practicable for moving the army.   Orders were at once given for putting this route in order. Porter had made a reconnoissance of the batteries at Grand Gulf, on the 22d, and being convinced that they should be

attacked before they became any stronger, he had called
upon McClernand for troops for this purpose. Osterhaus'
division had accordingly been embarked on the morning of
the 23d, but it was not thought that this was sufficient, and
it was dermined to await the arrival of more transports.   On
the 24th, Grant made a reconnoissance of the same batteries
in company with Porter.   He found the batteries to be very
strong, and the distance from Perkins' plantation to Grand
Gulf was so great (over twenty miles) that with his limited
transportation he did not feel justified in attempting an
attack from his present position.   It was necessary to seek
a point still farther down the river, near enough to Grand
Gulf to enable the transports to make frequent and rapid
trips in ferrying the troops across the river when a landing
should be effected.   McClernand was, therefore, directed to
reconnoitre in search of a road to such a point, and he discovered one leading around another bayou, called Lake St.
Joseph, to a hamlet, called Hard Times, just above the bend
on which Grand Gulf is situated.   While this route was
being examined, work on the bridges between Smith's and
Perkins' plantations was prosecuted with the utmost vigor,
so that on the 27th the whole of McClernand's corps was
assembled at Perkins'.   On the following day, two divisions
of this corps were moved down to Hard Times by the river,
the transports returning at once for the other two divisions.
At the same time, McPherson's two divisions, Logan in the
lead, were moving by the land route from Smith's around
Bayou Vidal to Perkins', and from Perkins' around Lake St.
Joseph to Hard Times.   On the 29th, everything was in
readiness for the long-expected crossing of the river, and on
that day an attack was made by the gunboats upon the batteries at Grand Gulf.

Before describing this, it will be necessary to refer to the

course of events on the Confederate side during this month
of April, in which Grant's army had been so laboriously
threading its way through the overflowed lands opposite
Vicksburg. On the last day of March, Pemberton's return
showed the paper strength of his command to be 82,318
men, of whom 61,495 were present, and 48,829 fit for duty
on that day. This effective force of 50,000 men, in round
numbers, was divided into three principal commands. The
first, consisting of about 22,000 effectives, commanded by
Maj.-Gen. C. L. Stevenson, occupied the main Vicksburg
position, extending from Haines' Bluff on the right to
Grand Gulf on the left. The second, consisting of over
16,000 effectives, commanded by Maj.-Gen. Frank Gardner,
garrisoned the fortifications at Port Hudson. The third,
consisting of 7,000 effectives, under Maj.-Gen. W. W. Loring, was stationed at Fort Pemberton, Grenada, and other
points in that immediate vicinity. In addition to these
three main bodies there were some 4,000 or 5,000 men stationed in Northern Mississippi, in observation of Hurlbut's
troops on the Memphis and Corinth Railroad. The distance
from Fort Pemberton to Port Hudson is two hundred miles
in a straight line, and this was certainly a long line for fifty
thousand troops to hold, even when well fortified ; but they
had some advantages in being on dry land, with railroad
and telegraph facilities, while their adversaries were in the
swamps, depending entirely on water transportation. The
left flank of the Vicksburg position was at Grand Gulf, a
point about thirty miles by land below Vicksburg, and possessed of very nearly the same natural features as that city.
Pemberton had given orders to occupy and fortify it on
March 5th, at a time when it seemed very probable that
Grant's canal would prove a success. The troops sent for
this purpose consisted of the Missouri brigade of six regi-

ments and four batteries, numbering in all about 2,500 men,
and commanded by Brig.-Gen. J. S. Bowen.   When McClernand's troops began to advance from Richmond to New
Carthage, skirmishing with a small detachment of cavalry,
Bowen sent three of his regiments across the river to hold
them in check, or at least observe their movements.   But
neither Bowen nor Pemberton attached much importance
to this operation and both discredited the rumors that it
was being conducted by a large force.   Pemberton's attention was principally directed to his right flank; the Yazoo
Pass expedition had hardly left the vicinity of Fort Pemberton before Steele's division made its appearance on Deer
Creek, and Pemberton feared a renewal of the attempts to
turn his right flank.   Rumors began to arrive, moreover,
from Memphis that Grant had determined to abandon his
operations against Vicksburg by the river, and was about to
return to Memphis and thence reinforce Rosecrans in Tennessee, or else begin another campaign southward on the
high land.   Pemberton, in fact, was very much in doubt as
to Grant's intentions; his telegraphic report of April 9th to
the Adjutant-General in Richmond stated that the enemy
was constantly in motion, that his principal efforts were apparently directed against Deer Creek on his right, for which
provision had been made, and that there were rumors of
a movement across the peninsula on the west of the river,
which were not credited.   A few days later he received renewed information that a large part of Grant's army had gone
up the river (Ellet's Marine Brigade, numbering about 2,000
men, had in fact been ordered to the Tennessee) and that
steamers had been sent down to bring the rest.   Pemberton
communicated this intelligence as a certainty to Johnston,
and quickly received in reply an order to send reinforcements
to Chattanooga.   There had just arrived at Jackson two bri-

gades, soon consolidated into one, numbering 4,000 men, who had been ordered from Port Hudson to Vicksburg, on receipt of intelligence that Banks had gone to the Red River country. These troops (Buford's brigade) were immediately put on the cars for Chattanooga, via Meridian and Mobile. On the next day, April 14th, Johnston ordered more troops to be sent to him, and Pemberton designated Vaughn's brigade from Vicksburg and Tilghman's brigade from Grenada. This force, numbering about 4,000 men, was ordered to proceed via Jackson as soon as transportation could be had. Hardly had Pemberton given his orders, however, before information began arriving from Vicksburg that the report of Grant's return up the river was a mistake. On the 15th, therefore, Tilghman's brigade was halted at Jackson, and Vaughn's near Vicksburg; the other two brigades were already on the way. Meanwhile some skirmishes had taken place across the river, and Bowen had reported from Grand Gulf that the movement there began to look serious; but Stevenson, who was in command at Vicksburg, was of a different opinion, believing that the attack would be made on the Yazoo. Pemberton himself was at Jackson, fifty miles from the river, and of course had to rely upon his subordinates for information. On the 17th, however, came the news of the passage of Porter's fleet. This quickly settled the question of any retreat up the river, and Johnston was at once appealed to for the return of the troops on the way to Tennessee. Green's brigade at Edward's Station was ordered to reinforce Bowen at Grand Gulf, and Bowen was ordered to withdraw his infantry detachment from across the river immediately, if it was not already too late. It succeeded in crossing the river that night. Johnston ordered the Port Hudson troops back to Pemberton, but some of them had already reached Chattanooga, and the rest were strung along

the road at Atlanta, Montgomery, and other points. It was
April 22d before they reached Meridian on their return.

By this time fresh complications had arisen, in consequence of the movement of Union columns, reported to be
very strong, southward from the Memphis and Charleston
Railroad. Pemberton was at this time very deficient in cavalry, nearly all of that arm in his department having been
sent, under command of Van Dorn, to Tennessee, where they
were operating in conjunction with Bragg's army. Pemberton's requests to have them returned had all been answered
to the effect that their services were indispensable in Middle
Tennessee. Consequently, he was unable to keep track of
the expeditions which were now reported to be rapidly advancing southward through the State.

In fact, one of the most thoroughly successful cavalry
raids of the whole war was now in progress. It was commanded by Col. B. H. Grierson, of the 6th Illinois Cavalry.
With his own and two other regiments, about 1,700 men in
all, he left La Grange on April 17th and moved directly
south. Northern Mississippi was at that time garrisoned by
about 1,000 men, under Brig.-Gen. Chalmers, who were
posted behind the Coldwater; and, in order to occupy their
attention and prevent them from interfering with Grierson,
a small force of infantry was sent out from La Grange and
another from Memphis.

Grierson thus got a good start, and moved rapidly through
Ripley and Pontotoc, following the roads about twenty
miles west of the Mobile and Ohio Railroad. On the 21st,
having reached a point midway between the villages of
Houston and Starksville, he detached one regiment, under
Col. Hatch, to break up the railroad between Columbus
and Macon, and then make his way back to La Grange.
Columbus was garrisoned by more than 2,000 men, and

Hatch had a very brisk engagement there, losing 40 men; after which he retreated up the railroad, destroying it at Okolona and Tupelo, thence returning through Ripley, where he had a brush with Chalmers, and reaching La Grange on April 26th. Grierson meanwhile continued his own movements without any delay, striking the Vicksburg and Meridian Railroad, at Newton Station, on April 24th, and destroying several miles of it west of Meridian. Thence he moved to the southwest, crossing Pearl River at Georgetown, and destroying the Jackson and New Orleans Railroad at various points between thirty and forty miles south of Jackson. On the 28th, a skirmish took place with a small detachment of cavalry sent out from Grand Gulf; after this had been driven off, Grierson moved rapidly down the New Orleans Railroad, skirmished with some of the troops sent out from Port Hudson, but avoided the main body of them, and, finally, on May 2d, reached the Union camp at Baton Rouge. With a force numbering barely 1,000 men (after Hatch had been detached), he had ridden entirely through the State of Mississippi, marching 600 miles in 16 days, had destroyed between fifty and sixty miles of railway and telegraph, and a large amount of other property, had captured a number of horses and mules, and had inflicted on the enemy a greater loss than he had himself suffered. But, far more important than all this, he had distracted the enemy's attention in an extraordinary degree at a most critical moment. Grierson had been in motion on Pemberton's rear at the very time that Grant was making the final preparations for the attack or crossing at Grand Gulf, *i.e.*, during the last ten days of April. Being so short of cavalry, Pemberton was unable to keep track of Grierson, and the most exaggerated rumors were current of his presence in a dozen places at once. At the same time, the slight de-

monstration from Memphis against Chalmers' force on the
Coldwater was magnified by rumor into an advance in large
force in the direction of Grenada. Pemberton was thus
obliged to send out expeditions in all directions to try to intercept this handful of bold troopers. One brigade was taken
from Fort Pemberton and sent toward Grenada ; Tilghman's
brigade, which had been stopped at Jackson en route to
Chattanooga, was also sent back toward Grenada; Buford's
brigade, which had just reached Meridian on its return
from Chattanooga, was sent up toward Columbus; Adams'
brigade was sent out from Port Gibson toward Jackson ;
Chalmers was sent across toward Okolona, with the idea of
intercepting Grierson when he should return; finally, a
large part of the garrison of Port Hudson moved out and
lay in wait for him. Not one of all these various expeditions succeeded in coming up with Grierson, more than to
exchange a few shots with skirmishers; and by calling out
so many men, and by cutting the railroad west of those at
Meridian, Grierson assisted very materially in diverting attention from Grand Gulf, and in delaying the movement of
troops to that place. Pemberton, however, had become
convinced, as we have seen, that the movement in that direction was serious, and he had ordered Green's brigade
from Edward's Station as a reinforcement. On April 28th,
he received word from Bowen that "transports and barges
loaded down with troops are landing at Hard Times." On
receipt of this, Tilghman was immediately recalled from the
direction of Grenada to Jackson ; Buford was directed to
march around the break in the railroad at Newton Station,
and come to the same place ; another brigade (Gregg's) was
ordered up from Port Hudson, and Stevenson was directed
to hold 5,000 men in readiness to move at a moment's notice
to Bowen's assistance, whose force, including Green's bri-

gade, numbered about 4,700 men. None of Stevenson's men were, however, actually sent, for Pemberton did not think that the movement was yet sufficiently developed, and was not entirely convinced that it was not a feint to cover an attack in the direction of Haines' Bluff. This was the condition of affairs on the Confederate side on April 28th.

At 7 A.M., on April 29th, Porter's squadron left its moorings at Hard Times, and slowly steamed down toward Grand Gulf. Immediately in rear of it were all the transports and flat-boats available, loaded with all the men they could carry, which was three divisions of McClernand's corps. These remained just out of range, above the point opposite Grand Gulf. Grant was on a tug in the middle of the stream, where he could follow closely the progress of the fight, and send in his troops whenever the favorable moment should arrive. Porter's squadron consisted of the following vessels:

Benton, Lieutenant-Commander J. A. Greer............... 16 guns.
Lafayette, Captain H. Walke............................ 10 "
Louisville, Lieutenant-Commander E. K. Owen............. 13 "
Tuscumbia, Lieutenant-Commander J. W. Shirk .... 3 "
Mound City, Lieutenant-Commander Byron Wilson......... 13 "
Carondelet, Lieutenant J. M. L. Murphy .... 13 "
Pittsburg, Lieutenant W. R. Hoel .... 13 "

Total.............. .... 81 guns.

The vessels averaged about six hundred tons each.

Grand Gulf was an insignificant village, the river terminus of a few miles of railway running to Port Gibson. But it was situated near the mouth of the Big Black River, which was navigable for several miles, and behind it rose a sharp line of bluffs, attaining a height of something over a hundred feet. Just above the village these bluffs come close to the water's edge. They were fortified by a strong line of earthworks, forming two principal sets of batteries, one above and one below the landing, the two being connected by a trench or covered way for infantry about a thousand yards in length. Work had been prosecuted diligently on the batteries during the seven weeks which had elapsed since the troops had occupied this point; they were now nearly completed but were only partially armed, containing in fact only thirteen guns, eight of which were of the calibre of thirty-pounder Parrots or less. They were but a poor match for Porter's eighty-one pieces, many of them 11-inch Dahlgrens or 9-inch rifles. The cannonade opened about 8 A.M., and kept up furiously and without intermission until 1 P.M. By that time the Confederate guns were silenced, and their batteries were somewhat ploughed up by the 2,500 projectiles which Porter had sent against them. But the troops had lost only 3 men killed (one of them being Col. Wade, Chief of Artillery) and 15 wounded. On the other hand, Porter had lost 19 killed and 56 wounded, and his vessels had received several hundred shots. The Tuscumbia had been hit 81 times, many of the shells penetrating her thin plating and bursting inside; she was so badly damaged as to be unfit for service for some time. The Benton had been struck 47 times and had lost 26 men, and the other vessels had received minor injuries.

It was very evident that although the few Confederate guns were temporarily silenced, the batteries were just as capable of resisting assault as before the bombardment began—their guns, in fact, resumed firing later in the day—and the infantry parapet was practically uninjured for defence. It was impossible to bring frail transports, loaded to the gunwales with men, in front of batteries which had held their own against iron-plated gunboats. Grant, therefore, determined to move still farther down the river and effect a landing which would turn the flank of these batteries; and as soon as Porter withdrew—about 2 P.M.—McClernand was ordered to land his men at Hard Times and march them across the point opposite Grand Gulf, coming out on the Mississippi at De Shroon's plantation, about three miles down the river. As soon as it was dark, Porter was requested to renew the bombardment, under cover of which the transports all slipped by with very little damage, and tied up at De Shroon's. McClernand's entire corps was in that vicinity at daylight the next morning.

Grant had at first intended to move down as far as Rodney, from which point it was known that a road led to Port Gibson, and thence to the various points in rear of Vicksburg, but during the night he learned from a negro that there was a good road leading to Port Gibson from a landing-place called Bruinsburg, just below the mouth of Bayou Pierre, and only five miles below De Shroon's. Grant determined to effect a crossing at this place. At daylight on April 30th the transports and gunboats were all brought into requisition to ferry the troops across, and by noon the whole of McClernand's corps—four divisions, numbering over 18,000 men—were on the east bank. There were no Confederates in sight, and it was most important to get possession of the bluffs, which are here about three miles back from the river, as quickly as possible. But for some unexplained reason rations had not been issued to McClernand's corps before landing; their wagons had been left away back at Perkins' two days before, and it was known that the first advance beyond the river would necessarily be made without them. Nevertheless the usual three days' rations in haversacks had not yet been issued, and a delay of four hours occurred on the bank just after landing in order to distribute them. This delay at such a critical period might have been disastrous, but fortunately it was not so ; and at four o'clock McClernand took up his line of march, Carr's division in the lead. At sunset he reached the bluffs, and finding no enemy, pushed on during the night toward Port Gibson. About one o'clock in the night Carr's leading brigade met the enemy about ten miles from Bruinsburg and four from Port Gibson ; a slight skirmish ensued, after which the whole division lay down on their arms until daylight should enable them to reconnoitre the ground and the force in front of them.

These troops were a portion of Green's brigade, which had been hastily dispatched from Grand Gulf by Bowen on the afternoon of the 30th. Immediately after the bombardment of Grand Gulf on the 29th, Bowen had telegraphed the result to Pemberton, and stated the urgent necessity for prompt reinforcement. The wires then failed to work, and nothing more was heard from Bowen until the afternoon of the 30th. Pemberton became alarmed at this, and telegraphed Stevenson to send at once the 5,000 men he had previously ordered to be held in readiness. These were Tracy's and Baldwin's brigades, and they left Vicksburg for Grand Gulf late on the afternoon of the 29th. Pemberton also ordered Tilghman to collect all available troops in Jackson—about a brigade—and proceed to Edward's Station, and there await further orders. Pemberton was at first somewhat disconcerted by reports from Stevenson of the presence of Union troops at Haines' Bluff, where Sherman with one division of his corps, escorted by eight gunboats, was making a vigorous demonstration, in pursuance of orders to that effect given by Grant on the 27th. But Stevenson expressed himself as being ready to meet any attack at that point, and it soon became evident

that the important move was at Grand Gulf. Late on
the afternoon of the 30th, Pemberton received word from
Bowen that 3,000 Union troops were within ten miles of
Port Gibson at 3 P.M. of that day, and that more were still
landing at Bruinsburg. On receipt of this, Pemberton gave
orders to his detachments at Grenada, Columbus, Meridian,
and other points to come at once to Jackson; after which
he took the train for Vicksburg. Tracy's brigade reached
Grand Gulf on the afternoon of April 30th, and Baldwin's
brigade came in during the night, the men of both brigades
in a jaded condition from hurried marching. Green's brigade, as already stated, had been sent from Grand Gulf to
Port Gibson on the afternoon of the 30th, and its advance
had met Carr's division on the road to Bruinsburg soon after
midnight. Tracy's brigade came to his assistance a little
before daybreak.

On the morning of May 1st, the Confederates were discovered posted across the roads, about three miles west of Port
Gibson. At this point the road from Bruinsburg divides
into two roads, which, diverging nearly at a right angle, curve
around and unite at Port Gibson. Green's brigade was
posted across the southern road and Tracy's across the
northern. The country was extremely rough and unsuitable for manoeuvres, being composed of short, steep hillsides,
following no regular system, and separated from each other
by ravines, filled with a dense growth of cane and underbrush. Carr's, Osterhaus', and Hovey's division of McClernand's corps were all on the ground at daylight, and A. J.
Smith's division was so close behind them that it reached
the field at 7 A.M. Logan's and Quinby's divisions of Mc-
Pherson's corps were crossing at Bruinsburg during the
night of the 30th and the following morning, so that it was
certain they could be relied on during the day, if necessary.

There was an abundance of force present ; the only difficulty was in bringing it into action on such difficult ground.

At 5.30 A.M., McClernand opened the battle by sending forward Osterhaus' division on the left along the northerly road. His leading brigade (Garrard's) was quickly met by a hot fire from Tracy's Confederate brigade, and its advance was checked. The other brigade (Sheldon's) having then come to its assistance the Confederates were slightly driven back, but soon made a stand, and Osterhaus' division was unable to make any further progress until late in the afternoon. On the right, Carr's division moved forward at 6.15 A.M., one brigade (Benton's) on the right of the southerly road, and the other (Stone's) on the left of it. Their routes lay through broken country covered with dense underbrush and their progress was slow. The enemy (Green's brigade) was posted in an advantageous position on a commanding ridge. In advancing, Benton's and Stone's brigades had diverged from each other, leaving a gap, into which Hovey's division was ordered about 7 A.M. The two brigades of this division worked their way laboriously forward through the cane and underbrush, and finally came within one hundred and fifty yards of the Confederate ridge, where a battery was posted, well supported by infantry. A determined assault was then made by Hovey's division, and Benton's brigade of Carr's division, and the ridge was carried, two pieces of artillery, three caissons, and 400 prisoners being captured. Green's brigade then fell back toward Port Gibson.

Bowen had sent a short report to Pemberton from Grand Gulf early in the morning, stating the probability of an engagement ; after which orders were given to Baldwin to move his brigade to Port Gibson, and to Cockrell (temporarily in command of Bowen's own brigade of Missouri troops) to move to Port Gibson with three regiments, leaving the other three posted respectively at Grand Gulf, at Thompson's Bluff on the Big Black, and at the Grindstone Ford on Bayou Pierre. Bowen then rode over to Port Gibson, reaching the battle-field at some time before 9 A.M. At the latter hour Baldwin's brigade passed through Port Gibson, and about a half hour later Green was driven back, as already stated. Baldwin was immediately ordered to form a new line about a mile in rear of Green's first position, and Green's brigade was re-formed and sent over to the assistance of Tracy on the northern road. Cockrell arrived about noon, and two of his regiments were sent to support Baldwin and one to support Tracy.

Hovey's and Carr's divisions pushed on as rapidly as the ground would permit in pursuit of Green's brigade, and early in the afternoon they came under the fire of Baldwin's brigade and a very severe contest ensued, lasting over an hour and a half. While this was in progress Bowen took two of Cockrell's regiments and made a desperate effort to turn McClernand's right flank. McClernand called up one brigade (Burbridge's) of A. J. Smith's division and sent it to meet this attack, and at the same time Hovey brought four batteries into position on a ridge from which they could enfilade Cockrell's regiments moving through the ravine toward the right. Under this combined fire Cockrell's attack was defeated, and he was driven to and across the southern road, where he joined Baldwin, who still held firm.

The other brigade (Landram's) of A. J. Smith's division now came up and joined Hovey's division and Stone's brigade of Carr's division in an attack on Baldwin. The odds were very great, even with the advantages of ground, and Baldwin made a most gallant defence, holding his ground until after the brigade on his right had been driven off the field, just before sunset, and then covering the retreat.

6*

Grant had left Bruinsburg early in the morning and had reached the field about ten o'clock, just as Hovey's and Carr's divisions had carried the first ridge on the right. Having examined the whole field on the right, he rode over to the left to inspect Osterhaus' position, and he remained there with the intention of using McPherson's corps on that flank as soon as it should arrive. Two brigades (J. E. Smith's and Stevenson's) of Logan's division of this corps were put in motion from Bruinsburg as soon as they landed, on the morning of the 1st. Hearing the sound of the battle, they marched as rapidly as possible through the heat, McPherson and Logan both being with the advance, and came on the field about noon. Owing to repeated requests for reinforcements from McClernand (although he had already three divisions under him opposed to about a brigade and a half), Grant ordered McPherson to send one brigade (Stevenson's) to McClernand, but to bring the other one (J. E. Smith's) to the support of Osterhaus on the left. McPherson accompanied this brigade in person and was ordered by Grant to move it in such manner as to turn the Confederate right flank. As soon as the ground was reconnoitred, a judicious position was selected by McPherson from which this movement could be effected, but owing to the tangled and broken character of the country it was several hours before the movement could be accomplished. Having finally got into position about 5 P.M., an attack was made by J. E. Smith's brigade in line on the enemy's right flank at the same time that Osterhaus renewed his front attack along the road. The result was the complete defeat of the enemy's right, soon followed by the rest of his line, Baldwin's brigade in the centre bringing up the rear. Green conducted the men from the right (Tracy having been killed early in the action) along the direct road to Grand Gulf, burning the bridge over

Bayou Pierre as soon as he had crossed, and taking a position on the hills north of that stream. Baldwin retreated through Port Gibson, destroying the bridge over the south fork of Bayou Pierre. The retreat was conducted in good order, every foot of the way being contested, so that darkness closed over the field before Grant's troops could reach Port Gibson. Under the circumstances, pursuit was impossible that night. Before daylight the next morning Baldwin continued his retreat to the Grindstone Ford, on the north fork of Bayou Pierre, crossed the bridge at that point and then burned it, and finally rejoined Bowen and Green by way of Willow Springs.

Bowen's force engaged in this action numbered about 8,500 men, according to the latest returns prior to the battle. In his official report, made three months later, he gave his strength at 5,500, although he stated to Loring, who joined him May 2d, that he then had 7,000 men, after deducting the losses in the battle. It is hardly necessary to figure down his strength; his defence was most gallant, even with 8,500 men, against the odds of a whole corps and two brigades of another, numbering in all 23,000 men. He reported his losses as follows:

	Killed.	Wounded.	Missing.
Cockrell's brigade	13	97	96
Green's "	17	83	122
Baldwin's "	12	48	27
Tracy's "	18	112	142
Total.........................	60	340	387
Aggregate...			787

According to the Union reports, the Confederates lost over 600 in prisoners alone. Grant's losses were as follows:

		Killed.	Wounded.	Missing.
Osterhaus' division		37	171	5
A. J. Smith's	"	2	16	0
Hovey's	"	'42	263	3
Carr's	"	42	222	0
Logan's	"	6	38	2
Total		129	710	10
Aggregate				849

During the whole of this day Pemberton had been in
Vicksburg, sending telegrams in all directions for the purpose of collecting his scattered forces.   Loring, who was in
Meridian, was directed to come by rail, via Jackson, to Edward's Station, bringing with him any troops that were ready
to move.   No troops were ready at Meridian or Jackson;
but at the railroad bridge over Big Black River there were
two regiments and a battery of Tilghman's brigade, which
were put in motion during the day.   Loring left the railroad
at the Big Black and proceeded on the road to Port Gibson,
overtaking these troops before night.   They did not arrive
within twenty miles of the field that day.   Finding that it
would be impossible for Loring to arrive in time, Pemberton ordered another brigade of Stevenson's division to move
from Vicksburg to Bowen's relief.   This brigade (Reynolds')
started on its march a little before dark.   The next morning
the two remaining brigades of Stevenson's division (Barton's
and Taylor's) started for Port Gibson with Stevenson in
command.

On the morning of May 2d, the Union troops entered
Port Gibson, and immediately began to construct a bridge
over the south fork of Bayou Pierre.   This was completed
at 4 P.M., and Crocker's (formerly Quinby's) division of Mc-
Pherson's corps, which had come up during the day from
Bruinsburg, took the lead, followed by Logan's division of

the same corps. They advanced as far as the north fork of
Bayou Pierre, eight miles, where the bridge was found still
burning. The fire was put out, and the bridge was repaired
during the night, so as to be ready for use at daybreak the
next morning.

Loring reached Rocky Springs with the two regiments
and battery of Tilghman's brigade on the morning of the
2d, and, hearing of Bowen's retreat to Grand Gulf, and fearing that he might be cut off from Vicksburg, he hastened
Tilghman forward to Grindstone Ford on the north fork of
Bayou Pierre, with instructions to hold that point at all
hazards. He then rode on himself to Grand Gulf, and,
learning the condition of affairs from Bowen, it was at once
determined to abandon Grand Gulf and retreat across the
Big Black. One regiment was left in Grand Gulf until
night, when the guns were dismounted, magazines blown
up, and the batteries abandoned. Porter's gunboats came
up and took possession on the morning of May 3d. Bowen
retreated in the direction of Hankinson's Ferry, where he
was joined by the three brigades of Stevenson's division
which had left Vicksburg that morning and the previous
evening. The total Confederate force now present consisted
of the whole of Stevenson's division (four brigades), and
Bowen's, Green's, Baldwin's, and Tilghman's brigades—in
all, about 17,000 men; but the men were worn out with
sudden and long marches and fighting, and were somewhat
demoralized. The retreat across the Big Black was begun
at Hankinson's Ferry on the evening of the 2d, a force
being left behind to protect the crossing. This force was
attacked by Crocker's division, of McPherson's corps, on
the morning of the 3d, near Willow Springs, but it stood
firm, contesting its ground, and retreating very slowly until
late in the afternoon, when Logan's division came upon its

flank, and caused it to hasten its progress toward the ferry.
The Confederate troops all crossed safely, but McPherson's
men were so close upon them that they were unable to destroy the boat bridge.

On the evening of the 3d, Grant took a dozen cavalrymen,
and, otherwise unattended, rode over to Grand Gulf, in
order to establish his base at that point, and make preparations for a speedy advance. Having issued the necessary
orders, he rejoined his troops at Willow Springs before daylight of the 4th. McPherson's corps was moved forward to
Hankinson's Ferry, and McClernand's to Willow Springs,
where they remained in bivouac for three days, awaiting the
arrival of Sherman's corps, and of rations and ammunition
necessary for an advance.

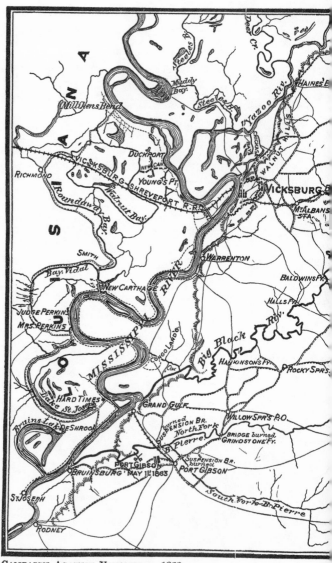

CAMPAIGN AGAINST VICKSBURG, 1863.

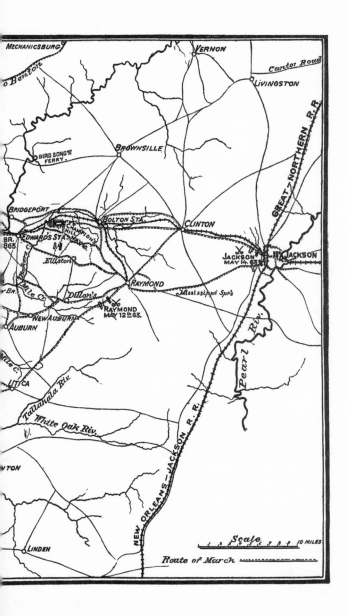

CHAPTER V.

THE CAMPAIGN IN REAR OF VICKSBURG.

GRANT'S army was at last on hard ground. A footing had been gained on the east bank of the river, the enemy had been in a measure surprised, his flank had been turned, and his troops were scattered. It was an opportunity to strike hard and strike quickly in order to gain decisive results— one of those opportunities, the seizure or neglect of which marks the difference between a great and an incompetent leader. It was no longer a question of going to Banks' assistance, or of diverting troops on any side issue; the opportunity could only be improved by a prompt movement between the enemy's forces, dividing them and beating them in detail. Grant was equal to the emergency; and eighteen days from the time the first regiment landed at Bruinsburg, the Confederate forces at Jackson had been defeated and driven off, while those-near Vicksburg had been routed and shut up within their fortifications, never to come out, except as prisoners. The deeds of these eighteen days challenge comparison with the most brilliant campaigns of history.

Pemberton's returns for the last day of March showed an effective strength, as already stated, of 50,000 men. This included the Port Hudson garrison, all of which, except 6,000 effectives, had now been recalled to Vicksburg. But at Pemberton's urgent request, Gist's and Walker's brigades,

numbering 5,000 men, from Beauregard's command, in
South Carolina, were ordered to his relief on May 5th, and
3,000 cavalry, from Bragg's army, were sent from Tennessee
to Northern Mississippi. He thus had an available force of
over 50,000 men for the defence of the short line from
Vicksburg to Jackson. Grant's return for the month of
April showed the effective strength of the force operating
against Vicksburg to be 50,068. These numbers were not
actually present on the east bank of the river. McArthur's division of McPherson's corps was still up the river,
one brigade being left at Lake Providence throughout the
campaign, and the other two not coming up in time to
be of service prior to the assaults at Vicksburg. Blair's
division of Sherman's corps was also left behind to guard
the roads from Milliken's Bend, but rejoined the army the
day before the battle at Edwards' Station. After deducting
these divisions, the force with which Grant began the campaign was about 41,000, and at no time prior to the siege
had he over 45,000 available. These divisions in rear, however, being occupied in guarding his communications, it is
proper that they should be counted as part of his effective
strength.

The numbers were therefore practically equal. The advantages of position were all on the side of the Confederates, they being in their own country, with which they
were perfectly familiar, and which afforded admirable opportunities for defence, while the Union forces were entirely
ignorant of the country, and were dependent for supplies
upon seventy miles of wretched road, through overflowed
lands, passing within a short distance of the Confederate
position, and thus open to attack at all times. On the
other hand, those who fought for the Union had an enormous advantage in their naval resources, which gave them

unquestioned command of the river navigation, and without which the campaign never could have been prosecuted in the manner that it was prosecuted. At the time of the Battle of Port Gibson, the armies on both sides were scattered, one corps of Grant's army being at Milliken's Bend, seventy miles from Bruinsburg, and one-third of Pemberton's being at or near Jackson, forty-four miles by rail from Vicksburg.

It was thus about an even thing on both sides, all things considered, except the quality of the commanders. Here the difference was enormous. On the Union side were the foremost chiefs—Grant, Sherman, and McPherson—which the Northern armies produced throughout the whole war. Johnston and Pemberton belonged to a different category. Johnston's abilities were undoubtedly great, and it is universally conceded that he showed great ability in extricating an army from a dangerous position ; but he seldom struck back, and he lacked that divine fire which gains battles. On the Peninsula, in Mississippi, in Georgia, and in North Carolina, he had as good opportunities as ever fell to Lee or Jackson, but he never dealt any such blows as those of Gaines' Mill, Chancellorsville, Manassas, and the Wilderness. His mind inclined more to disputatious writing than to bold and vigorous movements in the field, and, in the midst of his campaigns, he found time to write letters of interminable length, for the purpose of showing that the responsibility for his failures rested with Jefferson Davis, or with some one else, but not with himself.

Pemberton did not belong to the grade of second-rate generals even. He had seen no active service in the Civil War prior to his assignment in Mississippi, in October, 1862, and his appointment to that important command was then an anomaly; his conduct of that command made the anomaly only more striking, and he was never again employed as a general.

On the evening of April 29th, after the unsuccessful naval attack on Grand Gulf, Grant had written to Sherman that he felt confident of effecting a crossing the next day, and he therefore desired Sherman to cease his demonstration against Haines' Bluff and join him as quickly as possible with two divisions, leaving the third to guard the road for the present. Sherman received this near Haines' Bluff, May 1st, and immediately sent back orders for Steele's and Tuttle's divisions at Milliken's Bend to take up their march for Hard Times. During the night he withdrew down the Yazoo River with Blair's division, and the following day reached Milliken's Bend. Leaving Blair's division to guard the road, he went on in person, overtook his other two divisions, and reached Hard Times on the 6th. While on the march he received an order from Grant, dated at Grand Gulf, May 3d, directing him to organize a train of 120 wagons, bring them to Perkins' plantation and thence ferry them over the river to Grand Gulf, where they were to be loaded with 100,000 rations from the transports. This would give five days' rations for Sherman's corps after crossing the river, and two days' for McClernand and McPherson in addition to the three days' which they had already drawn. These five days' rations for the whole command were all that they received until a base was established at Chickasaw Bayou nearly three weeks later. The troops virtually lived on the country until Vicksburg was invested.

In order to avail himself of the services of McArthur's division of McPherson's corps and Blair's division of Sherman's corps, orders were sent, on May 5th, by Grant to Hurlbut at Memphis to send forward Lauman's division of the Sixteenth Corps to Milliken's Bend as soon as transports could be obtained.

On May 2d, at Port Gibson, Grant received a letter from

Banks, sent by Farragut on the ram Switzerland from the mouth of Red River. The whole subject of the projected co-operation between Grant's and Banks' armies will be fully discussed in a subsequent chapter. It is only necessary to say here that when Grant determined on March 29th to move across the peninsula from Milliken's Bend and turn the Confederate left flank, it was his intention to prosecute a campaign along the Big Black against Vicksburg after crossing the river. But on April 10th he received a letter from Halleck, dated April 2d, calling special attention to the necessity of co-operating with Banks. Halleck said: "If he cannot get up to co-operate with you on Vicksburg, cannot you get troops down to help him on Port Hudson?" This letter caused a modification of Grant's plans. He still determined to cross the river at or near Grand Gulf, but once across he proposed to send an army corps down the east bank of the river to Bayou Sara, near Port Hudson, to co-operate with Banks in the reduction of that place. McClernand was notified on April 12th that his corps would make such a movement, and on the 14th a despatch was sent to Banks informing him of the project. But Banks did not receive the despatch until May 5th, and the letter which was now received from him, and which was dated April 10th, was not in answer to this despatch, but to a previous letter of Grant's dated as far back as March 23d, in which Grant had proposed sending a corps by the Lake Providence route, which at that time seemed to be favorable. Banks stated that he intended to return to Baton Rouge by May 10th, in order to co-operate against Port Hudson, and that he had 15,000 men available for field service. It was now May 2d. To send troops to co-operate at Port Hudson on the 10th and to await their return, even if successful, was to lose a month at least in exchange for a reinforcement

of only 15,000 men. It was to wait for the enemy to collect his scattered troops and to draw reinforcements from
other points, as, according to rumors which Grant received,
he was already doing. To have carried out any such ar-
rangement would have been to throw away an opportunity
which Grant's army had been working for months to obtain,
and which was at last within their grasp. There could be
no question of Grant's duty in the premises ; it was to follow up promptly the advantage he had gained at Port Gibson, and to use all his force to beat the enemy nearest to
him. All idea of detaching any troops at present to Banks'
assistance was therefore abandoned.

From the 3d to the 6th of May McClernand's and McPherson's corps lay at Willow Springs and Hankinson's Ferry,
waiting for supplies and for Sherman's corps. On the 7th,
Sherman being across the river, the advance was resumed.
Reconnoitring had been carried on during the last three
days, but nothing definite had been developed. At that time,
Grant's information as to the enemy's position and movements
was simply that the force at Hankinson's Ferry had retreated
toward Vicksburg ; and there were rumors that a force was
being collected at Jackson. His intention, therefore, was
to advance along the line of the Big Black toward Edwards' Station, midway between Vicksburg and Jackson,
keeping a close watch of the ferries, so as to prevent any
attack on his left flank ; he would thus move with his main
body between the enemy's forces, and would be in a position
to attack either one of them as soon as their presence should
be developed. But while keeping his main force in the
centre of the theatre of operations, McPherson was to be
thrown out somewhat in advance on his right flank, so that,
without getting out of reach of supports, he could reach
Jackson as quickly as possible, break up any force in that

vicinity, destroy the railroad, and rejoin the main body between Edwards' Station and Bolton. McPherson was therefore ordered to take the road from Hankinson's Ferry, through Rocky Springs, Utica, and Raymond, to Jackson. McClernand was to follow the direct road to Edwards' Station, through Rocky Springs, Cayuga, and Auburn; one division being thrown out on a parallel road to the left, nearer the Big Black. Sherman was to follow McClernand, and, in case the roads permitted, to come up abreast of him. The troops marched forward under these instructions, halting for the nights as follows:

May 7th: 13th Corps (McClernand) at Rocky Springs; 15th Corps (Sherman) at Grand Gulf; 17th Corps (McPherson) at Rocky Springs.

May 8th: 13th Corps at Big Sandy; 15th Corps at Hankinson's Ferry; 17th Corps at Rocky Springs.

May 9th: 13th Corps at Big Sandy; 15th Corps at Hankinson's Ferry; 17th Corps 7 miles west of Utica.

May 10th: 13th Corps at Big Sandy; 15th Corps at Big Sandy; 17th Corps at Utica.

May 11th: 13th Corps at Five Mile Creek; 15th Corps at Auburn; 17th Corps 5 miles northeast of Utica.

May 12th: 13th Corps at Fourteen Mile Creek; 15th Corps at Fourteen Mile Creek; 17th Corps at Raymond.

On the night of the 11th Grant had his army well in hand, and the orders for the next day were to move forward into position on Fourteen Mile Creek, about seven miles south of the railroad, McClernand on the Telegraph road from Auburn to Edwards' Station, with one division thrown out to the Big Black at Baldwin's Ferry, and Sherman on the road from Auburn to Raymond; McPherson was to push forward rapidly into Raymond, in the hopes of capturing some commissary stores there, the army being in need of rations.

McPherson moved out accordingly before 4 A.M. on the 12th, Logan's division in the lead, followed closely by Crocker's. The enemy's videttes were soon seen falling back before them, and about 9 A.M. stronger bodies of the enemy were encountered. Logan thereupon formed one of his brigades (Dennis') in line of battle across the road, the other two brigades marching by the flank in rear of it. The only cavalry regiment present with the army accompanied McPherson's command, and it was now thrown out on the flanks, with orders to explore every lateral road on which the enemy might be posted. In this formation Logan continued his advance for about two hours. About 11 A.M., he came to a small stream crossing the road, about two miles from Raymond, and on the hills beyond it the enemy was discovered in force, the infantry drawn up in support of two batteries, which were posted in a position to enfilade the road and the bridge over the stream. A halt was made, and the ground was reconnoitred. It was evident that the enemy intended to dispute the passage. Logan was at once ordered to attack him, and orders were sent back for Crocker to hasten his march and come up as a reserve. The enemy's force consisted of Gregg's brigade, which had come from Port Hudson to Jackson, in pursuance of Pemberton's orders of April 28th, and had moved out to Raymond to cover Jackson, and to fall upon Grant's flank should he attack Edwards' Station. The brigade numbered, including some State troops picked up at Jackson, something over 3,000 men.

Logan's division was at once formed by deploying J. E. Smith's brigade on the right of Dennis', and placing De-Golyer's (8th Michigan) battery on the road in the centre. The infantry advanced, preceded by skirmishers, and a severe engagement was soon in progress. Stevenson's brigade

was then deployed on the right of Smith's, and the line continued to advance, passing over some open ground, and gaining possession of a piece of woods across the creek, in close
proximity to the enemy's position on the hills. The fight
continued for two or three hours, the line gradually advancing until, during the afternoon, the leading brigade of
Crocker's division came up and deployed in support of
Dennis' brigade. The enemy then abandoned the field
and retreated rapidly toward Jackson. Logan's division
followed in pursuit, passing through Raymond at 5 P.M.,
and pursuing the enemy for some distance beyond the town,
but being unable to overtake them the men were halted
and went into camp for the night. Crocker's division was
but slightly engaged in this affair, losing but two men.
Logan lost 65 killed, 335 wounded, and 32 missing; total
432. Gregg's loss, according to his own report, was 73
killed, 229 wounded, and 204 missing—total 505. Two disabled guns were captured.

The defence made by the enemy at Raymond induced
Grant to believe that their force in the vicinity of Jackson
might be stronger than he had supposed ; reports reached
him moreover that reinforcements were arriving at Jackson,
and that Johnston was daily expected at that point to take
command in person. He therefore decided, before moving
up against Edwards' station, to make sure of Jackson, which
would be a dangerous point on his flank or rear if it remained in the enemy's possession ; and as McPherson's
corps might not be strong enough to get possession of it at
once, single-handed—its fortifications being reported strong
—he determined to move his whole force in that direction.
On the evening of the 12th, therefore, orders were given
(countermanding previous orders of the same date, to move
up to the railroad) for McPherson to push forward at day-

light toward Clinton and thence to Jackson; Sherman to
move to Raymond and thence by Mississippi Springs toward
Jackson; and McClernand, with three divisions, to follow
Sherman by the road on the north side of Fourteen Mile
Creek, sending his other division back to Auburn to meet
and escort the trains which were coming up from the river
at Grand Gulf. The sharp skirmishing which both Mc-
Clernand and Sherman had had during the day in getting
possession of the crossings of Fourteen Mile Creek on their
respective roads was a strong confirmation of the numerous
reports that Pemberton was concentrating his Vicksburg
troops at Edwards' Station, but before attacking them Grant
desired to first dispose of the troops at Jackson and destroy
the railroad at that point.

Before following the manner in which the movement on
Jackson was executed, it is necessary to notice the Confederate movements during the past ten days. On May 1st,
Pemberton telegraphed to Johnston, then with Bragg's army
at Tullahoma, Tenn., that Grant's army had crossed the river,
and that a furious battle had been raging all day at Port
Gibson. Johnston answered on the following day: "If
Grant crosses, unite all your troops to beat him. Success
will give back what was abandoned to win it." Pemberton
however, was on the ground and his judgment of the situation was different from Johnston's. He coincided in the
opinion expressed by Jefferson Davis, that for lack of supplies Grant's army could not live more than a few days
away from the river and that it would soon return toward
Warrenton. He thought it probable, however, that a raid
might be made on Jackson. Acting upon this judgment
he made the following dispositions. The troops arriving from Port Hudson and any reinforcements that might
come from South Carolina were to stop at Jackson and de-

fend that place. The three divisions, Bowen's, Loring's, and Stevenson's, that had moved out toward Grand Gulf were to retire and take up a position as follows : Bowen's at Bovina Station to defend the railroad bridge ; Loring's on the Hall's and Baldwin's Ferry roads, to defend those ferries ; and Stevenson's from the Hall's Ferry road to Warrenton, to resist an attack along the river. These positions were taken up by May 7th, and were reported to Johnston and to Jefferson Davis. Grant's movements were watched as carefully as possible, but both sides were so remarkably deficient in cavalry that each was largely in the dark as to the other's movements. On May 11th, the presence of a considerable Union force (one of McClernand's divisions) at Baldwin's Ferry convinced Pemberton that Grant could live away from the river, and led him to believe that Edwards' Station was to be the point of attack. Pemberton therefore ordered Bowen to advance to Edwards' Station, and Loring and Stevenson to move up and join him. Walker, who had just arrived at Jackson, from South Carolina, was ordered to advance toward Raymond in support of Gregg, who had moved there the previous day. If the enemy attacked in heavy force they were to fall back within the fortifications of Jackson ; if he moved toward Edwards' Station they were to attack his flank and rear. Walker did not leave Jackson until the 12th, and on that day Gregg was entirely overpowered by McPherson. On the same day there was considerable skirmishing on Fourteen Mile Creek, only five miles south of Edwards' Station, between the heads of column of McClernand's and Sherman's corps, and a brigade sent forward in observation by Bowen. This convinced Pemberton that he was to be attacked in force the next morning between Fourteen Mile Creek and Edwards' Depot, and Loring and Stevenson were urged on

VIII.—7

and came up with Bowen, forming line of battle south of Edwards' Station on the morning of the 13th. Instead of attacking, however, Grant's whole force moved off toward Raymond and Jackson.

While these events were in progress Johnston had received orders from Richmond on May 9th to "proceed at once to Mississippi and take chief command of the forces there." He arrived at Jackson on the evening of the 13th and found the two brigades of Gregg and Walker just returning from Raymond. Gist's South Carolina brigade and Maxey's Port Hudson brigade were expected to arrive the next day. The total strength of these four brigades was about 12,000 men. He also learned that Pemberton was at Edwards' Station but that a large Union force was at Clinton, cutting off any communication with him. He hastened to telegraph a few words to Richmond conveying this information, and adding, "I am too late." He seemed to foresee disaster, and desired to clear himself in advance of any responsibility for it, rather than to bend his whole energy to avert it.

Meanwhile, in pursuance of Grant's orders of the night of May 12th, already referred to, McPherson had moved from Raymond to Clinton on the 13th, and from there toward Jackson on the 14th. Sherman had moved through Raymond to Mississippi Springs on the 13th, and thence toward Jackson on the 14th, communicating with McPherson on the other road, so as to approach Jackson about the same hour. McClernand had moved to Raymond on the 13th, and sent one division forward as far as Clinton on the 14th. Sherman and McPherson approached Jackson in a pouring rain, about 10 A.M. on the 14th. Hearing of their approach from his vedettes, Johnston posted one brigade on each road —Walker toward Clinton, and Gregg toward Raymond—in intrenchments which had previously been constructed on high ground commanding the approaches over open fields. He instructed them to make enough of a defence to gain time for him to remove stores and valuable property by the railroad leading northward toward Canton.

Gregg made but a feeble resistance. After some preliminary artillery firing, Sherman moved a portion of his men around the enemy's flank, and, at 1 P.M., they reached the enemy's intrenchments to find them deserted. About 250 prisoners were taken, together with all their artillery (18 guns), and much ammunition and stores. Sherman lost less than 30 men.

Walker made more of a fight. He occupied a fine position on the crest of a semi-circular ridge, his flanks protected by woods, and in front of him a gently sloping open field terminating, about one-third of a mile distant, in a boggy creek lined with thick willows. His artillery commanded the bridge over this creek. McPherson arrived in front of this position about 9.30 A.M., but the rain fell in such torrents that his attack was delayed for an hour and a half by the fear of spoiling their ammunition if the men opened their cartridge-boxes (this was before the days of metallic cartridges). Crocker's division had the advance this day, and, during this hour and a half, his men were moved into place, the three brigades being deployed in line, with one brigade of Logan's division in reserve. At 11 A.M., the rain having partially ceased, skirmishers were sent forward, and advanced as far as the creek, but were unable to move through the open field beyond it. They were then recalled, and a charge was ordered. The whole division moved forward in a superb line, driving the enemy's skirmishers out of the creek, and advancing under fire across the field. When they were about half way across it, the enemy broke from their intrenchments and made a hasty re-

treat. They were pursued about a mile and a half, during
which Crocker's men fell somewhat into disorder, and were
finally brought to a halt by some artillery posted in an inner
line of works close to the town. While they were re-form-
ing, the Confederates made their escape over to the Canton
road. In this engagement McPherson lost 265 men, and he
gives the enemy's loss at 845, a large portion of whom were
prisoners, and 17 guns. The Confederate reports make their
losses a little less than 400. McPherson's and Sherman's
troops entered Jackson about the same time, between 3 and
4 P.M. Pemberton's attempt to defend Jackson against a
"raid" by a detachment out of supporting distance had led
to complete disaster, viz. : the defeat of two brigades with
heavy loss, the loss of 35 guns, the capture of Jackson, and
the destruction of the railroads and all public property at
that place.

Grant entered Jackson with Sherman's troops, and there
learned that Johnston had ordered Pemberton to move out
to attack his rear. He immediately determined to attack
Pemberton before Johnston, circling around to the north,
could come to his assistance. His troops were in compact
shape, well in hand for such a movement. McClernand had
two divisions at or near Raymond, one at Clinton, and one
on the road between Auburn and Raymond, bringing up the
trains. Blair's division of Sherman's corps and one brigade of McArthur's division, of McPherson's corps, had
come up with these trains from Grand Gulf. This gave five
and a half divisions, all within ten miles of the railroad between Bolton and Edwards' Station. They were all ordered
to move on converging roads toward the latter point.
McPherson was to leave Jackson, at daylight on the 15th, for
Bolton, and Sherman was to complete the work of destruction at Jackson, and follow McPherson in the afternoon.

On the same day that Johnston's troops were driven out of Jackson (May 14th) most important events had transpired in Pemberton's camp. On his arrival the previous evening Johnston had sent a somewhat vague despatch to Pemberton, referring to the presence of Sherman's [McPherson's] corps at Clinton, stating the necessity of establishing communication between their forces, and saying: "If practicable, come up in his rear at once; to beat such a detachment would be of immense value. The troops here could co-operate." This despatch was carried by an officer around McPherson's flank, and delivered to Pemberton at Bovina about 7 A.M. on the 14th. Pemberton immediately replied: "In directing this move I do not think you fully comprehend the position that Vicksburg will be left in; but I comply at once with your order." The troops were ordered forward from Edwards' Station. Pemberton, however, continued to meditate on the order, and a fatal divergence of views between himself and Johnston was soon developed. Johnston's idea was that every man between Jackson and Vicksburg should be united, to fight a battle on which the fate of Vicksburg would depend, believing that any attempt to cover Vicksburg by a detachment would result in the loss of Vicksburg and detachment both. Pemberton's whole idea was to defend Vicksburg to the last, and to make no move which would uncover that place. About noon, therefore, before his troops had got in motion, under his orders of the morning, he suspended these orders, and called a council of war; read Johnston's letter to his generals and asked their views. The numerical majority of them were in favor of Johnston's proposition, but the two senior generals (Loring and Stevenson) preferred a movement against Grant's communications in rear of Raymond, in the hope of cutting off his supplies and compelling his retreat. Pemberton per-

sonally was in favor of making no movement at all, but of
awaiting an attack on chosen ground; but as his officers
were "all eager for an advance," he waived his judgment.
But the movement toward Clinton he would not make, for
he considered that "suicidal." He therefore determined to
move against Grant's communications. As Johnston says in
his "Narrative," "Although averse to both opinions, General Pemberton adopted that of the minority of his council,
and determined to execute a movement which he disapproved, which his council of war opposed, and which was in
violation of the orders of his commander." It was an awkward see-saw—Johnston moving out of Jackson toward the
north and west in the hope of joining Pemberton, and Pemberton moving from Edwards' Station toward the south and
east, against the communications of an army that was living
on the country. Conflicting plans and lack of leadership had
brought things to a bad pass for the Confederates, on this
night of May 14th. Pemberton had 23,000 men (his report
says 17,500, but his last previous returns give 23,701)—to wit,
Loring's, Stevenson's, and Bowen's divisions—at Edwards'
Station ; he had left 9,000—Forney's and Smith's divisions—
at Vicksburg, defending the batteries from Snyder's Bluff to
Warrenton, which batteries were now not threatened, nor was
this force strong enough to defend them if they had been
seriously attacked ; in the vicinity of Jackson were 12,000
men under Johnston, part of them just defeated in two engagements and part of them just arriving in railroad cars.
Reinforcements to the extent of 5,000 additional men had
just been ordered from the East, and double that number
were promised at an early day. Here, then, were 44,000 men
(and more to come) scattered over a territory 50 miles long
by 20 broad, and divided into three detachments, no two of
which were in supporting distance. Moreover, the enemy,

with an equal force of 44,000 men, all within a few hours'
march of each other, was between the two principal detachments, greatly outnumbering each of them, though not more
numerous than all the detachments combined.   There never
was a more striking instance of the wisdom of keeping an
army united and the folly of dividing it into detachments to
defend several points at once.

At 5.40 P.M. on May 14th Pemberton sent a despatch to
Johnston by an officer, stating his intention to move against
Grant's communications.   The orders for this movement
were immediately issued.   Loring's division was to form the
right, Bowen's the centre and Stevenson's the left.   The
troops were to move with the right in front, preceded by a
detachment of cavalry; they were to follow the roads leading from Edwards' Station toward Raymond as far as Elliston's plantation and then turn south so as to strike the Auburn and Raymond road at Dillon's.   Grant's wagon train
was in fact in the vicinity of Dillon's on this day, but it was
well guarded by McClernand's and Blair's troops.   Pemberton's order prescribed that the movement should take place
in the morning of the 15th, but the troops were not in motion before 1 P.M.   A considerable delay then followed in
consequence of the heavy rain of the day previous.   The
roads were muddy and the ford at Baker's Creek on the direct road to Raymond was not passable.   The troops were
therefore moved up the creek to the Clinton road, which
crossed the creek on a bridge.   Crossing this bridge and
moving forward about two miles to the forks of the road
south of Champion's Hill, the head of column turned to the
right through a cross road which brought them to the direct Raymond road near Elliston's.   Along this cross-road
Pemberton's army passed the night.   At 6.30 A.M., on the
16th, a courier arrived from Johnston, bringing an answer to

Pemberton's despatch sent after the council of war on the 14th. Johnston's reply was dated on the Canton road, ten miles from Jackson, 8.30 A.M., May 15th. It was as follows : "Our being compelled to leave Jackson makes your plan impracticable. The only mode by which we can unite is by your moving directly to Clinton, and informing me that we may move to that point with about six thousand." This was a reiteration of the previous order to effect a junction on the north of the railroad, which Pemberton had submitted to a council and had decided not to follow, because he considered it "suicidal." Having moved in an opposite direction for the purpose of attacking the enemy's rear, and having come into such proximity to the enemy that his advance was already skirmishing, Pemberton now determined to obey the order ! Directions were given to get his trains out of the road, countermarch his columns to Edwards' Station, and there take the road to Brownsville in order to join Johnston. The movement was, however, impossible, for the enemy was already upon him.

On the 15th McClernand's divisions had moved as follows : Hovey's from Clinton to Bolton, Osterhaus' from Raymond to the cross roads half way to Bolton, Carr's from Raymond to the first cross roads northwest of that town, A. J. Smith's (followed by Blair's of Sherman's corps) from Auburn to Raymond. On the same day McPherson's corps had marched from Jackson to within a few miles of Hovey's bivouac at Bolton. On the night of May 15th, therefore, Grant had seven divisions, about 32,000 men, in close supporting distance between Bolton and Raymond, occupying all the roads which converged from these points on Edwards' Station. Grant in person reached Clinton from Jackson at 4.45 P.M. on the 15th, and immediately sent orders to McClernand to move forward cautiously, feeling the enemy if

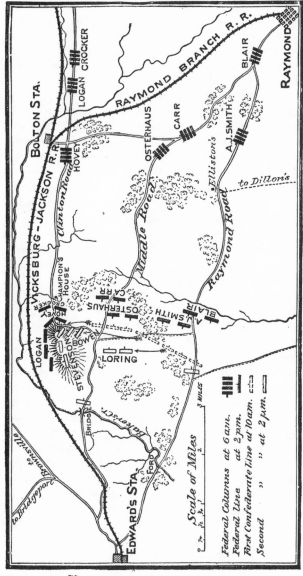

BOLTON STA.

RAYMOND BRANCH R. R.

RAYMOND

VICKSBURG — JACKSON R. R.

LOGAN CROCKER

HOVEY

OSTERHAUS

CARR

BLAIR

A.J.SMITH

Elliston's

to Dillon's

Clinton Road

Middle Road

Raymond Road

CHAMPION'S HOUSE

LOGAN CROCKER

HOVEY

CARR

OSTERHAUS

A.J.SMITH

BLAIR

STEVENSON

BOWEN

LORING

BRIDGE

Baker's Cr.

FORD

to Bridgeport

to Raymond

EDWARD'S STA.

Scale of Miles

0 ¼ ½ ¾ 1   2   3 MILES

Federal Columns at 6 a.m.
Federal Line   at 2 p.m.
First Confederate line at 10 a.m.
Second   „   „ at 2 p.m.

Champion's Hill. May 16, 1863.

7*

he encountered him, but not to bring on an engagement unless he felt entirely able to contend with him; also to order
Blair to move forward with him.

Grant passed the night at Clinton, and at daylight the
next morning two men, employees on the railroad, who had
passed through Pemberton's camp the day before, were
brought to his headquarters. They stated that Pemberton
had 80 regiments, estimated at 25,000 men in all, and that
he was moving to attack Grant's rear. Grant thereupon sent
a courier with an order to Sherman to bring one of his
divisions with the utmost possible speed to Bolton, and to
follow with the other as soon as possible. He also ordered
McPherson to move on rapidly beyond Bolton in support of
Hovey, and McClernand to establish communication between
the divisions of Blair and Osterhaus, and keep it up, moving
forward cautiously. He then rode to the front.

It will be seen by looking at the map that from the direct
road from Raymond to Bolton (about 8 miles long), there
are three roads leading to Edwards' Station. They were
known as the direct Raymond road, the middle Raymond
road, and the Clinton road. The first diverges about one
mile out from Raymond, and leads direct to Edwards' Station, crossing Baker's Creek at a ford; the second diverges
about two miles farther, and joins the third on the southern
side of Champion's Hill; the third passes half a mile south of
Bolton, and is the direct road from Clinton to Edwards' Station. Champion's Hill—then a portion of the plantation
of a Mr. Champion—is not more than 70 or 80 feet in
height, but it is quite a prominent feature in an otherwise flat landscape. Its northern side is abrupt, cut up
with steep ravines, and heavily wooded. The eastern and
southern slopes are more gentle and are partly open. The
Clinton road, coming in a westerly direction, strikes the

northeast slope of the hill near the point where Champion's
house then stood, then turns sharply to the south, passing
around the eastern slope of the hill till it meets the middle
road, then turns sharply to the west again and goes on to
the bridge over Baker's Creek, at the foot of the western
slope.   On the morning of the 16th the position was as follows : Hovey's division was on the Clinton road, moving
west from Bolton to Champion's Hill, with McPherson's
corps a few miles behind them; Osterhaus, followed by
Carr, was on the middle road, moving northwest to the same
point; and A. J. Smith, followed by Blair, was on the direct
Raymond road, near Elliston's, moving forward toward Edwards' Station.   On the Confederate side Loring was on the
Raymond road near Elliston's, skirmishing with A. J. Smith,
Bowen was in the centre, on a small cross-road leading to
Champion's Hill, and Stevenson was on the left, at the junction of the Clinton and middle roads.   All three were under
orders to countermarch to Edwards' Station.   It was soon
found, however, that the Union troops (McClernand's) were
pressing their rear so closely that the order to countermarch
could not be carried out.   It was necessary to stop and fight.
Orders were therefore given to form line of battle behind a
creek running in front of the cross road above mentioned.
This position was assumed between 9 and 10 A.M.   As the
skirmishing and artillery firing increased in amount on the
Raymond road as soon as the enemy made a stand, Mc-
Clernand sent word to Grant at 9.45 A.M. to ask if he should
bring on a general engagement.   Grant had ridden forward
from Clinton early in the morning, and near Bolton had
found McPherson's corps repairing a bridge, and the road in
front of them blocked with Hovey's wagons.   These were
quickly moved out of the way and McPherson's corps resumed its advance.   Grant came up with Hovey's division

not far from Champion's house about 10 A.M. Hovey's
skirmishers were already in contact with the enemy, and he
was forming his men in readiness to bring on an action at
any moment, but Grant directed him not to attack until he
heard from McClernand.

About noon McClernand's 9.45 A.M. despatch was received,
asking if he should bring on an engagement. From the
bearer Grant learned that McClernand was between two and
three miles distant. Grant sent a written reply at 12.35 P.M.,
directing McClernand to attack the enemy in force, if opportunity occurred. Subsequently verbal messages were sent,
directing him to push forward with all rapidity. These
orders did not reach McClernand until after 2 P.M. He immediately ordered Smith and Osterhaus to "attack the enemy vigorously, and press for victory." But the attack was
by no means vigorous.

On the other flank, McPherson's corps had reached the
field about 11 A.M., Logan's division in the lead, with
Crocker a short distance in the rear. As soon as Logan arrived, Hovey's two brigades were deployed on the left
(southeast) of the Clinton road, and two brigades of Logan's division formed on the right of the road, the third brigade being held in reserve. Hovey's men immediately
advanced, and, swinging their left flank forward, they
began climbing the eastern front of the hill under a heavy
fire. The troops opposed to them were two brigades of Stevenson's division. While Hovey had been forming his men
and waiting for the arrival of McPherson, Stevenson had noticed the concentration on his left flank, and had taken the
brigade (Barton's) on his extreme right and sent it in rear
of his line to the extreme left to take position in the woods
on Champion's Hill facing north; the other two brigades
(Lee's and Cumming's) had been marched by the left flank

along the road, and had taken position around the northeast
point of the hill, where the Clinton road ascends it, and
from there to the left; his fourth brigade (Reynolds') had
gone back with the trains toward Edwards' Station. Hovey's attack led against the right flank of Stevenson's new
position, and the men gradually fought their way up the
hill, driving back Cumming's brigade fully 600 yards, and
capturing 11 guns, the horses of which had nearly all
been killed by the well-directed fire of Hovey's batteries
posted near Champion's house. While Hovey was making
this attack, two brigades (J. E. Smith's and Leggett's) of
Logan's division had advanced against the northern slope of
the hill on Hovey's right. They gradually and steadily
drove the enemy before them as they climbed the wooded
slope ; and, when their attack was well advanced, the third
brigade (Stevenson's) of this division, which had been kept
in reserve for about an hour, was brought up on their right
and sent across a ravine, penetrating between Lee's and
Barton's brigades, cutting off the latter from all communication with the rest of his division, and capturing 7 guns.

Hovey maintained his position until about 2 P.M., when
the enemy was heavily reinforced, and he was driven back.
In moving over to the left during the morning, Stevenson
had notified Pemberton that the main attack was evidently
to be on his left flank, and, if successful, it would cut off
the line of retreat to Edwards' Station. He therefore intended to move as rapidly as possible to meet it, but, in so
doing, he would necessarily leave a gap between his division
and Bowen's. On receipt of this, Pemberton ordered Bowen
to follow Stevenson, and keep this gap closed. Shortly
after 2 P.M. Bowen closed up with Stevenson, and found
Hovey's men in possession of the crest of the hill and of the
captured guns. The leading brigade (Cockrell's) was imme-

diately sent into action against Hovey, followed quickly by
the other brigade (Green's).   Overpowered by superior numbers, Hovey's men were forced to give way ; they fell back
slowly, fighting desperately for every foot, but were gradually driven down the hill, and back through the open fields
around Champion's house, losing all but two of the eleven
guns which they had captured.   But by this time Crocker's
division had come up, and, on an appeal from Hovey to
Grant for reinforcements, this division was ordered to support Hovey.   These two divisions now moved forward again,
driving the Confederates before them, and for the third
time contesting the possession of the slope of the hill.   In
sight of this advance, Cumming's brigade, of Stevenson's
division, broke and fled; Bowen's Missouri troops made a
desperate fight, but were finally forced to give way, losing
five of the guns which had previously been lost and recaptured.   They made their retreat through a cross-road near
that where they had first formed in the morning, and, reaching the direct Raymond road, they retreated to the ford over
Baker's Creek.   Stevenson's division was completely routed
and broken up ; Barton's brigade retreated across Baker's
Creek by the bridge on the Clinton road, hotly pursued by
Logan's men, and Cumming's and Lee's brigades fled in
confusion to the Raymond road, and thence to the ford.

When the attack became so decided on the left flank,
Loring was at first ordered to send one, and then a second
brigade to the assistance of Stevenson and Bowen.   Buford's
brigade moved first, followed by Featherston's with Loring
in person ; the third brigade (Tilghman's) was left on the
lower road to confront Smith's and Blair's divisions.   The
two brigades did not reach the forks of the Clinton and
middle roads before the entire left flank was routed.   Loring
was then notified to form his men between the Clinton and

Raymond roads, to cover the retreat of Bowen's division and
pick up some of Stevenson's fugitives. In this position he
was attacked by Osterhaus' division and soon gave way.
He fell back again to the Raymond road, and there met
Tilghman's brigade, which had made a gallant attack against
Smith's division, in the course of which Tilghman had been
killed; the brigade had been repulsed and was now falling
back.   Loring then retreated along the Raymond road
toward the ford on Baker's Creek, having received word from
Stevenson and Bowen that they would hold the ford until
he arrived. But they were unable to keep their word, for
about sunset, a portion of Carr's division, which had moved
rapidly forward and crossed at the bridge on the Clinton road,
began taking a position which would command the Raymond
road. Stevenson and Bowen moved off hastily while there
was yet time, and when Loring reached the ford he found the
Union troops on the opposite bank. He then turned back
in search of another ford lower down the creek, and wan-
dered about on unknown roads during several hours of the
night, abandoning all his artillery—only to learn when he did
find a ford that the Union troops were already in Edwards'
Station, thus completely cutting him off from the rest of the
army. He therefore moved off to the south, and on the following day reported to Johnston his arrival, "without baggage, wagons, or cooking utensils," at Crystal Springs, on
the New Orleans Railroad, 25 miles south of Jackson.
Bowen's division, and the remnants of Stevenson's, made
their way back to the Big Black River.

The rout of Pemberton's army was complete. But if Mc-
Clernand had acted with the energy shown by McPherson,
and the three division commanders with him, Logan, Hovey,
and Crocker, every man in Pemberton's army would probably have been captured. Hovey's and Logan's divisions

brought on the battle by an energetic attack, and when
Pemberton threw his whole force upon them, the three
together bore the brunt of the battle. McClernand had
four divisions—more than half of the army—on the middle
and Raymond roads. Had he thrown his men in with the
vigor displayed by Hovey and Logan, he would have brushed
aside the small force in front of him, and cut off the retreat
by the Raymond road to the ford, in the same manner that
Logan cut off the Clinton road to the bridge. Pemberton
would then have been confronted with superior forces on
three sides, and an impassable stream on the fourth, and in
the demoralized condition of his men that evening, he
would have had no option but to surrender. That these four
divisions under McClernand's command were not energetically employed is abundantly shown by the following table
of losses.

	Killed.	Wounded.	Missing.	Total.
Hovey's division	211	872	119	1,202
Logan's "	48	326	29	403
Crocker's "	123	539	0	662
Osterhaus' "	14	76	20	110
Carr's "	1	0	2	3
A. J. Smith's division	0	24	4	28
Blair's division	0	0	0	0
	397	1,837	174	2,408

The Confederate losses were reported as follows:

	Killed.	Wounded.	Missing.	Total.
Stevenson's division	233	527	2,091	2,851
Bowen's "	131	430	307	868
Loring's "	16	61	43	120
	380	1,018	2,441	3,839

But if Pemberton's army was not captured it was very thoroughly routed, with the loss of 24 pieces of artillery ; its wagons were saved, owing to their early departure during the morning under the orders for a retrograde movement to join Johnston.

During the night of the 16th the demoralized troops kept arriving at the railroad bridge over the Big Black. Reynolds' and Barton's brigades went through Edwards' Station, closely pursued by Carr's division of McClernand's corps, which reached that point at 8 P.M., and passed the night there.   The rest of Pemberton's men avoided that place and moved straight from Baker's Creek Ford to the railroad bridge.   Pemberton was already there when they arrived, and directed the disordered regiments of Stevenson's division to move on as far as Mt. Alban's Station ; but the men gave out from exhaustion when they had gone as far as Bovina, and they were halted at that point between 1 and 2 o'clock in the morning.   Bowen's division was ordered into the trenches covering the bridge, and it was intended that Loring's division should form on the west bank.   But Loring never appeared.

When Pemberton first moved out from Vicksburg after the battle of Port Gibson, it was his intention to defend the line of the Big Black, and for this purpose he ordered *têtes-de-pont* to be constructed, covering the principal ferries and the railroad bridge.   Grant's troops arrived at the ferries so quickly that it was impossible to defend them, but a *tête-de-pont* had been constructed in front of the railroad bridge. At this point the river makes a wide bend in the form of a horseshoe, the distance in a straight line across the loop being about a mile.   The ground on the concave side of the bend was perfectly flat and entirely open, excepting some bunches of timber here and there ; a narrow but deep ditch or bayou ran across this ground in a nearly straight line. On the other side of the river the bluffs were 40 or 50 feet high, and the ground very broken. The line selected for the trenches ran straight across the open ground behind this ditch. Work was begun upon it on the 12th of May and finished on the 15th. This line would have served its purpose as a *tête-de-pont*, had it been occupied by a small advanced guard, supported by the main body in strong force, properly posted in its rear on the west bank. Unfortunately for Pemberton, the troops (Loring's division) which he had intended to post on the west bank, as they had been the least engaged at Champion's Hill, were cut off in that battle and never rejoined him. He was thus caught defending a bridge with nearly all his reliable troops in the *tête-de-pont*, and nothing in support. A complete stampede was the result.

In moving forward to Edwards' Station on the 13th and 14th with his field army, Pemberton had called up two brigades from those left in the defences of Vicksburg, and had stationed them at the Big Black bridge to secure that point in his rear against surprise. These were Vaughn's and Baldwin's brigades of Smith's division, the former of which was posted in the trenches on the east bank, and the latter at Bovina, a few miles in rear, in support. During the night of the 16th Bowen's division was halted and placed in the same trenches, Cockrell's brigade on the right and Green's brigade on the left of Vaughn. The object was to defend the position long enough to cover the crossing of Loring's division as soon as it should arrive. In order to facilitate the crossing, the ties of the railroad bridge were planked, and a second bridge was improvised by taking a steamer which happened to be there and mooring it athwart the stream. It was nearly as long as the stream was wide, and the vacant spaces at stem and stern were bridged over with plank.

Grant's army passed the night of the 16th between the battlefield and Edwards' Station, with the exception of Sherman's corps, which bivouacked at Bolton. At daylight the next morning the pursuit was resumed, McClernand's corps in the lead, moving toward Big Black bridge, followed by McPherson. Sherman's corps moved from Bolton direct to Bridgeport, in order to turn the position at the bridge. Carr's division, which was in the advance, came in sight of the trenches at the bridge about 8 A.M., and he immediately deployed his two brigades on the right of the road. Osterhaus was but a short distance behind him, and as soon as he came up his division was deployed on the left of the road. A few batteries were brought into position and some skirmishers sent forward, but the ground to the left of the road was completely open, and it was not deemed advisable to assault the works across such ground until more troops should come up. On the right of the road, however, there was a clump of woods extending nearly to the river, and Carr moved his men to these woods in order to gain an advantageous position for assault.

On the Confederate side everything was at odds and ends. There seemed to be no one in command, and the horses of the field guns that had been placed in the trenches had been removed across the river; if a retreat became necessary the guns must be abandoned. The distance from the point where the trenches crossed the road to the bridge was fully three-quarters of a mile; it was perfectly open ground, and there was no supporting force on the other bank of the river. Under such circumstances, in case of a retreat the men would be slaughtered. There were not more than 5,000 men in the trenches, and fully double that num-

ber now confronted them, with the prospect of more to arrive very soon. The "Missouri division" (Bowen's), was
renowned for hard fighting, both before and after this affair,
but this was a case to try the nerves of the steadiest veterans,
for every man felt instinctively that he was in a position
where he ought never to have been placed. As they observed the movement toward the woods on their left flank,
many of them slipped off one by one to the bridge in rear.

Meanwhile brisk firing was carried on opposite the centre
for about half an hour, during which Carr's division was
moving into the piece of woods on the right, and A. J.
Smith's division was coming up and forming on Osterhaus'
left. Just as Smith's division was coming into line Carr's
men emerged from the woods with a loud cheer, and rushed
forward upon the intrenchments. Vaughn's brigade in the
centre saw that they were cut off from the bridge and immediately turned and ran at full speed. Bowen's division
at first attempted to make a defence, but in a few minutes
saw that it was hopeless, and it then joined in the attempt
to reach the bridge. All the reports, Union and Confederate, speak of this as a precipitate flight, every man for himself. The 18 pieces of artillery were all abandoned, over
1,400 small arms were thrown away, and one-third of the
command (1,751 men) were cut off and made prisoners. The
rest reached the bridges in time, and immediately after
crossing set fire to them. As they had been previously prepared for this purpose by scattering loose cotton and tur-
pentine on them, they were quickly consumed. The losses
on the Federal side in this engagement were 273 in killed
and wounded, all but 30 of which were in Carr's division.
The whole affair was over soon after 9 o'clock in the morning.

The rest of the day and the night were consumed in

building bridges.   One was constructed near the site of the
railroad bridge for McClernand's corps.   McPherson's corps
reached the river about three miles to his right about 2 P.M.,
and immediately began the construction of two bridges, one
of solid timber, and the other of timber cribs filled with
cotton bales and floored with planks obtained by tearing
down a cotton-gin in the vicinity.   Sherman's corps (rejoined on this day by Blair's division) reached the river at
Bridgeport at noon.   The only pontoon bridge train accompanying the army was with Sherman, and his bridge
was ready by nightfall.   The others were not completed
until after midnight.

When the engagement opened in the morning, Pemberton, who was at Bovina, telegraphed to Vicksburg for a train
of cars ; as soon as it arrived, after sending a note by a
scout to Johnston to inform him of the disasters of the preceding and present day, and to state that Haines' Bluff was
now untenable, he hastened to Vicksburg, turning over the
command to Stevenson with orders to bring the army back,
and take post behind the fortifications.   The delay necessary to construct bridges gave the Confederates the whole of
the 17th in which to effect their retreat to Vicksburg (12
miles) unmolested.   On his arrival at the latter place, Pemberton telegraphed to Haines' Bluff, directing Hébert's
brigade of Smith's division, which formed the garrison at
that point to return forthwith to Vicksburg, leaving two
companies to spike the guns and blow up the magazines on
the approach of the enemy.   He then made arrangements
to dispose the troops, as they came in, for the defence of
Vicksburg.   Stevenson's division (four brigades) was placed
on the right, holding the line from Warrenton to the railroad, about five miles ; Forney's division (two brigades) was
in the centre, from the railroad to the graveyard road, a

distance of about two miles ; M. L. Smith's division (three
brigades) was on the left, from the graveyard road to the
river, about two miles; Bowen's division, and some small
detachments that had been called in from Fort Pemberton
and other points, were placed in reserve.[1]   During the two
weeks since he left Vicksburg Pemberton had lost the whole
of Loring's division, 8,700 men, in addition to the killed,
wounded, and missing in Stevenson's and Bowen's divisions
at Champion's Hill and Big Black, amounting to about
5,300 ; so that instead of 35,000, he now had about 21,000
effective men to guard his trenches, although doubtless his
rolls of men drawing rations at this time numbered over
33,000.   His troops all returned from the Big Black during
the afternoon of the 17th and were in their places early on
the 18th.   They had the whole of that day to recover their
composure before their pursuers could arrive.

Sherman crossed two divisions at Bridgeport during the
night of the 17th, followed by the other division the next
morning.   At break of day his leading divisions were on
the road to Vicksburg.   McClernand's corps, with the exception of Hovey's division, which was left at Edwards' Station
and Big Black, began crossing in the morning of the 18th
and was on the march by noon.   He followed the direct road
to Vicksburg until after passing Mt. Alban's Station, where
he turned into the Baldwin's Ferry road so as to give room
for McPherson between himself and Sherman.   McPherson's
corps, which had been joined on the evening of the 16th by
one brigade of McArthur's division, crossed in the morning
and moved up to the Bridgeport road, following in rear of
Sherman's corps.   By 10 A.M., Sherman had reached the
Benton road, thus interposing between Vicksburg and

---

[1] See map, Siege of Vicksburg.

Haines' Bluff. A regiment of cavalry was immediately sent
to take the batteries at the latter place from the rear. Sherman halted a couple of hours to allow his men to close up
and rest, and to receive instructions from Grant, who soon
came up. Sherman was directed to form the right of the
line, and at noon he resumed his march. About two miles
outside the intrenchments the road forked, the right hand
known as the Graveyard, and the left hand as the Jackson,
road; both leading into Vicksburg. Sherman took the
right hand and on approaching the defences moved two divisions toward the right along the ridge extending to the
Mississippi. Only one brigade of McPherson's corps came
up that night, Logan's and Quinby's[1] divisions being halted
a few miles back on the road at nightfall. About half of
Grant's army was in sight of the fortifications on the night
of the 18th. The cavalry regiment sent to Haines' Bluff by
Sherman arrived in rear of the batteries at that point during
the afternoon. The two Confederate companies left behind
to destroy the guns had fled without accomplishing their
purpose, and the cavalrymen rode in without opposition.
Signal was made to a gunboat lying in the Yazoo and it
came up and took possession. The magazine was full of
ammunition and the guns were all in good order. There
were 14 of them, of the heaviest calibre of that period.

The note which Pemberton had sent from Bovina on the
morning of the 17th was delivered to Johnston during the
succeeding night at a point on the road between Livingston
and Brownsville, whither he had moved in the hope of joining Pemberton. Johnston immediately answered in these
words: "If Haines' Bluff is untenable, Vicksburg is of no

---

[1] Quinby had been on leave of absence since May 1st, in consequence of severe
illness, but rejoined his command on the morning of the 17th. During his absence his division was commanded by Crocker.

value and cannot be held. If, therefore, you are invested in Vicksburg, you must ultimately surrender. Under such circumstances, instead of losing both troops and place, we must, if possible, save the troops. If it is not too late, evacuate Vicksburg and its dependencies, and march to the northeast." This was received by Pemberton at noon of the 18th. On reading it he was fairly aghast. He says in his report : " The evacuation of Vicksburg ! It meant the loss of the valuable stores and munitions of war collected for its defence, the fall of Port Hudson, the surrender of the Mississippi River, and the severance of the Confederacy. These were mighty interests, which, had I deemed the evacuation practicable, in the sense in which I interpreted General Johnston's instructions, might well have made me hesitate to execute them."

Much might be said on both sides of Johnston's proposition, but the question of the moment was, could the order be obeyed? Pemberton called a council of war, read Johnston's note, and asked the opinion of his generals if it were practicable to comply with it. Their opinion was unanimous, " that it was impossible to withdraw the army from this position with such morale and material as to be of further service to the Confederacy." While the council was deliberating, guns were heard booming outside the works. Sherman already held the road leading "to the northeast." Pemberton wrote a note to Johnston, stating the action of the council, and announcing his intention to hold Vicksburg to the last, as he " conceived it to be the most important point in the Confederacy." Having sent this by a scout, he resumed his occupation of giving orders for the defence.

A portion of Smith's division had occupied the ridge beyond Fort Hill, looking down into the Yazoo bottom on the north of the city. Pemberton thought that this gave too

great a development to his line for the number of troops on
hand, and he therefore ordered Smith to withdraw to the
Fort Hill ridge in rear of it. This was accomplished quietly
during the night. Steele's division, of Sherman's corps,
was working its way along this ridge at nightfall on the
18th, and in the morning he took possession of these deserted batteries, and extended his right to the Mississippi
River. At 8 A.M. on the 19th Sherman's corps was in position about 400 yards from the enemy's works, on the same
ground it occupied throughout the siege—*i.e.*, on the ridge
beyond Fort Hill, from the Mississippi River to the Graveyard road; Steele's division was on the right, Blair's on the
left, and Tuttle's in reserve. McClernand's corps came into
position about 2,500 yards from the enemy's works near
the Baldwin's Ferry road; Osterhaus's division on the left
of that road, A. J. Smith's on the right, and Carr's in reserve. McPherson's corps arrived only a short time before
noon, and took position on the Jackson road, between Sherman and McClernand; Logan's division on the right, and
Quinby's on the left, each with a brigade in reserve. Sherman was so close to the enemy's works that skirmishing
had been going on during the whole morning. The other
corps were hardly yet in position to attack, but Grant relied
upon the demoralization of the enemy, due to his constant
defeats in recent battles, and he therefore ordered a general
assault at 2 P.M. Sherman's corps made a vigorous effort
against the works near the Graveyard road, and his men
succeeded in reaching the ditch, but, being unsupported
by the other corps, they were repulsed. McClernand and
McPherson were so far from the works, that they had succeeded in accomplishing nothing more than an advance
for several hundred yards under a heavy fire, when darkness closed in upon them. The troops on the defence

VIII.—8

were intelligent veterans. They had been marched, and countermarched, and fought, with very little plan and system for the last two weeks, culminating in the affair at Black River bridge, where they had run like sheep. But now they were in intrenchments which had been prepared long before, and they felt at home. Their demoralization was all gone, and they stood up in their works, and poured out such a fire as beat back Sherman's troops with comparative ease. It was evident that Vicksburg was not to be taken by a mere *coup-de-main*.

It was now eighteen days since Grant had secured a footing on the east bank of the Mississippi by the battle of Port Gibson. In that time he had marched about 200 miles, and by keeping his army together had defeated the enemy's scattered detachments in four engagements, at Raymond, Jackson, Champion's Hill, and Big Black, all fought within six days; he had inflicted a loss upon them of 8,000[1] in killed, wounded, and missing, had captured 88 pieces of their artillery, and, finally, had driven them into the narrow defences of Vicksburg, causing their outworks at Haines' Bluff, Warrenton, and Grand Gulf to be abandoned, and establishing his own base on the Yazoo River in easy and safe reach of his gunboats and transports. He had not only prevented the junction of the enemy's detachments, but had still further scattered their forces, so that they had fully 14,000 less men available in Vicksburg at the close of this period than at the beginning. During these eighteen days Grant's men had had but five days' rations, having lived for the rest on the country; their own losses had been a little less than 3,500. We must go back to the campaigns of Napoleon to

---

[1] At Raymond, 800; Jackson, 1,100; Champion's Hill, 4,100; Big Black, 2,000. The number of prisoners which reached Memphis, May 29th, on their way North, was reported by Hurlbut at 4,500.

find equally brilliant results accomplished in the same space of time with such small loss.

His success was aided—as was Napoleon's in 1796—by the incapacity of his opponents. There can be little question that when Grant crossed the river, the proper movement for Pemberton was to abandon Jackson, and concentrate his whole force for a decisive battle. Yet such a movement involved a great sacrifice, for Jackson was the meeting-point of railroads by which reinforcements were arriving and were to arrive, and this sacrifice Pemberton was not prepared to make.

When Johnston reached Jackson on the night of the 13th, he was, perhaps, as he said, "too late." The situation was certainly full of danger, which he clearly foresaw. Yet a man of a more aggressive nature would hardly have con- tented himself with accepting the situation, and sending a vaguely worded order by a messenger, but would rather, at any risk of health, have joined Pemberton at once—leaving his detachments to follow—in order to fully understand the condition of affairs, and issue his orders advisedly. He would then, at least, have secured compliance with his orders, and there would have been no divided responsibility. For an emergency, such as then existed, a man of Johnston's temperament was peculiarly unsuited.

Pemberton's vacillation in first declining to obey John- ston's order to move from Edwards' Station to Clinton, and then attempting to execute it when in the presence of the enemy, cannot be defended. But it is quite possible that the effect of obeying the order would have been, as he says, "to abandon Vicksburg without striking a blow for its de- fence ;" for it may be safely said, without detracting in any way from Johnston's skill in defensive campaigns, that no decisive battle would have been fought under his command after the junction. It would have been "a skilful retreat" to Meridian, "owing to the insufficiency of his forces." Later, when Johnston ordered Pemberton to evacuate Vicksburg, if Haines' Bluff was untenable, and march to the northeast, there is much to justify Pemberton's idea of remaining, even had the evacuation been possible. For more than a year the Confederates had been defending Vicksburg, with uniform success; it was less than a month since Grant was still cooped up in the swamps, well-nigh dismayed at his lack of success in the various bayous. The Confederate President and Secretary of War had congratulated Pemberton on his success, and repeatedly urged him to stand firm, the possession of the Mississippi being vital to the success of the Confederacy. The Union gunboats had, indeed, run past the batteries, but the river was still closed as a line of commerce and communications, so long as the batteries at Vicksburg were intact. As Pemberton says, "these were mighty interests;" and to secure them, provisions and ammunition had been forwarded to stand a siege, and promises had been held out that every available man would be sent to raise it. Pemberton knew that Johnston had already a considerable force on the outside, and that it would rapidly be augmented; he had every reason to believe that Johnston, appreciating the vital importance of prompt and energetic action, would quickly strike a vigorous blow for his relief. The whole theory of the Confederacy was not to conquer the North, but to prove that the South could not be conquered; to remain on the defensive, beat back the Northern armies, and prolong the war until the North, in despair, should agree to a compromise. To hold Vicksburg and the Mississippi River to the last was probably more in accord with the general line of Confederate policy than to abandon it in the vain hope of regaining it after a battle.

Finally, the anomalous character of the command on the Confederate side was in itself a direct invitation to disaster, for which Jefferson Davis was personally responsible. Pemberton commanded the Department of Mississippi and East Louisiana, reporting directly to the authorities in Richmond and receiving orders from them. Yet Johnston commanded both Pemberton's and Bragg's armies, without the possibility of being really in charge of either. Hence Pemberton regarded himself as chiefly responsible for Vicksburg, and looked upon Johnston's instructions in the nature of advice rather than of positive orders.

Opposed to such divided responsibility and confusion of authority there was a united army with a single general in command, who had clearly defined plans and was in the midst of his troops to carry them out. Fortunately, he was at this time cut off from all communication with Washington, for on May 11th Halleck telegraphed him to unite his forces with those of Banks between Vicksburg and Port Hudson. Had this telegram been received and obeyed the whole campaign would have been wrecked. Of this no one was more convinced than Halleck and the President, both of whom were enthusiastic in their praises of the campaign when it was concluded.

CHAPTER VI.

THE SIEGE AND SURRENDER OF VICKSBURG.

VICKSBURG lies upon the river slope of a range of bluffs which extend for hundreds of miles along the eastern side of the alluvial valley of the Mississippi, and which are here washed by the river itself, though at other points of its winding course it is often from 50 to 100 miles distant from them. These bluffs are about 250 feet in height and are composed of a peculiarly tenacious, semi-indurated clay, which when cut vertically for roads or other purposes resists the action of the weather and retains its vertical sides for generations. In such a soil the action of running water in small streams has, in the course of centuries, resulted in cutting the bluff or plateau into deep ravines with remarkably steep sides, separated by very narrow ridges. The topography is thus extremely broken and complicated, and is of such a character that no manœuvres of troops are possible over it. On the other hand it lends itself admirably to the purposes of fortification, the narrow ridges having a complete command over the deep ravines in front of them, and their sinuous course enabling each point to bring a cross fire in front of adjacent points.

A careful study of the map is necessary to form even an approximate idea of the main features of this topography. It will be noticed that from the northeast corner of the town a ridge runs out to the eastward, on which is the Jack-

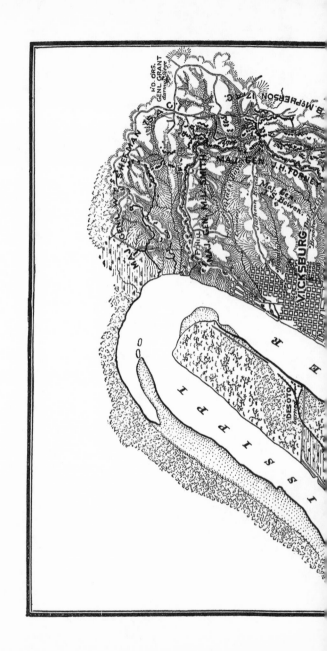

SIEGE OF VICKSBURG, 1863.

son road; about two miles from the outskirts of the town,
this ridge meets another ridge, which trends off to the southwest for several miles, following an irregular course, but having an unbroken crest nearly on the same level all the way.
Between the Jackson ridge and this second ridge there is a
collection of minor valleys, the drainage of which is finally
united into Stout's bayou, which empties into the Mississippi a few miles lower down, but is here separated from it
by another ridge, on which is the Warrenton road.   The
Confederate line began on the Warrenton ridge about three
miles south of town, crossed Stout's Bayou, and then followed the ridge without a break for five miles to the Jackson road.   Here the ridge turns to the east and subsequently to the north and west, reaching the Mississippi at
the point of the bend; but this ridge was considered as
giving too long a development to the line of defence, and
from the Jackson road the line ran due north, to a ravine
called Glass' Bayou, fully 150 feet deep, with precipitous
sides, and filled with a dense growth of vines and cane;
crossing this it continued along a lateral spur to the Graveyard road, where it intersected another narrow, level ridge,
running due west about two miles to the river at Fort Hill.[1]
This line had been selected for fortification in the autumn
of 1862, and during the winter and spring it had been most
thoroughly fortified.   At the salient and commanding points
of the ridge, at an average distance of perhaps two hundred
yards from one another, batteries were constructed for artillery in the form of redans, lunettes, or, in some places,

---

[1] The reports of the Engineer and other officers of the Seventeenth Corps, which
held the line at the Jackson road, speak of the crest of the ridge on that road as
"Fort Hill."   This is a mistake; Fort Hill overlooks the river about two miles
north of the city landing, as shown on the accompanying map.   It was so named
because the Spaniards erected a fort upon it as a defence against the Indians,
when they ascended the Mississippi, and it has retained the name to this day.

closed redoubts ; the parapets of these batteries were 25 feet thick and 10 feet high, and the ditch was 7 feet deep, making the top of the parapet 17 feet above the bottom of the ditch. Between the salient points there ran a line of intrenchments, which in the whole eight miles of line was broken only at two points, *i.e.*, at Stout's Bayou and Glass' Bayou ; this intrenchment was 10 feet thick and 5 feet high, and the ditch in front of it was 4 feet deep. In a few places, where cross spurs jutted out from the main ridge, advanced batteries were constructed, making a double or triple line, but in general there was only a single line of works.

They were defended when the siege began by 128 pieces of artillery, 36 of which were siege guns and the rest field pieces. In addition to these land defences, the circuit was made complete by a series of water batteries, extending from Fort Hill on the north, through the town, and along the Warrenton ridge till they met the land batteries on the south. They mounted 31 pieces of siege artillery of the heaviest calibre, and 13 pieces of field artillery.

The troops for the defence numbered about 20,000 effective men, divided into four divisions, under Generals Stevenson, Forney, Smith, and Bowen, and Waul's " legion." Stevenson's division held the right, beginning at the Warrenton road and ending at the railroad ; his four brigades were posted in the following order from right to left, viz. : Barton, from the Warrenton road about one mile north ; Reynolds, from Barton's right to the Hall's Ferry road ; Cummings, from the Hall's Ferry road to the square fort, about three-quarters of a mile south of the railroad ; Lee, from the square fort to the railroad.

Forney's division came next, with two brigades posted as follows : Moore, on both sides of the Baldwin's Ferry road, his right extending to the railroad, and his left nearly to the

Jackson road; Hébert from the Jackson to the Graveyard road, his troops occupying the main salients on both roads.

Smith held the left, with three brigades; Shoupe, from the Graveyard road about a mile westward; Baldwin on the left of Shoupe; and Vaughn on the extreme left, extending to Fort Hill.

Bowen's division and Waul's legion were in reserve.

Having failed to carry the works by a *coup-de-main* on the 19th, Grant devoted the next two days to perfecting his communications with the Yazoo. His depot was established between Johnson's and Lake's plantations near Chickasaw Bayou, on the identical ground where Sherman had landed and made his assault in the previous month of December. From this point roads were constructed to facilitate the hauling of supplies, and the army was firmly established within six miles of a base of supplies entirely secure from the enemy's attacks. On the 21st, the troops being now all in position, Grant determined to make a vigorous assault on the following day. Several reasons, the force of which cannot be denied, impelled him to this course. First of all he felt confident of success. Secondly, the troops desired the assault; they were flushed with an unbroken series of victories, and felt in the spirit of finishing the thing then and there; they were in no mood for the drudgery of pick and spade, until they had tried what they could do with their rifles. A third reason was found in Johnston's presence on the outside with a constantly increasing army, the sole object of which would now be to raise the siege. A successful assault before Johnston could be strong enough to attack, would enable Grant to at once turn on Johnston and disperse his forces, and then send a detachment against Port Hudson; and this without drawing any more troops from Memphis or other points. If a siege was begun reinforcements must be

8*   8

brought, to make sure both of holding Pemberton in Vicksburg and driving off Johnston on the outside. The orders
were consequently issued to make an assault at 10 A.M. on
the 22d, artillery fire and sharp-shooting to be kept up
from daylight. Admiral Porter was requested to bombard
the water batteries with his gunboats.

The investment was at that time by no means complete,
there being a gap of nearly four miles between McClernand's left, which was nearly opposite the square fort, and
the river. In this gap there were no troops, although one
brigade of McArthur's division of the 17th Corps, which had
been at Grand Gulf throughout the campaign, had reached
Warrenton on the night of the 21st, and was to move forward on the Warrenton road the next day. Grant had not
at that time enough troops to make a close investment of the
whole line, and he ran no risk in leaving this gap on the
south, because had Pemberton left his works and attempted
to escape in this direction he would have been caught in the
pocket between the Big Black and the Mississippi, and his
destruction would have been almost certain. The bulk of
Grant's troops were opposite that portion of the line between the square fort and the Graveyard road, and the three
roads—Baldwin's Ferry, Jackson, and Graveyard—which ran
along ridges, were the only practicable lines of approach;
the intermediate country being filled with steep, wooded
ravines, through which troops could not advance in any sort
of order. It was along these roads that the main efforts
were made, the troops moving in narrow columns. Watches
had been compared so as to insure a simultaneous movement, and at precisely ten o'clock the three columns sprang
forward.

On the right, Sherman had placed Blair's division near
the Graveyard road, supported by Tuttle's, leaving Steele's

division to make an assault nearer to the river. A storming party of 150 volunteers had been formed, provided with boards and poles to cross the ditch; Ewing's brigade was immediately behind these, followed by Giles Smith's and Kilby Smith's brigades. All these troops were sheltered in a ravine which led up to the road about 200 yards in front of the bastion. Four batteries had been placed in a position from which their fire could be concentrated on the bastion. At ten o'clock the signal was given; the storming party jumped up on the road, and ran forward at full speed, with Ewing's brigade just behind them. Until this time not a man had been seen on the Confederate parapet, but as these troops came forward in full view, the regiments of Hébert's brigade and a portion of the Missourians, which garrisoned this part of the lines, stood up, and the parapet fairly blazed. Some of the storming party reached the ditch, followed it a short distance, climbed the parapet and firmly planted their flag; it waved there till nightfall, all efforts of the Confederates to step forward and seize it being frustrated by the fire of the assailants. The greater part of the storming party were killed, and their bodies, together with those of the troops immediately following, soon obstructed the narrow road so as to make it almost impassable. In passing over them under the terrible fire, Ewing's brigade wavered, halted, and sought shelter on the slope of a ravine about seventy yards from the works. Giles Smith's brigade, which came next, turned down this ravine to the left, and deployed opposite a point of the works about three hundred yards south of the road; Kilby Smith's brigade followed it in the same direction but deployed close to Ewing. The troops were thus partly sheltered, and opened a withering fire upon any object which showed itself above the parapet, not a stone's throw distant; but they could not

advance an inch. Affairs remained in this condition until
2 P.M.

In McPherson's corps, Ransom's brigade of McArthur's
division was on the right, in the ravines south of the Graveyard road ; Logan's division in the centre, on the Jackson
road ; and Quinby's division on the left, between the Jackson
and Baldwin's Ferry roads. Neither Quinby nor Ransom
was in a position to do more than make a strong demonstration, as each was opposite a re-entrant portion of the line
where, in an advance, they would be mowed down under a
cross fire from the salients. Logan's division, however, was
opposite the salient, J. E. Smith's brigade on the Jackson
road, Stevenson a little to his left, and Leggett in reserve.
At the appointed hour two brigades rushed forward, Smith's
by the road, and Stevenson's up the slope south of it, both
being directed against the main fort just north of the road.
Smith's troops were brought to a halt by the severe fire
across the road, but Stevenson's pressed on, and two regiments reached the ditch of the work, where the colors of
the 7th Missouri were planted, and six standard-bearers
killed in as many minutes. These regiments were unable
to maintain themselves in this position, and soon withdrew
to find shelter about 200 yards from the works, where they
remained until ordered to withdraw at nightfall.

In McClernand's corps, Carr's division was on the right
with one brigade, Benton's, on the Baldwin's Ferry road, and
one, Lawler's, just south of the railroad ; A. J. Smith's division was in his rear, one brigade in support of each of Carr's
brigades ; Osterhaus' division was on the left, opposite a
salient about half-way between the railroad and the square
fort ; and Hovey, with one brigade of his division, the other
being at Big Black Bridge, was on the left of Osterhaus.
At the same hour, 10 A.M., Benton's and Lawler's brigades

moved forward. Lawler's attack was directed against a fort on a very prominent hill a few yards south of the railroad. Two regiments of Lawler's brigade, the 22d and 21st Iowa, charged up this hill and reached the ditch of the fort, where the principal part of them were brought to a halt. A small body, however, led by Sergeant Joseph Griffith, entered the work and engaged in a hand to hand fight with the defenders, in which nearly all but the sergeant were killed. This work was for a short time deserted by the Confederates, but it was commanded by a second work on higher ground, 100 yards in rear, which prevented the Iowa troops from retaining possession of its interior. The colors of the 22d Iowa were, however, planted on its parapet, and remained there for nine hours. Landram's brigade, of A. J. Smith's division, followed close behind Lawler's brigade, and the 77th Illinois came up and planted its colors alongside those of the 22d Iowa. The main body of these two brigades was not able to penetrate the work, but remained in the ditch, where hand-grenades were thrown upon them by the defenders, causing considerable loss.

On the Baldwin's Ferry road, Benton's brigade, followed by Burbridge's, made the attack in the same gallant style and met the same experience. They reached the ditch, planted their colors on the parapet, but could not enter the work. The enemy used hand-grenades against them also.

On the left, Osterhaus' and Hovey's men moved forward and came within a short distance of the works, but they were subjected to a heavy cross-fire from the square fort on their left and were unable to make any farther advance.

Within half an hour after the assault began the condition of affairs was substantially the same at all three of the principal points of assault; at each of these points the Union flags were flying on the works, and the men were in the ditch, but unable to go any farther. A most unfortunate misunderstanding now occurred, which resulted in a large and unnecessary increase of the loss of life. Grant had taken a position in the morning on a high point on the Jackson road, from which he had a clear view of the principal points of assault; McPherson was a few hundred yards in his front, Sherman less than a mile on his right, and McClernand about a mile and a half to his left. From this point he had observed the assaults, had witnessed the flags planted on the parapets, and had seen the men halt at the ditches under the terrible fire. By half-past eleven, an hour after the troops had first reached the works, it became apparent to him that the assault could not succeed. He was just starting over to Sherman's position to confer with him as to the prospects of success by further efforts, when he received a note from McClernand, dated 11.15 A.M., saying that he (McClernand) was hotly engaged with the enemy, who was massing on his right and left, and that a vigorous blow by McPherson would create a diversion in his favor. Grant answered at 11.50 A.M., directing him to strengthen his advance by drawing from his reserves or from other parts of the line. He then rode over to Sherman. Just as he arrived there, he received a second despatch from McClernand, dated 12 M., which was in these words: " We are hotly engaged with the enemy. We have part possession of two forts, and the stars and stripes are floating over them. A vigorous push ought to be made all along the line." Grant answered: " McArthur advanced from Warrenton last night; he is on your left. Concentrate with him and use his forces to the best advantage." He also showed the despatch to Sherman, who immediately ordered a renewal of the attack. Grant then started back to see McPherson and order him to make the diversion which McClernand desired. While on his way

he met a messenger with a third despatch, written about 1
P.M., although the exact hour was not given. It was as follows : " We have gained the enemy's intrenchments at several points, but are brought to a stand. I have sent word to
McArthur to reinforce me if he can. Would it not be best
to concentrate the whole or a part of his command at this
point ? P. S.—I have received your despatch. My troops are
all engaged, and I cannot withdraw any to reinforce them."

Grant was somewhat doubtful as to the extent of these
successes of McClernand, as he had seen nothing of the
kind up to the time he left his point of observation on the
Jackson road. But there was not time to ride over to con-
sult with McClernand, it being already after two o'clock, and
he therefore ordered Quinby's division to move immediately
to McClernand's support ; he also showed the despatches to
McPherson, and directed him to renew the assault.

In consequence of these orders, Sherman sent Tuttle's
division forward to the assistance of Blair's division, which
still remained in the position it had gained in the morning,
and directed both of them to attack with vigor. At the
same time Giles Smith's brigade united with Ransom's brigade of McPherson's corps to make an assault between the
salient on the Graveyard road and Glass' Bayou ; Steele's
division on the right, which had been working its way forward since morning, was now near the enemy's works, and
assaulted them at about the same hour as Tuttle and Ransom.   The result was simply a repetition of the morning's
experience ; everywhere the troops reached the enemy's
works, but could not enter them. Logan's division on the
Jackson road also moved forward again; it did not reach
the works, but suffered heavy loss.   McArthur did not
arrive from Warrenton until the next morning. Quinby's
division did not reach McClernand's position until a short

time before dark. The men were nearly exhausted with fighting and marching through difficult ground all day, but they were at once ordered by McClernand to attack the curtain of trench lying between the two salients (Baldwin's Ferry road and railroad), where his men had been since morning. The attack was made, was entirely unsuccessful, and resulted in heavy loss, Colonel Boomer, one of the brigade commanders, being among the killed. Just at dark the Confederate troops occupying the redoubt on the Baldwin's Ferry road, having been reinforced by a portion of Bowen's division, made a sortie from their work and drove off the men in the ditch. About the same time McClernand's troops near the railroad also retired from the ditch of the work where they had been since morning.

The result of the assault was therefore unsuccessful at all points. Of the 40,000 infantry present for duty in Grant's army that day all but about 5,000 had been brought into action. The length of line assaulted was about two and a half miles, and it was held in the morning by two Confederate brigades (Moore's and Hébert's), and by parts of two others. As soon as the attack was begun, Bowen's division and a part of Smith's division were sent to the threatened points, Green's brigade going to the Baldwin's Ferry road and the railroad, Cockrell's to the Jackson road, and Vaughn's on the Graveyard road. The entire force of defenders actually engaged did not number more than 13,000, but the nature of the ground was such that the works could only be approached at three principal points; these points were salients which covered the line between them with cross-fires, and by holding them the entire line was secure. A force of 4,000 men at each of these points was all that the works would hold, and any more men would have been superfluous. The Confederate loss is not known; it prob-

ably did not much exceed 500. In Forney's division, which
bore the brunt of the assaults of Sherman's and McPherson's
corps, the loss was only 42 killed and 95 wounded. Grant's
loss in the two assaults of May 19th and 22d were over 4,000,
as follows, more than three-fourths of them being on the 22d :

	Killed.	Wounded.	Missing.	Total.
Thirteenth Corps :				
Carr's division............	109	559	57	725
A. J. Smith's division.....	69	400	30	499
Osterhaus' "	35	233	1	269
Hovey's "	....	....	....	50
Seventeenth Corps :				
Logan's division...........	33	378	6	417
Quinby's "	52	295	2	349
Ransom's brigade	70	375	31	476
Fifteenth Corps :				
Blair's division............	173	708	9	890
Tuttle's "	22	185	43	250
Steele's "	....	....	....	150
	....	....	....	4,075

In his official report Grant blamed McClernand very
severely for the misleading character of his despatches,
which induced him to renew the assault, "and resulted in
the increase of our mortality list fully 50 per cent., without
advancing our position or giving us other advantages." Mc-
Clernand wrote a long reply, dated Springfield, Illinois, September 25, 1863, which is on the files of the War Department,
and will be published with the records. In this McClernand endeavored to show, among other things, that his despatches were less glowing as to his success than those he
received from his subordinates, that he was in a position to
see clearly what took place in his front, that if he had been
reinforced early in the afternoon he would have broken

completely through the enemy's line, and that he never
wrote that "he was in possession of, and still held, two of
the enemy's forts," as stated in Grant's report. It is hardly
necessary to follow out the details of this controversy.
McClernand's despatches did undoubtedly mislead his commanding general, and did cause the latter to renew the assault at heavy sacrifice and without success, which he would
not have done had he been distinctly advised as to the actual
state of affairs. McClernand's despatch (previously given)
reads: "We have part possession of two forts." Had he
said plainly that his men were in the ditch but could not
carry the works, he would have stated the exact fact, and
there would have been no second assault.

It was now apparent to every one that the Confederate
troops had recovered from the demoralization of Champion's
Hill and the Big Black, and that their works were too strong
to be carried in open assault. A regular siege was unavoidable, and every one was willing to perform the necessary
labor to carry it on. The orders for beginning the siege
were issued on May 25th, Captains F. E. Prime and C. B.
Comstock, of the Engineers, being in succession the Chief
Engineers in charge.

It was, however, important to guard at once against any
attack from the rear by Johnston. Osterhaus' division of
the 13th Corps had been sent back to guard the Big Black
Bridge immediately after the assault of May 22d; and on the
26th, an expedition was formed, to consist of six brigades,
three each from the 15th and 17th Corps, the whole under
command of Blair. This expedition was to march to the
northeast, between the Yazoo and Big Black Rivers, dis-
cover what force Johnston had in that region, and, if possible, break it up. Blair reached Mechanicsburg, in the
vicinity of Liverpool, on the 28th, where he had a slight

skirmish with a small party of the enemy, but he reported
that he was satisfied there was no large body between the
Yazoo and the Big Black. Johnston was said to be organizing his army in the vicinity of Canton, and it was rumored
that A. P. Hill had joined him from the east, and that their
united forces numbered 45,000 men, but this Blair did not
credit.   Blair then returned to Haines' Bluff, by way of
the Yazoo Valley, destroying all supplies that could be of
use to the enemy. A gunboat expedition was also sent up
the Yazoo about this time, as far as Yazoo City, destroying
all boats in the river.

The certainty that Johnston was organizing as large a
force as possible in his rear, induced Grant to order Hurlbut, at Memphis, to " strip his district to the lowest possible
standard," and send him all available men.   Just after he
crossed the river, Grant had ordered Hurlbut to send him
one division to take the place of the troops that had been
left to guard the road from Milliken's Bend to Perkins's.
Lauman's division had accordingly been sent ; it had
reached Milliken's Bend, 6,000 strong, about May 18th, and
had been moved across to Grand Gulf, and thence up to
Warrenton. On the 28th, it took position on the Hall's Ferry
road, partially filling up the gap between McClernand's left
and the river.   On receipt of the further call from Grant for
reinforcements, Hurlbut made up another division of twelve
regiments, under Brig.-Gen. N. Kimball, and sent them below ; and later still, a third division, under Brig.-Gen. W. S.
Smith.   On May 29th, Grant also sent a telegram, via Memphis, to Halleck, stating that if Banks did not come to his
assistance, he must be reinforced from elsewhere.   Halleck
was in daily communication with Hurlbut, and knew exactly
what troops he had sent.   On receiving Grant's telegram on
June 2d, Halleck immediately telegraphed to Schofield, at

St. Louis, and to Burnside, at Cincinnati, stating Grant's situation, and asking if they could send any troops to his assistance; also to Rosecrans in Tennessee, saying that Johnston was reinforced from Bragg's army, and if he (Rosecrans) could do nothing himself, a portion of his troops must be sent to Grant. Rosecrans replied with a long despatch, expressing the opinion that none of his troops should be taken, and that he was about to execute a movement. Burnside and Schofield replied that they could spare troops for temporary service, and two divisions of the 9th Corps, under Maj.-Gen. J. G. Parke, were at once sent from Ohio, and one division, under Maj.-Gen. F. J. Herron, from Missouri.

The result of these prompt measures was that Grant was reinforced almost as rapidly as Johnston, and in as large numbers, and the opportunity when Johnston could have attacked was soon lost. At the close of the siege, there were 17,000 men from Hurlbut's corps present at Vicksburg, and these, with Parke's corps and Herron's division, carried the total strength of Grant's army to 71,141 men, and 248 guns, on June 30th.

Kimball's division of the 16th Corps arrived on June 3d and was sent up the Yazoo to Haines' Bluff, and thence along the Benton road, with orders to destroy the railroad bridge over the Big Black near Canton. Kimball found, however, on arriving at Mechanicsburg that a large force was in front of him at Yazoo City and Liverpool, and as the Yazoo River on which he depended for his supplies was rapidly falling he returned to Haines' Bluff, where he received orders to fortify a position and hold it against any force coming from the northeast.

Herron's division arrived on June 8th and was immediately marched across the peninsula and ferried over the river below Warrenton. He came up on the south side of Vicksburg and took post on the Warrenton road, enabling Lauman to close up on McClernand's left. The investment on the south side was thus perfected. Hitherto it had been imperfect on account of the insufficiency of Lauman's force to close the entire gap between McClernand and the river.

W. S. Smith's division of the 16th Corps began arriving on June 11th, and was at once sent to Haines' Bluff, this and Kimball's division being united under command of Maj.-Gen. C. C. Washburne.

Parke's 9th Corps arrived on the 14th. It was at first intended to move it to the south of the city as a reserve behind Lauman and Herron, but in view of the threatening aspect of affairs along the Yazoo, it was moved to Haines' Bluff.

Meanwhile Johnston was slowly organizing an army at Canton. The difficulties were very great, for Loring's troops had joined him without guns, wagons, or camp equipage, the troops arriving by rail were also without wagons, and though the country was full of food, there were no supplies available, Pemberton having moved his own supplies to Vicksburg; the railroads were still out of repair from Grierson's raid, and were fully occupied at present in bringing up troops. These difficulties could only have been surmounted, if at all, by a man of extraordinary energy, boldness, and resource. In spite of his undoubted abilities in command of an army on the defensive, Johnston was hardly the man for such an emergency as that in which he was now placed. After sending the order to Pemberton to march to the northeast he remained in the vicinity of the Big Black until he received, on May 19th, Pemberton's answer saying that he could not make the movement ordered; he then marched back to Canton in order to assemble and organize his army. While he was doing this, Grant organized a still

larger force to use against him, and so it came about that
Pemberton lay for 47 days in his trenches, before he finally
gave up in despair, during which time Johnston organized
an army of over 31,000 men, but never came within musket-
shot of his enemy.

Johnston arrived at Canton on May 20th, and the next day
was joined by Gist's brigade from South Carolina and
Ector's and McNair's from Chattanooga. Loring's division
reached Jackson on the 20th, and was joined by Maxey's
brigade from Port Hudson on the 23d. Between that date
and June 3d there arrived in addition, Evans' brigade from
South Carolina, Breckenridge's division from Chattanooga,
and a cavalry division from Bragg's army, commanded by
W. H. Jackson, one of the most energetic cavalry leaders in
the South. Johnston organized his command into four
divisions, commanded by Loring, Breckenridge, W. H. T.
Walker, and French. There was subsequently much controversy between himself and the authorities in Richmond as
to the strength of his command, and therefore the following
statement is given in full, taken from the return signed by
himself on June 25th, and now among the archives of the
War Department. There were no reinforcements received
between June 3d and 25th.

FIELD RETURN.

	Present for duty.	Aggregate present.	Present and absent.
Loring's division...................	6,451	7,427	13,375
Breckenridge's division............	6,107	6,884	9,688
Walker's division	8,049	9,571	13,452
French's ''	6,498	7,466	10,559
Jackson's cavalry	3,606	4,373	6,797
Miscellaneous.....................	515	594	881
Total.........................	31,226	36,315	54,747

Constant correspondence was maintained between Johnston and the Richmond authorities during the months of May and June, the latter urging him to attack at almost any risk, as the disparity in numbers would probably increase rather than diminish with time. Johnston at first replied (May 28th) that, although he would have only 23,000 men when all his reinforcements arrived, he must try to beat Grant with that number if no more could be sent. But on June 7th, he telegraphed that when he thought of trying to accomplish anything in aid of Pemberton the case seemed "desperate." On the 8th the Secretary of War asked if more reinforcements should be drawn from Bragg's army. Johnston replied that to draw more troops from Bragg would "involve yielding Tennessee; the Government must decide between this State and Tennessee." On the 15th he telegraphed that he considered "saving Vicksburg hopeless"; and on the 16th received a reply that "Vicksburg must not be lost without a desperate struggle. . . . If better resources do not offer, you must hazard attack. It may be made in concert with the garrison, if practicable, but otherwise without, by day or night as you think best." Johnston answered that he could not attack Grant because Grant was covered by the Big Black, which would cut off his retreat if defeated. The Secretary of War then telegraphed (June 21st), reiterating, in the most urgent language, his orders for active movements, of which he assumed all the responsibility, and suggesting that if a movement against Grant's army was not feasible it might be possible to raise the siege of Port Hudson. Johnston replied that this would involve abandoning Jackson and with it the State of Mississippi. Johnston saw nothing but difficulties whichever way he turned; to save Mississippi was to lose Tennessee, and to save Port Hudson was to lose Mississippi; while he was still meditating on the dilemma Vicksburg surrendered, followed immediately by Port Hudson and Jackson; and thus everything was lost.

While this correspondence was in progress Johnston had observed the movements of Osterhaus near Big Black Bridge, and of Blair toward Mechanicsburg, in the last week of May, and he had sent Walker's division to Yazoo City, and Loring's to Benton. These troops simply remained in observation, and were confronted by a larger number of Union troops, extending from Mechanicsburg to the Big Black Bridge. On June 14th Johnston sent a courier to Pemberton, who penetrated the lines and delivered his letter on June 20th. In this Johnston said to Pemberton that the utmost that both armies could accomplish was to save the troops at Vicksburg; to raise the siege was impossible. He therefore asked Pemberton to indicate what point should be attacked. Pemberton replied, under date of the 21st, proposing that Johnston should attack on the north of the railroad, while he (Pemberton) cut his way out to Hankinson's Ferry on the south; he added, "I await your orders." On the 22d Johnston wrote (in answer to a despatch of the 15th just received), saying that he feared he would be unable to accomplish anything with his small force, and suggesting to Pemberton that, in the last extremity, he might try to cross the river and join the Confederate forces operating in that quarter. This was the last letter received by Pemberton from Johnston prior to the surrender; no definite instructions were ever received in answer to the former's despatch of June 21st. Johnston, however, received one further letter from Pemberton, dated June 23d, suggesting that Johnston should propose to Grant the surrender of Vicksburg, but not of the troops. Johnston's reply did not reach Pemberton. It was to the effect that any such propositions must be made by Pemberton himself.

On June 28th, Johnston finally considered his army ready to advance ; and orders to that effect were issued. Walker's division had already been withdrawn from Yazoo City to Vernon ; and Loring's from Benton to Canton. Walker was now ordered to move down the Big Black, while Loring advanced from Canton, and French and Breckenridge from Jackson. On July 1st, Walker's, Loring's, and French's divisions were at Birdsong's Ferry, and Breckenridge's near Edwards' Station. Johnston states that this movement "was not undertaken in the wild spirit that dictated the despatches from the War Department of June 16th and 21st." He intended simply to examine the enemy's lines, and see if there was any prospect of breaking them in order to save the garrison ; there was no hope of saving the place. Consequently he devoted July 2d, 3d, and 4th to reconnoissances, which convinced him that no attack was practicable north of the railroad. Such was unquestionably the fact, for at that time Sherman had been detached from the blockading force, and placed in command of a large force on the outside. These consisted of Parke's 9th Corps, Washburne's two divisions of the 16th Corps, Tuttle's division of the 15th, McArthur's of the 17th, and Osterhaus' of the 13th. This force numbered nearly 30,000 men, and another division of McPherson's corps was in readiness to move at once on Sherman's order. These troops were posted from Haines' Bluff on the left to Black River Bridge on the right ; they had fortified and barricaded every road in the interval between these points, and were ready to hold them against double their numbers.

Having found no opening on the north of the railroad, Johnston intended to move on the 5th by Edwards' Station to the south of the railroad, and examine the prospect in that vicinity. But on the night of the 4th he received the news of the surrender. He countermarched his columns forthwith toward Jackson. He was none too quick, for Sherman was on his heels in pursuit with nearly 50,000 men, before sunset of the day on which the garrison laid down its arms.

While the negotiations for the surrender were in progress on July 3d, Grant was in constant telegraphic communication with Sherman, and it was arranged that the moment the surrender took place, Sherman should move out to attack Johnston, pursue him to Jackson, and effectually destroy the railroads north and south of that point. In addition to the troops already mentioned, the remaining divisions of the 13th and 15th Corps were ordered to join Sherman, so that his force consisted of the 9th, 13th, and 15th Corps, with one division of the 16th attached to the 9th, and one of the 17th attached to the 15th. The other division of the 16th was left with Washburne at Haines' Bluff. The entire force under Sherman's orders consisted of 12 divisions, and numbered about 48,000 men, over two-thirds of the whole army at Vicksburg.

Sherman was in motion on the afternoon of the 4th, and the additional troops from Vicksburg started during the night. On the 5th they all approached the Big Black, Ord with the 13th Corps at the railroad bridge, Steele with the 15th Corps at Messenger's Ferry, a few miles above Bridgeport, and Parke with the 9th Corps, at Birdsong's Ferry, on the Brownsville road. Bridges were constructed at each of these points, and the crossing was completed on the 6th. On the 7th the advance was continued, the 13th and 15th Corps reaching Bolton that day, and the 9th Corps being slightly in rear.

On the 8th, the 15th Corps reached Clinton, and on the 9th, passed through that place on the direct Jackson road, while the 13th Corps went through Raymond, and the 9th on a road north of the railroad. On the night of the 9th, the troops approached Jackson, skirmishing with the enemy's outposts, and on the morning of the 10th, they closed in around that city. Johnston, as we have seen, had retreated from the Big Black on the 5th and reached Jackson on the 7th. The fortifications of that place extended in a semicircle on the west of the town, from the Pearl River on the north to the same river on the south. Loring's division was placed on the right, on the Canton road; Walker's and French's in the centre; and Breckenridge's on the left, across the New Orleans Railroad. Jackson's division of cavalry was directed to observe the fords on the river north and south of the fortifications.

As Sherman closed in on the 10th he placed Parke's corps on the left, Steele's corps in the centre, and Ord's on the right, both flanks extending to the river. The heat and dust had been intense during the march, and the troops were fatigued; the fortifications were strong, and Sherman determined not to assault them, but to invest the place, and throw up a few batteries to guard against any sortie. It was not probable that Johnston had enough stores to stand a siege, and he would soon be obliged to abandon the place, and it was hoped to fall upon him as soon as he left his works. Artillery fire was opened on the 11th, and during the following day one of the divisions of the 13th Corps, which had been ordered to make a reconnoissance, pressed closer to the works than had been intended, and it was driven back with a loss of nearly 600 men. After this the siege was confined to artillery firing. Expeditions were sent out on either flank to destroy the railroad for several miles.

Johnston sent a detachment of cavalry to break Sherman's communications near Clinton, but it was intercepted and driven off by McArthur's division.

Johnston had hoped and expected that Sherman would make an assault. When he saw that preparations were making for a siege, he telegraphed to Richmond (July 15th), that he had no provisions for a siege, and that it would be madness for him to make an attack. He therefore issued orders on the 16th to withdraw across the bridges over Pearl River within his own lines, and during the night this movement was skilfully executed. It was not detected until 6 A.M. of the 17th, by which time he was well on his way. Sherman sent a detachment in pursuit, but his instructions did not contemplate an advance beyond Jackson in any force. He telegraphed to Grant for further instructions, and received orders to discontinue the pursuit, complete the thorough destruction of the railways, and then return to Vicksburg.

Johnston was therefore pursued no farther than Brandon Station, a dozen miles from Jackson. He halted at Morton, on the railroad, about half way between Jackson and Meridian, and there went into camp. Sherman returned leisurely to Vicksburg, arriving there between the 25th and 27th of July. His losses during the expedition were a little over 1,100 men. Johnston reported his losses as 71 killed, 504 wounded, and only 25 missing—but Sherman captured and sent to Vicksburg, by actual count, 765 prisoners.

Johnston's efforts for the relief of Vicksburg thus came to an end. He had been forestalled by his enemy in every move. The railroads at Jackson, the point he considered essential for the defence of the State of Mississippi, were so thoroughly destroyed that that point lost all its strategic importance for the rest of the war.

While Grant had been thus active in guarding against any attack in his rear, he had prosecuted the siege in his front with equal vigor. Just after the assault of May 22d, it was thought that by bringing gunboats to enfilade the batteries on Fort Hill, that position might be carried. At Sherman's request Porter gave the necessary orders, and on the morning of May 27th the Cincinnati came down to engage these batteries ; at the same time four vessels which were below the town engaged the batteries near the Marine Hospital. The Cincinnati was shot through and through by the plunging fire from Fort Hill, and in less than half an hour five of her guns were disabled, and she was in a sinking condition. She was run toward the shore about a mile north of Fort Hill, and sank in three fathoms of water; 36 of her crew were killed, wounded, or drowned. After this the efforts of the navy during the siege were confined to bombardment, which was kept up almost incessantly from the gunboats and from mortar-boats. Several large guns were landed from the vessels, and took their place in the besiegers' lines, where they were worked by naval crews.

As soon as the siege was ordered lines of sap were begun at various points. There was great lack of engineer officers to direct these technical works, and hence they did not progress as rapidly as would otherwise have been possible. The labor was furnished by pioneer companies, by the troops, and by negroes hired in the vicinity. Materials for fascines, gabions, and sap rollers were found in abundance in the cane and underbrush of the ravines. Twelve miles of trenches, and 89 batteries were constructed, armed at the close of the siege with 220 guns, all but 12 of which were field pieces.

There were ten lines of approach, the four most important being on the Graveyard, Jackson, Baldwin's Ferry, and

Warrenton roads.   These approaches were all within a few yards of the enemy's works when the place fell.   Mining was employed on the Jackson and Graveyard roads, and was met by countermining on the part of the besieged.   On the Jackson road a mine was exploded on June 25th, under the enemy's parapet, just north of the road.   It was loaded with a ton of powder, and fired with complete success.   The troops rushed into the crater and held it for twenty-four hours, but were then driven out by hand-grenades and returned to their own trenches.   A second gallery was then run, and another mine exploded on July 1st, blowing about 25 of the defenders into the air ; but no attempt was made to occupy the crater, owing to the failure of the preceding attempt.   Small mortars were improvised by shrinking iron bands on logs of tough wood and boring out the core.   With these, shells were constantly thrown across the small space separating the two lines.   When the lines were so close the casualties on each side were from 10 to 100 each day.

On July 1, the approaches were all within from 5 to 100 yards of the defenders' works.   Any farther advance by digging resulted in hand-to-hand fighting.   The time had come for the final assault, and orders were issued for this to take place on July 6th.   The approaches were to be widened so that troops could easily move in columns of fours, and artillery could pass ; planks, and sand-bags stuffed with cotton, were to be prepared for crossing the ditches.   The troops were to be assembled in the approaches during the night, and at daylight were to rush forward across the few yards separating them from the enemy's works, and endeavor to carry the place at every point of approach.   The assault, however, was unnecessary, for the place surrendered on July 4.

On June 7th an attack was made upon a detachment of

white and black troops, guarding Milliken's Bend, by J. G.
Walker's division numbering 4,000 men.   These troops had
been ordered from Arkansas by Gen. E. K. Smith, who commanded the Trans-Mississippi Department, in response to
urgent requests from Johnston that he would come to the
assistance of Vicksburg.   It is stated that the object of this
movement was to throw supplies and possibly troops into
the place ; or, failing in that, to cover Pemberton's escape
across the river.   Of this Pemberton was not informed, so
that the scheme fell through.   It would have been doomed
to almost certain failure in the presence of Porter's fleet of
gunboats.   Walker's division was marched down to Alexandria, where it reported to Maj.-Gen. R. Taylor, commanding
the district of West Louisiana.   It was then placed on transports and carried up the Washita and Tensas Rivers until
abreast of Vicksburg, where it was disembarked and marched
across to Richmond, La., which was unoccupied except by
an outpost.   From Richmond the attack was made upon
Milliken's Bend.   The troops of this garrison were at first
driven out of their works by the Confederates, and forced
back to the levee on the river bank.   But here two gunboats
came to their assistance, and the Confederates were in turn
driven back and retreated to Richmond.   Mower's brigade
of the 15th Corps was sent across the river the next day, and
was soon reinforced by the Marine brigade under Ellet.
These troops advanced against Walker's division, and he
then retreated along the Shreveport Railroad to Monroe.
This expedition had no effect whatever upon the course of
the siege.

On June 18th, Gen. McClernand was relieved from the
command of the 13th Corps, and succeeded by Maj.-Gen.
E. O. C. Ord.   He had published to his troops a vainglori-
ous order, filled with insinuations against the troops of the

other corps, and with indirect reflections upon the Commanding General. A copy of the order was published in the Memphis papers, and thus came to the notice of Sherman and McPherson, who vigorously protested against it. Grant asked McClernand if the newspaper slip was a correct copy, and why the order had not been forwarded to his headquarters as required by the regulations. McClernand replied that the newspaper slip was a correct copy, and that he was "prepared to maintain its statements;" it was owing to the carelessness of his adjutant that a copy had not been forwarded. On receiving this reply, Grant issued an order directing McClernand to repair to his home in Illinois, and assigning Ord to the command of the 13th Corps, subject to the President's approval. McClernand complied with the order under protest, and appealed the case to Washington, but without success; although in the following year he was assigned to a command in Texas, where he served a few months and then resigned.

This was the termination of a long-standing controversy, in which the majority of his officers thought that Grant had shown more patience than was necessary or proper. Whatever McClernand's talents may have been, he was certainly lacking in subordination, and his relief caused no dissatisfaction, to say the least, in his own corps or in other parts of the army.

As the month of June wore on, Pemberton's hopes of relief began gradually to diminish, and then to disappear. His men were on reduced rations, but were not at starvation point; his ammunition was deficient, but it had been carefully husbanded during the siege, and he had enough for a battle. Every man capable of doing duty was in the trenches, and many of those previously wounded had recovered, so that their numbers now amounted to nearly 22,000, as shown by their returns—a little more than when the siege began; about 7,000 were in the hospitals. In his report Pemberton vehemently denies that either lack of food or of ammunition induced his surrender. He says he surrendered because his men were enfeebled by long exposure in a cramped position in trenches, and because there was no prospect of relief. It is probable that the most potent cause of surrender was the temper of the men. They were physically exhausted and mentally discouraged, and they saw no object in a continuation of the present state of affairs, and no issue from it except in surrender.

It has already been stated that on June 20th Pemberton received a note from Johnston, asking for suggestions of a plan of attack by which he might be enabled to cut his way out, and that Pemberton answered on the next day, giving a plan for such an attack. It is a singular coincidence that in a conversation between the Union and Confederate pickets, on the night of the 20th, the Confederate said that they had expected an assault, and were prepared for it, but as it had not been made, the feelings of the troops had been canvassed to see if they could be induced to make an attack for the purpose of cutting their way out. The troops all declined, and some of them threatened to mutiny if their officers did not surrender. They were only persuaded to continue on duty by the assurance that there were enough supplies to last a week, and, by that time, 2,000 boats would be made by which they could cross the river. Houses were being torn down—so said the Confederate—to make the boats. Three days after this canvassing, i.e., on June 23d, without having received any further letters from Johnston, Pemberton wrote to him suggesting that he propose to Grant a surrender of Vicksburg.

9*

On the 28th Pemberton received the following very curious document:

APPEAL FOR HELP.

IN TRENCHES NEAR VICKSBURG,

June 28, 1863.

GENL. J. C. PEMBERTON

Sir! In accordance with my own feelings and that of my fellow soldiers with whom I have conferred I submit to your consideration the following note:

We as an army have as much confidence in you as a Com'd'g. Gen'l. as we perhaps ought to have; we believe you have displayed as much generalship as any other man could have done under similar circumstances; we give you great credit for the stern patriotism you have evinced in the defence of Vicksburg during a protracted siege—

I also feel proud of the gallant conduct of the soldiers under your command in repulsing the enemy at every assault, and bearing with patient endurance all the privations and hardships incident to a siege of forty odd days' duration.

Everybody admits that we have all covered ourselves with glory, but alas! alas! Gen'l. a crisis has arrived in the midst of our siege.

Our rations have been cut down to 1 biscuit, and a small bit of bacon per day, not enough scarcely to keep soul and body together, much less to stand the hardships we are called upon to stand. We are actually on sufferance, and the consequence is, as far as I can hear, there is complaining and general dissatisfaction throughout our lines. We are and have been kept close in the trenches day and night, not allowed to forage any at all, and even if permitted there is nothing to be had among the citizens.

Men don't want to starve and don't intend to, but they call upon you for justice, if the Commissary Department can give it, if it can't you must adopt some means to relieve us very soon. The emergency of the case demands prompt and decided action on your part.

If you can't feed us, you had better surrender us, horrible as the idea is, than suffer this noble army to disgrace themselves by desertion. I tell you plainly men are not going to lie here and perish; if they do love their country, self-preservation is the first law of nature, and

hunger will compel a man to do almost anything. You had better
heed a warning voice, though it is the voice of a private soldier.

This army is now ripe for mutiny unless it can be fed.

Just think of one small biscuit and one or two mouthfuls of bacon
per day. Genl. please direct your inquiries in the proper channel, and
see if I have not stated stubborn facts, which had better be heeded before we are disgraced.

From

MANY SOLDIERS.

This document was preserved by Pemberton, and its existence was probably not publicly known until it was found
among the "Pemberton papers" received by the War Department a few months since. How much or how little importance he attributed to it no one can say.

The above facts are not cited for the purpose of reflecting
in any way on Pemberton, but to show what was probably
the temper of his men. They, as well as himself, knew that
the case was hopeless, and that he had but two alternatives,
viz.: to surrender or to make a vain effort to cut his way
out; in other words, surrender or suicide. He chose the
former, his own statement of the case being as follows:
"When forty-seven days and nights had passed, with the
knowledge I then possessed that no adequate relief was to be
expected, I felt that I ought not longer to place in jeopardy
the brave men whose lives had been entrusted to my care."
Hoping that on the great national holiday he might obtain
the most favorable terms, he opened negotiations on the eve
of the Fourth of July.

Before taking the final step, however, Pemberton asked
his division commanders, by circular letter dated July 1st,
their opinion as to the ability of their troops " to make the
marches and undergo the fatigues necessary to accomplish a
successful evacuation." Three of them—Forney, Smith,
and Bowen—reported unequivocally, on the following day,

that their troops were unable to undergo such fatigues : and two of these advised an immediate capitulation. The fourth —Stevenson—said that his men were much enfeebled, but he believed that the most of them, rather than be captured, would exert themselves to the utmost to accomplish an evacuation. Smith stated that an evacuation was almost impossible, on account of the temper of his troops. The opinion of the brigade and regimental commanders was almost unanimous against the idea of cutting their way out. After receiving these answers, Pemberton assembled his four division commanders for consultation. The minutes of the meeting show that they unanimously advised a capitulation.

On the morning of the 3d, therefore, Pemberton sent a flag of truce by Bowen, with a letter to Grant, proposing that three commissioners be appointed on each side to arrange terms for capitulation. Grant replied that he did not favor the proposition of appointing commissioners ; that his only terms were an unconditional surrender of the city and garrison, and that Pemberton might feel assured that men who had shown so much endurance and courage as those now in Vicksburg would be treated with all the respect due to prisoners of war. Bowen expressed a desire to converse with Grant, which was refused ; but Grant sent word that if Pemberton desired to see him he would meet him in front of the lines at 3 P.M. At that hour Grant, with his two corps commanders then present, Ord and McPherson, and the division commanders nearest that part of the line, Logan and A. J. Smith, besides several members of his staff, went forward to a point just south of the Confederate works on the Jackson road. Here he was met by Pemberton, Bowen, and some of the former's staff. Pemberton asked what terms he would be allowed, and Grant answered those indicated in his letter that morning. Pemberton replied that then the conference might terminate, and hostilities be resumed. Grant said "Very well." Some further conversation ensued, when the proposition was made—by whom is a matter of dispute—that Bowen and A. J. Smith should retire for consultation. Grant made no objection to this, except that he would not consider himself bound by anything they might agree upon. These officers then stepped to one side, but came to no conclusion. Finally the conference broke up with the understanding that Grant would formulate his terms in detail, and send them to Pemberton at 10 P.M.

The letter which Grant sent that evening conveyed the same idea of unconditional surrender, although those words were not used. He proposed to take possession of the city the next morning, have rolls made out as soon as possible, and individual paroles signed by every officer and man, after which the Confederate troops were to march out ; the rank and file taking no property but their clothing, and officers retaining their side arms and one horse for each mounted officer. Thirty wagons and any desired amount of rations could be taken from their own stores.

These terms would not only insure a complete surrender, but they would save the trouble of transporting and feeding the prisoners until exchanged.

Pemberton accepted these terms in the main but proposed that he should first march out with his colors and arms, before Grant took possession ; also that officers should retain their personal property and " the rights and property of citizens to be respected." This proposition was received after midnight, and Grant at once answered, declining to make any stipulations about citizens, and agreeing to the officers retaining their private baggage and side arms, which was already included in his first letter. As to the proposition to march out with colors and arms, he had no objection, provided that, as soon as the arms were stacked, the troops marched back again and remained within the lines until duly paroled.   Pemberton was notified that unless his acceptance of these terms was signified by 9 A.M. they would be regarded as rejected, and measures taken accordingly.   He immediately replied accepting them.

In these negotiations Grant had waived the technical point of not offering any terms further than the words " unconditional surrender," as in his position of conqueror it was very easy for him to do.   But he had kept the negotiations in his own hands, instead of delegating them to commissioners, and he had yielded nothing of the principle for which he contended, *i.e.*, the surrender of the whole force, with their arms and munitions, as prisoners of war, not to take arms again until properly exchanged.

At 10 A.M. on July 4th, the Confederate troops marched out, each division in front of its works, stacked arms, laid their colors upon them, and then returned toward the town. Logan's division was marched in to take possession.   Paroles were made out and signed as quickly as possible, and the prisoners were meanwhile fed from the Union stores.   On July 11th, they marched out without arms, and proceeded to the vicinity of Enterprise, Miss., and Demopolis, Ala., where they remained until they were declared exchanged in the following month of September.[1]

---

[1] On July 10th, Jefferson Davis telegraphed to Pemberton that all the general officers had been exchanged, and were released from their parole ; and that they should return to duty at once.   He also desired to know what portion of the troops were really effective, and was informed that Stevenson's, and Bowen's, and a part of Forney's division were fit for service, *i.e.*, about two-thirds of the whole force. On September 11th, the Confederate Agent of Exchange notified the United States Agent that on the following day the divisions above named would be de-

The number actually paroled, as certified by the U. S. Commissioner of Exchange, to whom the rolls were forwarded, was 29,391—viz., 2,166 officers, and 27,225 men. In addition, 790 refused to be paroled, and were sent North as prisoners of war, and several hundreds escaped, or died in the hospitals before they could be paroled, so that the total force surrendered was, in round numbers, 31,000. The artillery found in the place numbered 172 pieces, 67 of which were siege guns, and the rest field pieces.

Grant's losses in the entire campaign, including the expedition against Jackson, were a little less than 10,000, some of which, being men slightly wounded, were only temporary. Of the army which, on Pemberton's return for March, numbered 61,495 actually present, all had now been lost except about 6,000 who escaped with Loring from Champion's Hill, 4,000 who were operating in the northern and eastern

---

clared exchanged, and on the 12th the order was issued. It was notorious that at this time—just prior to the battle of Chickamauga—the Confederates were sorely in need of troops. The Confederate agent gave no statement of numbers, nor any description of the Union prisoners against whom they were exchanged; but merely stated " I have in my possession more valid paroles of your officers and men than would be an equivalent for the officers and men herein enumerated." It was, however, an unquestioned fact, which had been the subject of correspondence among the Confederate authorities at this very time, that the capture of the troops at Vicksburg placed the balance of prisoners largely in favor of the United States. Against this extraordinary proceeding the United States agent at once protested, but without avail, and some of the paroled Vicksburg prisoners were taken in arms at the battle of Chattanooga in November following. Both sides then declared all paroled prisoners exchanged, which threw the subject of exchanges into hopeless confusion. A voluminous correspondence was carried on for months with reference to the subject, during which the Confederates advanced the proposition that the paroles at Vicksburg and Port Hudson were all invalid on technical grounds. This was submitted to General Grant, then in command of all the armies, in April, 1864, and he directed that no further exchanges be made of any character unless the paroles at Vicksburg and Port Hudson were fully recognized. In consequence, no more exchanges were made during the war, except in special cases of sickness. It was not, as has been represented, from a desire to cripple the South that the exchange of prisoners was stopped, but from a belief that the Confederate authorities had deliberately acted in bad faith.

part of the State, and 7,000 from Port Hudson, who had joined Johnston at Jackson. The losses in the battle of Raymond and the two battles at Jackson, among Johnston's troops, were about 2,000. The net total of losses to the Confederates was therefore over 46,000 men, 60,000 small arms, and 260 cannon, which they had but poor means of replacing; add to this the loss of the Mississippi River and the resources of the fertile region beyond it.

The events of July 4, 1863, at Vicksburg and Gettysburg, sounded the death-knell of the Confederacy. There was desperate fighting thereafter, but it was without hope; it was the fighting of men who saw defeat and ruin staring them in the face, but were determined to fight until nothing should be left, and in their downfall to create as much havoc as possible.

CHAPTER VII.

PORT HUDSON.

In the month of November, 1862, Maj.-Gen. N. P. Banks sailed from New York with a force of between 15,000 and 20,000 men.[1] His instructions, conveyed in a letter from Halleck, dated November 9, 1862, were to proceed to New Orleans, relieve General Butler in command of the Department of the Gulf and, uniting the forces brought with him with those already serving on the Gulf, advance up the Mississippi in co-operation with General Grant, in order to gain complete possession of that river; after the river was cleared he was to advance sufficiently far into the interior to hold an unbroken line of communication by land from New Orleans to Vicksburg, and then, turning to the west of the Mississippi, he was to occupy the Red River country as a protection for Louisiana and Arkansas and a basis of future operations against Texas.

Banks arrived at New Orleans about the middle of December, 1862, and assumed command on the 16th of that month. A portion of his command, numbering 10,000 men, under Brig.-Gen. C. Grover, was not disembarked at New Orleans, but proceeded directly up the river to Baton Rouge. Grover reached this point at daylight on

---

[1] The War Department Records contain no data as to the exact strength of this force.

the 17th, and immediately landed and took possession, driving off a small force of Confederates which was stationed there as an outpost. Baton Rouge is but twenty-five miles by land south of Port Hudson, and was a convenient base of operations against that stronghold. But Grover did not consider his division sufficiently strong to make any advance at that time; it was not thoroughly organized and equipped for the field, the troops were new—this being their first service—and they were deficient in transportation and other essentials for active service.

The entire force under Banks' command consisted of 56 regiments, nearly one-half of which were enlisted for nine months only, numbering in all 31,253 officers and men for duty, out of a total of 36,508 present, as shown on his return of December 31st. They occupied positions along the Gulf, stretching from Florida to Western Texas, and up the Mississippi from the forts below New Orleans to the vicinity of Port Hudson. It was necessary to hold all these points, as those on the Gulf were of material assistance in maintaining the blockade, and those in the vicinity of New Orleans were necessary to protect that city from capture, either from the direction of Texas, or from Mobile, or other points in Alabama. Banks' troops were designated as the 19th Army Corps, and were divided into four divisions, commanded by Maj.-Gen. Augur and Brig.-Gens. T. W. Sherman, Emory, and Grover.

Almost immediately after Banks' arrival, his attention was directed to the condition of Galveston, which had been captured in the previous month of October, and was now held by the navy. It was reported to be threatened by a considerable force moving against it from the north, and, although his instructions did not include the defence of that place, yet Banks considered it of such importance that, at the request of Admiral Farragut and of Brig.-Gen. Hamilton, who had come with Banks to assume the duties of Military Governor of Texas, he sent a regiment of infantry to assist in the defence of the place. A portion of this regiment reached Galveston on December 28th, just in time to be captured. The place was attacked on January 1st by a force of Confederates, numbering over 2,000 men, under Magruder, and it was captured with its little garrison and the gunboat Harriet Lane, whose commander (Wainwright) was killed. The gunboat Westfield was blown up to escape capture.

Galveston remained in the possession of the Confederates from this time until the close of the war, and Banks had no further opportunity for efforts in this direction.

The most important duty entrusted to Banks by his instructions was an advance up the Mississippi River against Port Hudson, in co-operation with Grant's operations against Vicksburg. But after deducting the garrisons of all the positions before referred to, he found that he could not take the field with more than 15,000 men. The garrison of Port Hudson, according to the information which Banks received, numbered 18,000 men, and the position was one of considerable strength, thoroughly fortified by a continuous line of works, each flank of which rested on the river. Rumors even reached Banks that the garrison numbered over 30,000 men, but without crediting this exaggerated report it was evident that his force was entirely insufficient to assault the works at Port Hudson. He therefore turned his attention to the project of passing it or reducing it by other means.

This post, as well as Vicksburg, drew its supplies mainly from Western Louisiana and Texas, by way of the Red River. If this river could be reached and held, these supplies could

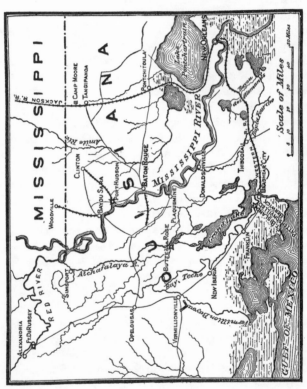

Operations in Louisiana. February to July, 1863.

be cut off and communication opened with the troops under Grant near Vicksburg. At this time the Confederate forces in Louisiana consisted of about 4,000 men under Maj.-Gen. R. Taylor. Their principal point of defence was at Alexandria, but their outposts extended down as far as the railroad from New Orleans to Brashear City. Just below Alexandria they had an earthwork called Fort de Russy, intended to block the passage up Red River. On the Bayou Teche, at Pattersonville, a few miles west of Brashear City, they had another work, called Fort Bisland, extending from Grand Lake to the impassable swamps south of the Teche. On the Atchafalaya there was a third work at Butte-à-la-Rose, about twenty miles north of Grand Lake.

The whole country, for 50 miles west of the Mississippi, in this region is alluvial land filled with countless bayous, lakes, rivers, and swamps, crossing and connecting with each other in such manner that the country is almost impassable; but there is a road along the Teche from Brashear City through Opelousas to Alexandria; and in high water the Teche is navigable to Opelousas, and the Atchafalaya to Red River. Along these two streams, therefore, lay the routes of any advance to the Red River. The Confederate forts were intended to defend these lines of approach, and Fort Bisland was, in addition, to be used as a base of operations against the La Fourche and New Orleans.

In the latter part of January, Banks organized two expeditions, one of which, consisting of 4,000 men under Brig.-Gen. Weitzel, was to move up Bayou Teche from Berwick, and the other, of 3,000 men under Brig.-Gen. Emory, was to leave the Mississippi at Plaquemine, and pass through a bayou into the Atchafalaya. The two columns were then to unite and advance upon the fort at Butte-à-la-

Rose, after taking which they were to move up to the Red River. This expedition came to nothing—beyond a small skirmish on the Teche—because it was found impossible to penetrate through Bayou Plaquemine. Before it had been completely abandoned, information was received of the capture by the Confederates, on the Red River, of the ram Queen of the West, and the gunboat De Soto, which had run past the batteries at Vicksburg and descended the river early in February. On hearing of this, Admiral Farragut determined that it was necessary to patrol the river at once above Port Hudson with his vessels. He requested Banks to make a demonstration with his troops against Port Hudson, while he ran past the batteries for this purpose.

Banks gave his assent, and immediately withdrew Emory from the west bank of the river, and taking all the force available from New Orleans—excepting Weitzel's command on the Teche, which was essential for the defence of the city from that direction—he moved to Baton Rouge early in March. His force numbered about 17,000 men. A delay of ten days then occurred, owing to the necessity for repairs to the machinery of some of the vessels, but on March 13th Farragut arrived at Baton Rouge with his fleet. On the same day Grover's division moved out from Baton Rouge for Port Hudson, followed, on the morning of the 14th, by Emory's and Augur's divisions. These troops, whose effective strength was reported by Banks as only 12,000—a considerable force having been detached to guard the points in his rear—took position on the roads east of the Port Hudson works, intending to make a demonstration against them, and to advance close enough to use their artillery in order to create a diversion during the passage of the fleet. The time for this latter had been fixed at a little before dawn on the 15th, but

late in the afternoon of the 14th Banks received a despatch
from Farragut saying that he found it more favorable to pass
during the evening, and he intended to start soon after dark.
Banks' advance was delayed by erroneous maps and by the
necessity of constructing some bridges, and it was impossible for him to approach near enough to the works to use
his artillery with any effect. Beyond exchanging a few
shots with the enemy's pickets, his troops accomplished
nothing on this expedition. He was still engaged in
building bridges when, at 11.30 P.M., on the 14th, the noise
of Farragut's guns was heard from the direction of the
river.

Farragut brought with him from New Orleans, for the purpose of passing Port Hudson, the following vessels :

Hartford, Capt. J. S. Palmer	28	guns.
Richmond, Comdr. James Alden	25	"
Monongahela, Capt. J. P. McKinstry	11	"
Mississippi, Capt. Melancton Smith	19	"
Essex, Comdr. C. H. B. Caldwell	7	"
Albatross, Lt.-Com. J. E. Hart	7	"
Genesee, Comdr. W. H. Macomb	8	"
Kineo, Lt.-Com. John Waters	6	"
Sachem, Lt. Amos Johnston	5	"
5 mortar-schooners	5	"
Total	121	guns.

The first four were sloops of war, the Essex a river iron-
clad, the other four were gunboats. The order of battle
prescribed that each of the large vessels—except the Mississippi, which was a side-wheeler—should take a gunboat
firmly lashed on the port side, away from the batteries, and
that they should proceed up the river in the order named
above, the Hartford in the lead. The mortar-boats were

anchored near the east bank, about a mile below the batteries. The captains were reminded that the object of the movement was to pass the batteries with the least possible damage to their vessels, so as to secure as efficient a force as possible for patrolling the river above. The vessels were trimmed by the head, so that in case of grounding they would not swing around with the current.

At 9 o'clock, the signal was made for the ships to get into line, and as soon as this was accomplished, the Hartford slowly steamed ahead. At 11.20 P.M. two rockets were fired on the east bank, and almost immediately the batteries opened fire. The fleet and the mortar boats immediately answered, and from this time till long after midnight, the noise of 150 guns firing as rapidly as possible was incessant.

The fleet moved forward steadily under the fire. As the Hartford reached the upper batteries, the smoke was so dense that the pilot could see nothing, and the firing was ceased. It was immediately found that the strong current had deflected the ship from her course, and she was heading for the shore. While the Albatross backed, the Hartford's engines drove forward, and thus the two ships were turned into the current again, the Hartford grounding for a moment only. Just as she was free, the Richmond came upon her from the stern, and a collision was barely avoided. Once in the right direction, the Hartford, and her consort, the Albatross, went forward at full speed, and were soon out of range above the bend, where they came to anchor, having been under fire an hour and ten minutes.

None of the other ships were able to follow. Their various mishaps will be described in turn.

The Richmond reached the bend just after getting clear of the Hartford, and then received a shot on the safety-valves, upsetting them, and allowing the steam to escape. Her engines were thus useless, and all the efforts of the Genesee, her consort, were insufficient to carry both ships forward against the strong current. They were therefore forced to turn back, and came to anchor below the batteries.

The Monongahela ran too close to the west shore, and grounded in turning the point at 11.20 P.M. Her consort, the Kineo, broke adrift with the shock, and went ahead a short distance, and also grounded. Her rudder had previously been destroyed. Just after grounding, the bridge of the Monongahela was shot away, and her captain thrown violently to the deck, injuring him so that he was unable to take further part in the action. The Kineo having floated, she backed to the Monongahela, and made fast again; both vessels then backed with all steam, and finally got off after being aground under fire for twenty-five minutes. The Monongahela then started up stream again, but in a few minutes the engine stopped, and the engineer reported that the crank pin of the forward engine was so heated that he could not go ahead. The ship thus became unmanageable, and drifted down below the batteries.

The Mississippi also grounded at 12.30 A.M. on the west bank just at the point of the bend. She grounded hard and fast, and lay there for thirty-five minutes under fire, firing her starboard guns, and backing her engine with all the steam the engineer deemed safe. But it was of no avail. The captain then determined to abandon the ship; her engine was destroyed, small arms thrown overboard, the sick and wounded landed on the shore, and fires kindled in several parts of the ship. When these were well under way the captain left the ship, and with his crew in open boats went past the batteries to the fleet below. The Mississippi floated at 3 A.M. and came down the river in full blaze. At

5.30 the flames reached the magazine and she was blown to atoms.

The Essex acted in connection with the mortar boats at the lower batteries and did not come up to the bend. At the close of the action she picked up the boats of the Mississippi and embarked the wounded from the west shore.

Of the Mississippi's crew of 297 men, 64 were missing at the close of the action and, it was supposed that 25 of these were killed. The casualties on the other ships were 11 killed and 38 wounded; the total loss was thus 113. One ship had been destroyed, four had been disabled, and two had succeeded in passing. It is doubtful if the Confederates lost a dozen men, and their works were practically uninjured.

It was an extremely gallant fight, conducted against great odds in spite of the naval superiority in number and weight of guns; for a successful shot from the ships merely threw up a cloud of dirt, while a successful shot from the shore destroyed an engine or a rudder and rendered a ship helpless if it did not sink her. The object of the fight was to pass the batteries and patrol the river above, especially at the mouth of the Red River, whence the Confederates drew their supplies. Although five out of seven of Farragut's ships met with disaster, yet he fully accomplished his purpose, and the Red River route was completely blockaded from this time forward. This object may seem small as compared with the capture of a great city like New Orleans, yet it was a most important object in the operations then in progress.

Banks received word from his signal officers on the 15th that Farragut had passed the batteries with the Hartford and Albatross, and that the other vessels were disabled. The object of his expedition being merely to make a demonstration while the vessels were passing, his men at once returned to Baton Rouge.[1] Leaving Augur's division there, Banks returned in person to New Orleans, giving orders for Emory and Grover to move down the river to Donaldsonville, and thence march across to Thibodeau, on the railroad, in order to join Weitzel at Brashear City, and resume the movement up the Atchafalaya and Teche, which had been suspended by the demonstration against Port Hudson. Lack of transportation both on the river and on land delayed these movements so that it was the 10th of April before the troops were united and ready for action at Brashear City. They numbered about 17,000 men.

Banks arrived in person from New Orleans on the 8th, and on the morning of the 11th the movement began, Emory's division and Weitzel's brigade crossing Berwick's Bay and moving forward toward Pattersonville, and Grover's division moving up Grand Lake in transports, and landing opposite the bend in Bayou Teche, just above Franklin, so as to cut off the enemy's retreat. On the 13th the Confederates were met in front of Pattersonville and driven into their works at Fort Bisland after a sharp contest. It was intended to make an assault on the following morning, but during the night the Confederates evacuated Fort Bisland, retreating toward Opelousas. Grover reached Franklin on the following day (14th), having been greatly delayed in disembarking in consequence of shallow water extending out a mile from the shore. He had succeeded in landing on the evening of the 13th, and the next morning was attacked by a detachment which had been sent against him from Fort Bisland, in

---

[1] In his annual report for 1863, Halleck says: "Had our land forces invested Port Hudson at this time, it could easily have been reduced, as its garrison was weak." In this Halleck was mistaken. The garrison of Port Hudson was at its maximum—16,287 for duty out of 20,388 present—at this time. See p. 227 post.

order to keep open the line of retreat. He beat off this de-
tachment, but was unable to head off the main body of the
Confederates, who made good their retreat to Opelousas.
During the affair at Fort Bisland the ram Queen of the
West was finally destroyed by the gunboats Estrella, Ari-
zona, Clifton, and Calhoun, under command of Lt.-Com.
A. P. Cooke, U. S. Navy. Two other gunboats were blown
up by the Confederates to prevent their capture.

Banks followed up the retreating force of the Confederates and occupied Opelousas on April 20th. On the same
day the gunboats, under Lt.-Com. Cooke, after a short engagement, captured the fort at Butte-à-la-Rose on the Atchafalaya, with its garrison of 60 men. Remaining two weeks
at Opelousas, Banks moved forward on May 5th, and on the
9th occupied Alexandria, the Confederates retreating toward Shreveport. The vessels of Farragut's fleet above
Port Hudson, reinforced by four gunboats under Porter,
who had come down from Grand Gulf on the Mississippi,
had all ascended the Red River and appeared at Alexandria
simultaneously with the troops. In these operations from
Brashear City to Alexandria, Banks had captured a large
number of prisoners and 22 guns, and had destroyed three
Confederate gunboats and a considerable amount of property. His own loss had been about 600.

It was, however, nearly five months since Banks had arrived at New Orleans, and during that time nothing of any
importance had been done against Port Hudson or in co-operation with Grant. For this Banks was sharply called to
account by Halleck as soon as the latter heard of the occupation of Alexandria, but Banks seems to have been perfectly justified in his movements against the Red River
forces prior to any action against Port Hudson, for had his
troops besieged Port Hudson before driving back Taylor's

forces, the latter would possibly have been able to capture New Orleans, the safety of which exceeded in importance all other considerations.

During the months of March, April, and May, considerable correspondence took place between Grant and Banks as to the co-operation of their forces, which, as it has been much quoted and misinterpreted, is given in full, with dates of receipt, in the Appendix. The first letter is from Banks to Grant, dated March 13th, the day before the passage of the batteries at Port Hudson. In this Banks announced his arrival at Baton Rouge with 17,000 men, for the purpose of making a demonstration, while Farragut passed the batteries. After this he hoped to communicate with Grant as to the best means of co-operation between the two armies under their respective commands.

Farragut carried this up the river, and delivered it to Grant on March 20th. A few days later Farragut prepared to go down the river again, and Grant took advantage of the opportunity to send word to Banks. He wrote him a despatch, dated March 23d, explaining the condition of affairs at Vicksburg, and his various attempts to reach dry land on the east bank of the river. On the same day he wrote a letter to Farragut, in the nature of a postscript to the letter to Banks, and with a request that it might be sent to that officer, saying that the Lake Providence Canal promised success, and that he had sent to the Ohio River for light-draught steamers. If they arrived, he stated that he could send 20,000 men to Banks on the Red River by that route.

Farragut started down the river with these two letters on March 28th, and arrived above Port Hudson on April 6th. Here his secretary, Mr. Gabaudan, volunteered to slip past the batteries in a skiff, and convey the letters to Banks. But for fear of accident or capture, it was thought best not to take the letters with him but, to commit them to memory. He arrived safely at Baton Rouge on April 8th, and thence took steamer down the river, and reached Banks' headquarters at Brashear City on April 10th. From the verbal message which he conveyed, Banks gathered the information that Grant positively intended to send 20,000 men by the Lake Providence route. The contingency of receiving suitable transports (which, in fact, never arrived) was either not reported or not noticed. Banks immediately wrote Grant in reply that he was advancing toward Opelousas, but had no intention of remaining west of the Mississippi; that he would return to Port Hudson by May 10th, and that his available force for field operations was 15,000 men. Mr. Gabaudan took this letter, returned to Baton Rouge, and made his way across the wooded swamp opposite Port Hudson, reaching the Hartford on April 15th. Farragut had no opportunity to forward the despatch until May 1st. On that day he sent the Switzerland up the river with the letter, which reached Grant on May 2d, just after he had crossed at Bruinsburg. It was this despatch which has previously been referred to as convincing Grant that he could receive no co-operation from Banks during his campaign behind Vicksburg, and as causing him to retain all his own troops for that campaign instead of sending a corps to Port Hudson as he had intended before crossing the river. Grant wrote Banks to that effect on May 10th, as will be subsequently explained. It will be noticed that it took 40 days, from March 23d to May 2d, for Grant to receive a direct answer from Banks, and in the course of that time the whole condition of affairs had changed around Vicksburg. It was hopeless to effect any co-operation between two armies with such delay in communicating intelligence.

In this interval several other despatches had been sent on both sides, crossing each other on the road ; they had but little effect on the campaign, and what little they had was in the direction of creating confusion rather than of assisting in co-operation.

In the first place, the two letters of March 23d from Grant to Banks, which Farragut brought down the river with him, were sent across the peninsula opposite Port Hudson, and delivered to General Augur at Baton Rouge, who forwarded them by an officer of his staff. They did not reach Banks until April 21st, eleven days after Mr. Gabaudan had conveyed his verbal message. Banks was then at Opelousas. The letters themselves, instead of conveying the positive information that 20,000 men were to be sent by Lake Providence, made the sending of them depend on the arrival of light-draught steamers. The letters were a month old when received, and nothing had meantime been heard of any troops coming down the Tensas. Banks was therefore uncertain as to Grant's intentions, and he wrote in reply, asking for definite information as to the method and time of co-operation, and as to Grant's facilities for supplying any troops he might send. This letter was sent to Farragut, who received it on the evening of May 1st, and forwarded it a few days later. It reached Grant about May 10th.

Still another despatch was sent by Grant from Milliken's Bend, April 14th. At that time, as we have seen, Grant had just received a despatch from Halleck, urging his co-operation at Port Hudson, and Grant had made his plans for such a movement as soon as he could cross the river. In the despatch Grant communicated these plans, said he would send a corps to Bayou Sara " by the 25th," and asked if Banks would send troops to Vicksburg after Port Hudson had fallen. The despatch was delayed in transmission ; it did not reach Banks till May 5th, at Alexandria. It was forwarded from New Orleans by telegraph, in cipher and without date. Banks supposed it was only a few days old, and that "the 25th" meant May 25. He replied May 6th in the following words: "By the 25th, probably, by the 1st, certainly, I will be there." This referred to being at Port Hudson, and said nothing about coming to Vicksburg. The reply reached Grant on May 10th.

Finally, however, Banks received a despatch, only two days old, giving him information which caused him no little disappointment, but at least enabled him to form definite plans. This was Grant's despatch of May 10th, dated at Rocky Springs. In this, Grant explained to Banks the circumstances under which the campaign had opened in earnest behind Vicksburg, the necessity for prompt action, and the impossibility of detaching any troops to go down the river. On the contrary, Grant asked Banks to come to Grand Gulf with all his effective force, or to send such portion of it as could be spared, to take part in the operations at Vicksburg, on which everything on the Mississippi depended. In order to insure safety in the delivery of this despatch, Grant sent it by one of his staff on a special steamer, and by chance this officer met one of Banks' staff at Natchez, who immediately took charge of it, and delivered it to Banks at Alexandria, on the 12th, two days after it was written.

Banks was greatly disappointed at receiving information that no reinforcements would come to him from Grant's army. Under these circumstances, he deliberated whether he should pursue the enemy in his front to Shreveport, or go to Vicksburg, as requested by Grant, or invest Port Hudson with such troops as he already had. Nothing could be gained by advancing beyond Alexandria, for the enemy was reported to have already dispersed. To go to Vicksburg would consume weeks of time, for he had only enough steamers to transport a few regiments at a trip; moreover such a movement left New Orleans comparatively defence-less and open to attack from the forces at Port Hudson should he be detained long at Vicksburg. To march to Port Hudson was the only feasible plan, and orders were at once issued to put it in operation. Two days later (May 14th), Grover's division left Alexandria, for Simsport, on the Atchafalaya, followed on the 16th by Emory's division, and a few days later by Weitzel's brigade, which had been sent forward on a reconnoissance, nearly seventy miles toward Shreveport, but was now recalled. The whole force was united at Simsport on the 19th, crossed the Atchafalaya at that point by means of transports, thence marched down the west bank of the Mississippi to opposite Bayou Sara, where it was ferried across the river by the same boats, and marched to the vicinity of Port Hudson. It arrived there on May 24th, and effected a junction with Augur's division, which meanwhile had moved up from Baton Rouge, in pur-suance of orders to that effect.

It has already been narrated in the first chapter how the Confederates came to select Port Hudson for a fortified point, after their unsuccessful attack upon Baton Rouge in August, 1862. Slave labor was then abundant and time was not pressing, as they were not molested for several months. In that interval they constructed a series of works around Port Hudson of remarkable strength, the parapets having an average thickness of 20 feet, and the depth of the ditch below the top of the parapet being not less than 15 feet. They consisted of a series of batteries, in all mounting 20 siege guns, along the bluff at an elevation of about 80 feet above the river. The land defences consisted of a

10*

continuous line of parapet of strong profile, beginning at a
point known as Ross's Landing, about one mile below Port
Hudson, thence running eastwardly through a slightly broken

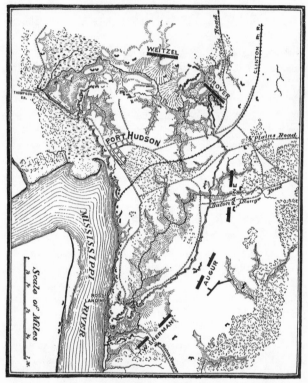

Port Hudson. 1863.

country for about a mile, gradually coming into a broad
plain, dotted here and there with clumps of trees; thence
the line turned to the northward, following a general direction paral'el to the river, and finally turning westward

through a rough country much cut up by ravines, and meeting the river bank at the mouth of Thompson's Creek, about half a mile north of Port Hudson. Near Ross's landing on the river bank the line began in an enclosed bastion work; at the southeast salient of the line was another work; a third was situated at the forks of the roads leading to Baton Rouge and Bayou Sara, and there was a fourth facing Thompson's Creek. The entire length of the line was between three and four miles; it was of strong profile throughout, was defended by about 30 pieces of field artillery, and the ground in rear of it afforded admirable facilities for prompt movement of troops from one point to another.

Brig.-Gen. Beall constructed the works, and commanded the garrison, which gradually increased from 6,000 to 12,000 men during the autumn of 1862. Maj.-Gen. Frank Gardner succeeded him in command on December 28, 1862, and remained in command until the surrender of the place. In the months of January and February, rumors of Banks' arrival with a large force at New Orleans and his advance to Baton Rouge were communicated by Gardner to Pemberton with the request for reinforcements. In response to this, on February 22d, Pemberton sent Rust's brigade, which carried the total strength of the garrison to 16,287 for duty and 20,-388 present as shown by the returns of March 31st. Subsequently Pemberton became alarmed for the safety of Vicksburg, and on April 5th, he ordered Gardner to send Rust's and Buford's brigades back to him. On April 29th, when Pemberton heard that Grant was crossing the river, he ordered Gardner to send Gregg's and Maxey's brigades to Jackson, and the garrison was then reduced to 4,652 effective out of a total of 5,715 present, as shown on a return dated May 19th. But this return is manifestly erroneous, as the number actually paroled, the sick not paroled, and the acknowledged losses during the siege, make up a total of a little over 7,000; which was the force present when Banks arrived in front of the place on May 24th. On May 19th, Johnston sent Gardner an order to evacuate the place and bring whatever force he had to Jackson. But just as the courier arrived with this order the place had been invested.

Banks brought with him from the Red River country the divisions of Grover and Emory (the latter under command of Brig.-Gen. Wm. Dwight, Emory being sick) and the brigade of Weitzel. He was joined by Augur's division and a part of T. W. Sherman's from Baton Rouge. His returns for April 30th and June 30th, show a force of 33,000 men for duty out of over 40,000 present.[1] Of these 33,000 all but about 2,300 appear on the return as being at Port Hudson. The rest were at New Orleans, Brashear City, or elsewhere in small detachments.

The troops were all united on the road a few miles east of Port Hudson on May 25th, and after some skirmishing with the outposts, the place was invested. Preparations were immediately made for an assault. The troops of Grover, Dwight, and Weitzel were on the right; Augur's division was in the centre; and T. W. Sherman was on the left. Orders were issued for a simultaneous assault along the whole line early in the morning. Between 5 and 6 o'clock the artillery opened briskly, and at 10 o'clock the troops on the right moved forward to the assault. The ground was very broken and progress was difficult; severe fighting was kept up on this part of the line until 4 o'clock

---

[1] Banks' final report, dated April 6, 1865, states that his effective force before Port Hudson was "less than 13,000, including Augur's command." His official returns, however, are as above given, without counting Grierson's cavalry, which was defending his rear from cavalry raids of the enemy.

in the afternoon. In the centre and on the left there
was some delay in the assault, which did not take place
until 2 P.M. It was then made with great determination, and the troops reached the ditch, but were unable
to cross the parapet. At nightfall they were withdrawn.
The assault in general was entirely unsuccessful, and it
entailed a loss of 293 killed, 1,545 wounded, and 157 missing, total 1,995. General T. W. Sherman was severely
wounded, losing a leg in this assault. The defenders lost
probably less than 300. Some siege guns were then brought
up and constant skirmishing ensued for several days, during
which the Union troops slightly advanced their position,
and intrenched their line. This line was parallel to that of
the Confederates, and between seven and eight miles in
length. On June 13th, Banks summoned the garrison to surrender, and this being refused, another assault was ordered.
Dwight's division was now on the left, and it was ordered to
push forward at daylight under cover of a ravine, and attack
the large bastion, called the "Citadel," while the main attack was made on the right by Grover and Weitzel. Neither
columns were successful, although the lines were advanced
from 50 to 200 yards, the troops intrenching themselves on
the new ground and permanently holding it. On the left
an eminence was gained, from which an approach was subsequently run to within ten yards of the citadel.[1]

In this assault the loss was 203 killed, 1,401 wounded,
and 201 missing—total 1,805. Nearly 4,000 men, therefore
were lost in the two assaults.

The usual siege operations were then resumed and the
approaches were carried forward within a short distance of

[1] The War Department Records contain no reports of division commanders for
either of these assaults. The above account, which is necessarily very meagre, is
taken from Banks' reports.

the defender's works. On July 7th a letter was received
from Grant communicating the intelligence of the surrender
of Vicksburg. Salutes were fired and loud and prolonged
cheers were given along the Federal lines. The news
quickly spread among the Confederates, and in the afternoon of that day Gardner asked Banks to give him an official
assurance that the news was true. Banks replied during
the middle of the night, sending a copy of Grant's letter.
Gardner immediately announced his willingness to surrender, and proposed the appointment of three commissioners on each side to arrange the details. Banks acceded to
this, and the commissioners met at 9 A.M. and drew up the
articles of capitulation, by which the entire garrison was
surrendered as prisoners of war, together with all arms, munitions, public funds, and material of war at the post. The
garrison laid down its arms on the morning of the 9th, and
was paroled a few days later. The number actually paroled
was 5,953, exclusive of about 500 sick and wounded in the
hospitals. The losses during the siege of 45 days were
about 800. The artillery numbered 51 pieces, and the small
arms over 5,000; there were also large quantities of ammunition, but almost no commissary stores, the defenders having lived on mules and rats for several days.

While the siege had been in progress a small body of
cavalry had been hovering in the rear between Clinton and
Camp Moore, but they were easily beaten off by Grierson.

A very serious danger had, however, arisen in the return
of Taylor's forces from Alexandria to the lower Teche and
La Fourche Bayous, from which they now threatened the city
of New Orleans as well as Banks' communications on the
river. After Banks had left Alexandria for Port Hudson in
May, Taylor had been ordered, as we have seen, to accompany
Walker's division from Arkansas on its bootless expedition

against Milliken's Bend. After this expedition had retired
from the vicinity of Vicksburg to Monroe, Taylor had asked
to take this division to Alexandria and unite it with his
own troops, which would give him a force of between 7,000
and 8,000 men. With these he proposed to move down the
river and either raise the siege of Port Hudson or capture
the city of New Orleans—according to the disposition of
Banks' forces. In this plan Taylor was overruled by Kirby
Smith, who ordered Walker's division to remain in the
vicinity of Vicksburg. Taylor then returned to Alexandria
alone and there recruited and reorganized his own forces,
which numbered about 3,000 men. He divided them into
two detachments, the first of which, consisting of the infantry brigades of Mouton and Thomas Green, was to move
down the Teche to its mouth and attack Brashear City in
front; while the other detachment, consisting of three cavalry regiments under Col. Major, was to move from Opelousas by way of Plaquemine and Thibodeau and attack Brashear
City in the rear. Small detachments of Union troops were
at this time posted at Plaquemine, Donaldsonville, and New
Orleans on the river, and at Brashear City and Thibodeau
on the Western Railroad. All the rest of Banks' troops
were at Port Hudson.

The detachments moved as ordered, and Major's command
reached Plaquemine on June 18th, capturing its little garrison of 70 men and burning two steamers; thence Major
hurried on, avoiding Donaldsonville, to Thibodeau, where
he attacked and was defeated on the 20th and 21st; thence
he moved westward on the railroad toward Brashear City.
Mouton and Green had meanwhile marched down the Teche,
and near its mouth had collected some small boats and rafts.
With these they crossed Grand Lake on the 22d, and attacked Brashear City simultaneously with Major's command.

The place was captured, with everything in it. Taylor
states that his prisoners numbered 1,700 and the captured
guns 12; Banks gives the strength of the garrison as "about
300," and the guns lost as 8. Taylor says that, with this
capture, he had supplies for the first time since he arrived
in Western Louisiana, which is not disputed.

Taylor collected his captured property as rapidly as possible, and on the 24th he sent Green with his own and
Major's men to Donaldsonville, while Mouton moved along
the railway to the La Fourche, whence he sent his pickets as
far as Bayou des Allemands, within 25 miles of New Orleans, creating no little excitement in that city, which was
practically without defenders. There can be little doubt
that, had Walker's division been sent to Taylor as he requested, he would have captured New Orleans, though he
would have been unable to hold it for more than a short
time.   In regaining it, however, Banks might have felt
obliged to raise the siege of Port Hudson. It was still two
weeks before Port Hudson surrendered.

Green arrived in front of Donaldsonville with a force of
about 1,400 men on the afternoon of the 27th. There was a
small earthwork at the place, garrisoned by 180 men of the
28th Maine, under command of Maj. J. D. Mullen.   At
1.30 A.M. of June 28th the Confederates assaulted the work,
but in the darkness there was a good deal of confusion in
their movements, and they were completely defeated by the
combined action of the little garrison and of three gunboats
in the river. The affair lasted until daylight. There is
the usual discrepancy as to the losses, Taylor stating the
Confederate loss at 97 in all, whereas the Union reports
speak of burying 69 Confederate dead and taking 120 prisoners.   Being repulsed in this assault, the Confederates
moved down the river a few miles, and there erected bat-

teries commanding its navigation. The situation was now
very serious, one force of Confederates in front of the La
Fourche directly threatening New Orleans, and another on
the river cutting off all communication by transports with
Port Hudson. Gen. Emory, then in command at New Orleans, wrote to Banks, on July 4th, that he must come to
the assistance of New Orleans at once or it would be lost;
that the choice lay between New Orleans and Port Hudson.
Banks, however, wisely determined to remain at Port Hudson, as he felt confident it must fall in a few days, when he
would have abundant force to drive Taylor off.

His confidence was justified. Port Hudson was surrendered on the morning of July 9th, and on the same afternoon all the transports available were loaded with Weitzel's
and one of Grover's brigades and sent down to Donaldsonville, where they arrived the same afternoon. Other troops
followed, and on the 13th Grover attacked Green's force on
the La Fourche and a sharp engagement followed, which
was indecisive in its results. A day or two later, however,
Green withdrew to Brashear City, and Mouton was called in
to the same point from the Bayou des Allemands. Banks
overestimated Taylor's force, and did not pursue vigorously,
so that Taylor had a week longer in which to remove all the
stores for which he had means of transportation. On July
21st he ran all the captured cars and heavy guns into Berwick's Bay, and on the following day began his retreat up
the Teche. Banks' troops arrived at Brashear City on the 22d
but did not continue the pursuit. Taylor retreated, without
molestation, to Opelousas, where he remained, skirmishing
occasionally on the Teche, until the opening of Banks' Red
River campaign in the spring of 1864.

CHAPTER VIII.

CONCLUDING OPERATIONS.

As soon as the Richmond authorities learned that Pemberton had been invested in Vicksburg, the Confederate Secretary of War sent a despatch (May 25th) to Johnston suggesting that the troops in the Trans-Mississippi Department should advance toward Vicksburg, in order to make a diversion in favor of Pemberton. Johnston forwarded this to E. K. Smith on May 31st, with a letter requesting compliance with this suggestion. The first result was the fruitless expedition of Taylor and Walker against Milliken's Bend, which has already been narrated. After this had failed Lt.-Gen. T. H. Holmes, who commanded the District of Arkansas in E. K. Smith's department, sent the following telegram, dated Little Rock, June 15th, to Smith at Shreveport: "I believe we can take Helena; please let me do it." To which Smith replied: "Most certainly do it." Holmes then had in his entire district, according to his returns of May 1st, 31,933 men, of whom 14,508 were "estimated" as fit for duty. For his expedition to Helena he collected about twenty regiments, consisting of Price's and Marmaduke's divisions and Fagan's and Walker's brigades. In his report Holmes states that these troops numbered 7,646 men. With their officers the whole force was probably between 8,000 and 9,000; it was estimated by the Union officers at 15,000.

Holmes' object in this expedition was to capture Helena, by which he hoped to raise the siege of Vicksburg, or if

Vicksburg fell to still keep the river closed and perhaps make a new Vicksburg on the west bank.

Helena had been occupied by the Union troops ever since Curtis arrived there from Western Arkansas, in July, 1862. It had been considerably fortified by a redoubt, called Fort Curtis, just west of the town, and by four outlying batteries— named Batteries A, B, C, and D—which commanded the roads on the west of the town, as shown on the accompanying sketch.

The garrison at this time consisted of Ross' division of the 13th Corps (temporarily in command of Brig.-Gen. Salomon) and a brigade of cavalry. The entire force num-

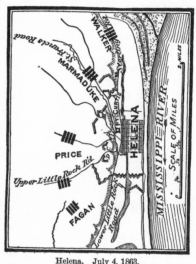

Helena.   July 4, 1863.

bered 4,129 men, and was commanded by Maj.-Gen. B. M. Prentiss.

Holmes arrived in front of the place on the evening of July 3d. His orders were to assault at daylight, Fagan's brigade on the right against Battery D, Price's division in the centre against Battery C, Marmaduke's division on the left against Batteries A and B, and Walker's cavalry brigade covering the extreme left. Prentiss was expecting an attack, and his troops were under arms all night in order to be prepared for it.

At daylight Fagan and Marmaduke moved forward. The latter's attack was feebly made, and was not supported by Walker's cavalry on his left as had been ordered. It accomplished nothing all day. Fagan, however, attacked with great determination and carried all the outer intrenchments in front of Battery D, but was unable to enter that work. His men were subjected to a severe cross-fire from the other batteries, and were forced to fall back; the four regiments of this brigade lost over 400 men. Price also made a most vigorous assault, although he did not come into action until an hour later than Fagan. He carried all the intrenchments in his front and Battery C also. He then ordered one brigade to move forward toward the town and the other to assault Battery D in rear. But there was a great deal of confusion among his men, and the orders were not obeyed. In the midst of the delay he was energetically attacked by the Union troops, and Battery C was recaptured. Seeing that his attack had no chance of success, Holmes gave the order to withdraw at 10.30 A.M. His troops returned to Little Rock without molestation, Prentiss having too small a force to attempt a pursuit.

The Confederate losses, as stated by Holmes, were 173 killed, 687 wounded, and 776 missing, making a total of 1,636. Prentiss certifies that he buried 400 dead, paroled 108 wounded, and sent North 993 prisoners, about one-fourth of whom were wounded, making a total of 1,501 left in his hands. The Union loss was 57 killed, 127 wounded, and 36 missing; total, 230.

This battle of Helena was the last expiring effort on the part of the Confederates to retain control of the Mississippi River; and it was a hopeless, and to some extent a discreditable defeat, the mortification at which is not concealed in their reports. It occurred on the same day that Vicksburg fell, and was followed in a few days by the fall of Port Hudson; the last hostilities at various points on the river being thus almost simultaneous. The great river was finally free, and free forever. On July 16th the steamer Imperial arrived at New Orleans direct from St. Louis, thus showing that the Mississippi was once more a highway of commerce.

Garrisons were retained until the end of the war at various points between Cairo and New Orleans, and the banks were infested by partisan and guerilla bands, supplemented now and then by a cavalry raid of larger proportions. But no serious effort was ever made to again bring the Mississippi within Confederate control or to permanently blockade it against commerce. These cavalry raids were of importance, because they occupied the attention of a large force of Union troops, but they accomplished no other purpose; they would have been long since forgotten but for the indelible stain left by Forrest when he slaughtered the captive negro garrison of Fort Pillow, in April, 1864.

The Union armies on the Mississippi turned their attention to other fields. Banks' troops assembled at New Orleans, and afterward operated on the Red River and in the direction of Texas. Grant's army was broken up, the 9th Corps returning to Ohio and Herron's division to Missouri; the 13th Corps was sent to Texas, and the 15th, followed eventually by the 17th and part of the 16th, to Chattanooga. Grant remained at Vicksburg until October, 1863, when he was assigned to the command of all the troops in the West and ordered to Chattanooga to retrieve the defeat at Chickamauga, and to prepare the way for the eventual advance to Atlanta and thence through the heart of the Confederacy.

APPENDIX A.

SUMMARY OF PRINCIPAL EVENTS.

1861.

May 10th.	Capture of Camp Jackson, near St. Louis, by U. S. Troops.
July 28th.	New Madrid, Mo., occupied by C. S. Troops.
Aug.	Fort Henry, Tenn., occupied by C. S. Troops.
Aug.	Fort Donelson, Tenn., occupied by C. S. Troops.
Sept. 1st.	Cairo, Ill., occupied by U. S. Troops.
Sept. 4th.	Columbus, Ky., occupied by C. S. Troops.
Sept. 6th.	Paducah, Ky., occupied by U. S. Troops.
Sept. 18th.	Bowling Green, Ky., occupied by C. S. Troops.
Nov. 7th.	Engagement at Belmont, Mo.

1862.

Feb. 6th.	Fort Henry captured by U. S. Troops.
Feb. 15th.	Bowling Green evacuated by C. S. Troops.
Feb. 16th.	Fort Donelson surrendered by C. S. Troops.
Mar. 3d.	Columbus, Ky., evacuated by C. S. Troops.
Mar. 8th.	Chattanooga occupied by C. S. Troops.
April 6th, 7th.	Battle of Pittsburg Landing.
April 24th.	Battle of Forts St. Philip and Jackson below New Orleans.
April 25th.	New Orleans captured by U. S. Navy.
May 1st.	New Orleans occupied by U. S. Troops.
May 10th.	Naval Engagement at Fort Pillow, Tenn.
May 12th.	Vicksburg occupied by C. S. Troops.
May 18th.	Farragut's fleet arrives at Vicksburg.
May 29th.	Farragut's fleet returns to New Orleans.
May 30th.	Corinth evacuated by C. S. Troops.
June 4th.	Fort Pillow evacuated by C. S. Troops.
June 5th.	Memphis evacuated by C. S. Troops.
June 6th.	Naval engagement near Memphis, Tenn.
June 10th.	Buell's army moves from Corinth toward Chattanooga.
June 25th.	Farragut's fleet arrives at Vicksburg.

June 28th.   Farragut's fleet passes the batteries at Vicksburg and joins Davis' flotilla above.

July 24th.   Bragg's army moves from Tupelo, Miss , toward Chattanooga.

July 29th.   Farragut's fleet returns to New Orleans, and Davis' to Helena.

Aug. 5th.   Battle of Baton Rouge, La.

Aug. 7th.   Port Hudson, La., occupied by C. S. Troops.

Aug. 21st.   Baton Rouge, La., evacuated by U. S. Troops.

Sept. 19th. Battle of Iuka, Miss.

Oct. 3d, 4th. Battle of Corinth, Miss.

Oct. 5th.   Engagement on Hatchie River, Miss.

Nov. 24th.   Grant's army moves southward into Mississippi.

Dec. 11th to Jan. 3d. Forrest's raid into Western Tennessee.

Dec. 14th.   Banks' expedition arrives at New Orleans.

Dec. 17th.   Baton Rouge reoccupied by U. S. Troops.

Dec. 20th.   Grant's dépôt at Holly Springs destroyed by Van Dorn.

Dec. 20th.   Sherman's river expedition leaves Memphis.

Dec. 28th.   Grant's army returns to Tennessee.

Dec. 29th.   Battle of Chickasaw Bluffs.

1863.

Jan. 1st.   Capture of Galveston by C. S. Troops.

Jan. 11th.   Capture of Arkansas Post by U. S. Troops.

Jan. 11th to Feb. 28th. Expedition on Bayou Teche.

Jan. 16th.   McClernand's river expedition returns to vicinity of Vicksburg.

Jan. 20th to March 7th. Work on canal opposite Vicksburg.

Jan. 29th.   Grant takes command of river expedition.

Feb. 1st to April 5th. Yazoo Pass expedition.

Feb. 5th to Mar. 18th. Work on Lake Providence project.

Mar. 14th.   Farragut's fleet passes the batteries at Port Hudson.

Mar. 16th to Mar. 27th. Steele's Bayou expedition.

Mar. 25th to May 14th. Expedition on Bayou Teche.

Mar. 29th to April 30th. Movement from Milliken's Bend to Bruinsburg.

April 12th. Engagement at Fort Bisland, La.

April 14th. Engagement at Franklin, La.

April 20th. Capture of Butte à la Rose, La.

April 29th. Engagement at Grand Gulf.

April 30th. Grant's army crosses the Mississippi.

May 1st.   Battle of Port Gibson.

May 2d.   Evacuation of Grand Gulf.

May 7th.   Occupation of Alexandria, La.

May 12th.   Battle of Raymond.

May 14th.   Battle of Jackson.

May 16th.   Battle of Champion's Hill.

May 17th.   Battle of Big Black Bridge.

May 19th.   Assault at Vicksburg.

May 19th.   Evacuation of Haines' Bluff.

May 22d.   Assault at Vicksburg.
May 22d to July 4th. Siege of Vicksburg.
May 24th to July 9th.   Siege of Port Hudson.
May 27th.   Assault at Port Hudson.
June 14th. Assault at Port Hudson.
June 23d.   Capture of Brashear City by C. S. Troops.
June 28th. Engagement at Donaldsonville, La.
July 4th.   Battle of Helena.
July 4th.   Surrender of Vicksburg.
July 9th.   Surrender of Port Hudson.
July 9th to 15th. Investment of Jackson, Miss.
July 13th. Engagement at Donaldsonville, La.
July 16th. Evacuation of Jackson, Miss.
July 22d.   Recapture of Brashear City by U. S. Troops.

DEPARTMENTS AND COMMANDERS.

AT the outbreak of the war, the territory between the Mississippi River and the Rocky Mountains constituted the Military Department of the West. Brig.-Gen. W. S. Harney was in command until May 31, 1861, when he was succeeded by Brig.-Gen. N. Lyon. On July 3, 1861, the title was changed to Western Department, the boundaries remaining substantially the same, with the addition of Illinois, and Maj.-Gen. J. C. Frémont was assigned to the command. On November 9, 1861, this department was discontinued, and a new department constituted, consisting of the States of Missouri, Iowa, Minnesota, Wisconsin, Illinois, Arkansas, and Western Kentucky. This was styled the Department of the Missouri, and Maj.-Gen. H. W. Halleck was assigned to the command. On the same date the Department of Kansas was formed, consisting of that State and the neighboring territories, under Maj.-Gen. D. Hunter; and the Department of Ohio, consisting of the States of Ohio, Michigan, Indiana, Tennessee, and Eastern Kentucky, under Brig.-Gen. D. C. Buell. On March 11, 1862, these three departments were consolidated into one, styled the Department of the Mississippi, and General Halleck was assigned to the command. The three field armies within the department were the Army of the Tennessee, under Maj.-Gen. U. S. Grant; the Army of the Ohio, under Maj.-Gen. D. C. Buell, and the Army of the Mississippi, under Maj.-Gen. John Pope. These three armies were united at Corinth, and separated again in June, 1862, into two armies, under Generals Grant and Buell, the Army of the Mississippi being divided between them; one army acting on the line of the Mississippi, and the other on the line from Nashville to Chattanooga.

General Halleck was appointed General-in-Chief, July 11, 1862, but no successor was appointed to the command of his department. In September and October, 1862, this department was gradually broken up, and four new departments formed out of it, viz., Department of the Missouri, under Maj.-Gen. S. R. Curtis, succeeded in May, 1863, by Maj.-Gen. J. M. Schofield; Department of the Tennessee, under Maj.-Gen. U. S. Grant; Department of the Cumberland, under Maj.-Gen. W. S. Rosecrans; and Department of the Ohio, under Maj.-Gen. H. G.

Wright, succeeded in 1863 by Maj.-Gens. A. E. Burnside and J. G. Foster, and in 1864 by Maj.-Gen. J. M. Schofield.

These four departments remained independent until October 16, 1863, when the three which were east of the Mississippi (Tennessee, Cumberland, and Ohio) were grouped into the Division of the Mississippi, and General Grant was assigned to the command. This division continued in existence until August, 1866, General Sherman succeeding General Grant on March 18, 1864, when the latter was placed in command of all the armies.

On the Confederate side, the Mississippi Valley was divided at the outbreak of war into two departments, known as Departments No. 1 and No. 2. The first embraced the State of Louisiana and the lower part of Mississippi, and was commanded by Maj.-Gen. D. E. Twiggs from May 27th to October 7, 1861, and then by Maj.-Gen. Mansfield Lovell. The capture of New Orleans virtually abolished the Department, and it was merged into Department No. 2, on June 25, 1862. Department No. 2, sometimes called the Western Department, comprised the Mississippi Valley north of Louisiana. Maj.-Gen. L. Polk was assigned to the command on June 25, 1861, and was succeeded by General A. S. Johnston on September 10, 1861. At his death, April 6, 1862, the command devolved on General G. T. Beauregard, who was succeeded on June 17, 1862, by General Braxton Bragg. In May, 1862, that portion of this department which was west of the Mississippi was formed into a new department, called the Trans-Mississippi Department, which was commanded by Maj.-Gen. T. H. Holmes until February 9, 1863, when he was succeeded by Lt.-Gen. E. K. Smith, who retained the command until the close of the war. In October, 1862, still another department was formed from a portion of the original No. 2. It was called the Department of Mississippi and East Louisiana, and embraced the territory named in its title. Lt.-Gen. J. C. Pemberton was assigned to the command, and retained it until the surrender of Vicksburg.

The various armies and districts which were embraced in these departments have been indicated in the text.

APPENDIX B.

Abstract from Returns of the Armies of the Mississippi and of the Tennessee, and of the District of the Ohio, MAJOR-GENERAL H. W. HALLECK *Commanding, for May 31 and June 1, 1862.*

COMMANDS.	Present for Duty. Officers.	Present for Duty. Men.	Aggregate present.	Aggregate present and absent.
Army of the Mississippi (Pope):				
Right wing (Rosecrans)	525	10,356	13,050	16,018
Left wing (Hamilton)	527	10,317	1 ,544	15,318
Cavalry division (Granger)................	114	2,408	3,153	4,135
Engineers (Bissell)........................	6	105	762	865
Reserves (Carlin).........................	71	1,736	2,033	2,228
Total..............	1,243	24,922	31,542	38,564
Army of the Tennessee—Right wing (Thomas):				
2d Division (Davies)......................	283	5,246	6,745	10,343
4th " (Hurlbut)	290	5,629	7,094	9,861
5th " (W. T. Sherman)...............	344	6,060	7,867	11,873
6th " (McKean)	255	5,401	6,989	10,251
7th " (T. W. Sherman)[1].............	368	7,066	8,365	11,306
Total..............	1,540	29,402	36,950	53,634
Reserve Corps (McClernand):				
1st Division (Judah).......................	319	5,537	7,159	11,355
3d " (Wallace).....................	264	5,540	7,029	9,370
Total..............	583	11,077	14,188	20,725
Total Armies of the Tennessee and Mississippi	3,366	65,401	82,680	112,923
District of the Ohio (Buell):				
2d Division (McCook)......................	370	7,785	9,225	11,902
3d " (Mitchel)[2]......................	339	6,072	8,672	11,687
4th " (Nelson)......................	299	6,212	7,641	10,693
5th " (Crittenden)	199	3,460	4,298	6,556
6th " (Wood)	349	6,220	7,458	10,455
7th " (Morgan)[3]......................	442	8,240	10,154	12,780
7th Brigade (Negley) [4]...................	134	2,927	3,320	4,228
23d " (Lester)	110	2,411	2,853	3,367
Dumont's command	95	1,683	2,019	2,447
Cavalry (Jackson)	90	1,798	2,379	3,151
Artillery reserve (Barnett)	17	453	490	564
Unattached artillery........................	13	315	364	437
" cavalry	119	2,419	2,841	3,405
" infantry	227	5,157	6,007	7,019
Total..............	2,803	55,152	67,781	88,636
Grand Total	6,169	120,523	150,461	201,559

[1] Formerly 1st Division (Thomas), Army of the Ohio.
[2] In Northern Alabama.   [3] At Cumberland Gap.   [4] At Nashville.
All of Buell's troops, except those commanded by Mitchel, Morgan, and Negley, were at or near Corinth.
NOTE.—The above was compiled in the War Records Office, and will appear on page 235 of Vol. X., Part II., of the Records of the War of the Rebellion.

APPENDIX C.

Field Return of the Confederate Forces prior to the Evacuation of Corinth [about May 28, 1862].

COMMAND	PRESENT											ABSENT									PRESENT AND ABSENT	
	For duty Officers	For duty Enlisted Men	Sick Officers	Sick Enlisted Men	Extra duty Officers	Extra duty Enlisted Men	In arrest Officers	In arrest Enlisted Men	Effective total	Total	Aggregate	Detached duty Officers	Detached duty Enlisted men	With leave Officers	With leave Enlisted men	Without leave Officers	Without leave Enlisted men	Sick Officers	Sick Enlisted men	Total	Aggregate
INFANTRY.																						
Army of the Mississippi	2,870	32,168	611	12,697	60	2,488	18	99	34,750	47,447	51,006	170	2,721	570	11,019	83	2,738	244	5,897	69,882	74,547
Army of the West	1,093	11,531	209	3,456	27	827	4	18	12,381	15,867	17,170	81	1,669	220	7,286	12	676	1	9	25,475	27,122
Total	3,963	43,699	820	16,153	87	3,315	22	117	47,131	63,294	68,176	251	4,388	790	18,305	94	3,474	245	5,906	95,357	101,669
ARTILLERY.																						
Army of the Mississippi	80	836	6	301	1	91		1	955	1,256	1,348	6	109		212		92	7	243	1,913	2,021
Army of the West	47	488	13	140	1	31		1	520	660	721	2	32	8	3	1	3	7	324	1,022	1,092
Total	127	1,351	19	441	2	122		2	1,475	1,916	2,064	8	141	8	215	1	95	14	567	2,935	3,113
Cavalry	236	3,868	25	824	4	232	1		4,100	4,924	5,189	31	540	36	715	9	119	24	657	6,955	7,315
Grand Total	4,326	48,918	864	17,418	93	3,669	23	119	52,706	70,124	75,429	290	5,069	834	19,235	104	3,688	283	7,164	105,227	112,092

Respectfully submitted.

[BRAXTON BRAGG, *General Commanding*].

NOTE.—The above is a copy of the return on file in the War Department. It will be published on page 791 of Vol. X. of the Records of the War of the Rebellion. It will be noticed that the "effective total" is made up of enlisted men present, for duty, extra duty, and in arrest, but does not include officers. The number of these latter must be added to the "effective total," in order to find the actual fighting strength.

APPENDIX D.

CORRESPONDENCE WITH REFERENCE TO THE DISPERSION OF HALLECK'S ARMY AFTER THE CAPTURE OF CORINTH.

No. 1.

LINCOLN TO HALLECK.

WASHINGTON, June 5, 1862—9.30 P.M.

I have received the following despatch from General McClellan, which I transmit for your consideration:

"MCCLELLAN'S HEADQUARTERS, June 5, 1862—4 P.M.

"May I again invite your Excellency's attention to the great importance of occupying Chattanooga and Dalton by our Western forces? The evacuation of Corinth would appear to render this very easy. The importance of this move in force cannot be exaggerated."

No. 2.

HALLECK TO LINCOLN.

CORINTH, June 7, 1862.

Your telegram of yesterday just received. Preparations for Chattanooga made five days ago, and troops moved in that direction. Mitchel's foolish destruction of bridges embarrassed me very much, but I am working night and day to remedy the error, and will very soon reinforce him.

[NOTE.—Mitchel had written orders from Buell to destroy the bridges referred to.—F. V. G.]

No. 3.

HALLECK TO STANTON.

CORINTH, June 9, 1862.

. . . General Buell, with four divisions, has been directed to move East, to form a junction with Mitchel. . . . It is absolutely necessary to reinforce General Curtis. I hope the navy will assist me in supplying him by White River. I am pushing forward troops and opening the road to Memphis.

No. 4.

STANTON TO HALLECK.

WASHINGTON, June 9, 1862.

Your despatch of this date has just been received, and your proposed plan of operations is cordially approved. I suppose you contemplate the occupation of Vicksburg and clearing out the Mississippi to New Orleans. If it should in any contingency become necessary, can you lend a hand to Butler?

No. 5.

STANTON TO HALLECK.

WAR DEPARTMENT, June 28, 1862.

The enemy have concentrated in such force at Richmond as to render it absolutely necessary, in the opinion of the President, for you immediately to detach 25,000 of your force, and forward it by the nearest and quickest route by way of Baltimore and Washington to Richmond. . . .

No. 6.

HALLECK TO STANTON.

CORINTH, June 30, 1862.

Your telegram of 28th is just received . . . and measures will be immediately taken to carry it out. . . . I think, under the circumstances, the Chattanooga expedition better be abandoned, or at least be diminished. If not I doubt our ability to hold West Tennessee after detaching so large a force as that called for. . . .

No. 7.

STANTON TO HALLECK.

WAR DEPARTMENT, June 30, 1862.

Your telegram of this date just received. The Chattanooga expedition must not on any account be given up. The President regards that and the movement against East Tennessee as one of the most important events of the war, and its occupation nearly as important as the capture of Richmond. . . . He directs that no force be sent here if you cannot do it without breaking up the operations against East Tennessee. . . .

No. 8.

LINCOLN TO HALLECK.

WASHINGTON, June 30, 1862.

Would be very glad of 25,000 infantry—no artillery or cavalry; but please do not send a man if it endangers any place you deem important to hold, or if it forces you to give up, or weaken, or delay the expedition against Chattanooga. . . .

No. 9.

HALLECK TO STANTON.

CORINTH, July 1, 1862.

Telegram suspending orders for troops is received. If order had been carried out we should have been either defeated or forced to retreat. No forces can be spared at present. . . .

No. 10.

HALLECK TO LINCOLN.

CORINTH, July 1, 1862.

Your telegram just received saves Western Tennessee. . . . If these troops had been sent East we should have been defeated or forced to retreat.

At the time this correspondence took place, McClellan was withdrawing his army to the James River, and his secret service agents were reporting that the Confederate army in front of Richmond numbered 180,000, its actual strength being under 80,000. See Vol. III. of this Series, page 182.

APPENDIX E.

ORGANIZATION OF THE ARMY OF THE TENNESSEE,

COMMANDED BY MAJOR-GENERAL U. S. GRANT, AS SHOWN ON THE RETURN DATED APRIL 30, 1863.

THIRTEENTH ARMY CORPS.

MAJOR-GENERAL J. A. McCLERNAND.

Escort—3d Illinois Cavalry, Co. L.

NINTH DIVISION (OSTERHAUS).

First Brigade (GARRARD).

49th Indiana.
69th Indiana.
120th Ohio.
118th Illinois.
7th Kentucky.

Artillery.

1st Wisconsin Battery.
7th Michigan Battery.

Second Brigade (SHELDON).

16th Ohio.
42d Ohio.
114th Ohio.
54th Indiana.
22d Kentucky.

Cavalry.

3d Illinois Cavalry, Co.'s A, E, and K.

TENTH DIVISION (A. J. SMITH).

First Brigade (BURBRIDGE).

16th Indiana.
60th Indiana.
67th Indiana.
83d Ohio.
96th Ohio.
23d Wisconsin.

Artillery.

Chicago Mercantile Battery.
17th Ohio Battery.

Second Brigade (LANDRAM).

19th Kentucky.
77th Illinois.
97th Illinois.
108th Illinois.
130th Illinois.
48th Ohio.

Cavalry.

4th Indiana Cavalry, Company C.

TWELFTH DIVISION (A. P. HOVEY).

First Brigade (McGINNIS).

11th Indiana.
24th Indiana.
34th Indiana.
46th Indiana.
29th Wisconsin.

Second Brigade (SLACK).

47th Indiana.
24th Iowa.
28th Iowa.
56th Ohio.

Artillery.

2d Illinois, Battery A.
2d Ohio Battery.
16th Ohio Battery.
1st Missouri, Battery A.

Cavalry.

1st Indiana Cavalry, Company C.

THIRTEENTH DIVISION (ROSS).

First Brigade (SALOMON).
43d Indiana.
35th Missouri.
28th Wisconsin.

Second Brigade (FISK).
29th Iowa.
33d Iowa.
36th Iowa.
33d Missouri.

Artillery.
3d Iowa Battery.

FOURTEENTH DIVISION (CARR).

First Brigade (BENTON).
1st United States.
8th Indiana.
18th Indiana.
33d Illinois.
99th Illinois.

Second Brigade (LAWLER).
11th Wisconsin.
21st Iowa.
22d Iowa.
23d Iowa.

Artillery.
1st Indiana Battery.
1st Iowa Battery.

Cavalry.
3d Illinois Cavalry, Co. G.

SECOND DIVISION, CAVALRY (BUSSEY).

First Brigade (WILEY).
5th Illinois Cavalry.
1st Indiana Cavalry.

Second Brigade (CLAYTON).
2d Arkansas Cavalry.
3d Iowa Cavalry.
5th Kansas Cavalry.

2d Illinois Cav. (5 Co.'s).
Kentucky Infantry, Patterson's Co.
6th Missouri Cav. (7 Co.'s).

FIFTEENTH ARMY CORPS.

MAJOR-GENERAL W. T. SHERMAN.

ELEVENTH [FIRST] DIVISION (STEELE).

First Brigade (MANTER).
13th Illinois.
27th Missouri.
29th Missouri.
30th Missouri.
31st Missouri.
32d Missouri.

Second Brigade (C. R. WOODS).
25th Iowa.
31st Iowa.
3d Missouri.
12th Missouri.
17th Missouri.
76th Ohio.

Third Brigade (THAYER).
4th Iowa.
9th Iowa.
26th Iowa.
30th Iowa.

Artillery.
2d Missouri, Battery F.
4th Ohio Battery.

Cavalry.
Kane Co. Illinois Cavalry.
3d Illinois Cavalry, Co. D.

FIFTH [SECOND] DIVISION (BLAIR).

First Brigade (G. A. SMITH).
6th Missouri.
8th Missouri.
113th Illinois.
116th Illinois.
13th United States.

Second Brigade (T. K. SMITH).
55th Illinois.
127th Illinois.
54th Ohio.
57th Ohio.
83d Indiana.

Third Brigade (EWING).
30th Ohio.
37th Ohio.
47th Ohio.
4th West Virginia.

Artillery.
Battery A, 1st Illinois Artillery.
Battery B, 1st Illinois Artillery.
Battery H, 1st Illinois Artillery.

Cavalry.
Thielemann's Cavalry.
10th Missouri Cavalry, Co. C.

EIGHTH [THIRD] DIVISION (TUTTLE).

First Brigade (BUCKLAND). *Second Brigade* (MOWER). *Third Brigade* (MATTHIES).

72d Ohio.
95th Ohio.
114th Illinois.
93d Indiana.

47th Illinois.
5th Minnesota.
11th Missouri.
8th Wisconsin.

8th Iowa.
12th Iowa.
35th Iowa.

Artillery.

2d Iowa Battery.   1st Illinois Artillery, Battery E.

SEVENTEENTH ARMY CORPS.
MAJOR-GENERAL J. B. McPHERSON.

Escort—4th Co. Ohio Cavalry.

THIRD DIVISION (LOGAN).

First Brigade
(J. E. SMITH).
20th Illinois.
31st Illinois.
45th Illinois.
124th Illinois.
23d Indiana.

Second Brigade
(DENNIS).
30th Illinois.
20th Ohio.
68th Ohio.
78th Ohio.

Third Brigade
(J. D. STEVENSON).
8th Illinois.
81st Illinois.
7th Missouri.
32d Ohio.

Artillery.

1st Illinois Artillery, Co. D.
2d Illinois Artillery, Co. G.

2d Illinois Artillery, Co. L.
8th Michigan Battery.

3d Ohio Battery.

Cavalry.

2d Illinois Cavalry, Company A.

SIXTH DIVISION (McARTHUR).

First Brigade (REID). *Second Brigade* (RANSOM). *Third Brigade* (HALL).

17th Illinois.
95th Illinois.
1st Kansas.
16th Wisconsin.

11th Illinois.
72d Illinois.
14th Wisconsin.
17th Wisconsin.
18th Wisconsin.

11th Iowa.
13th Iowa.
15th Iowa.
16th Iowa.

Artillery.

2d Illinois Artillery, Co. F.
1st Minnesota Battery.

1st Missouri Artillery, Co. C.
10th Ohio Battery.

Cavalry.

11th Illinois Cavalry, Company G.

SEVENTH DIVISION (QUINBY).

First Brigade
(ALEXANDER).
48th Indiana.
59th Indiana.
4th Minnesota.

Second Brigade (HOLMES).
56th Illinois.
17th Iowa.
10th Missouri.
24th Missouri, Co. E.
80th Ohio.

Third Brigade (BOOMER).
93d Illinois.
5th Iowa.
10th Iowa.
26th Missouri.

Artillery.

1st Missouri Artillery, Co. M.
11th Ohio Battery.

6th Wisconsin Battery.
12th Wisconsin Battery.

Cavalry.

2d Illinois Cavalry, Co. E.   5th Missouri Cavalry, Co. C.

SIXTEENTH ARMY CORPS.

Major-General S. A. HURLBUT.

FIRST DIVISION (W. S. SMITH).

First Brigade (Loomis).
26th Illinois.
90th Illinois.
12th Indiana.
100th Indiana.

Second Brigade (Hicks).
40th Illinois.
103d Illinois.
6th Iowa.
46th Ohio.

Third Brigade (Cockerell).
97th Indiana.
99th Indiana.
53d Ohio.
70th Ohio.

Fourth Brigade (Sanford).
48th Illinois.
49th Illinois.
119th Illinois.
15th Michigan.

Artillery.

1st Illinois Artillery, Co's. F, I, and M.
2d Illinois Artillery, Co. D.

4th Indiana Battery.
1st Missouri Artillery, Co. K.

Cavalry.

7th Illinois Cavalry, Co. B.

2d West Tennessee Cavalry.

DISTRICT OF CORINTH (DODGE).

First Brigade (Sweeny).
52d Illinois.
2d Iowa.
66th Iowa.

Second Brigade (Mersy).
9th Illinois.
12th Illinois.
122d Illinois.
81st Ohio.

Third Brigade (Bane).
7th Illinois.
50th Illinois.
57th Illinois.
39th Iowa.
18th Missouri.

Fourth Brigade (Fuller).
37th Ohio.
39th Ohio.
63d Ohio.

Artillery.

1st Missouri Artillery, Co. B.

2d U. S. Artillery, Co. F.

Siege Batteries.

Cavalry (Cornyn).

1st Alabama Cavalry.
15th Illinois Cavalry.

10th Missouri Cavalry.
5th Ohio Cavalry (3d Battalion).

THIRD DIVISION (KIMBALL).

First Brigade (Brayman).
43d Illinois.
61st Illinois.
106th Illinois.
12th Michigan.

Second Brigade (Richmond).
18th Illinois.
54th Illinois.
126th Illinois.
22d Ohio.

Third Brigade (True).
62d Illinois.
27th Indiana.
50th Indiana.
1st West Tennessee.

Artillery.

3d Illinois Artillery, Co. A.
14th Indiana Battery.

14th Ohio Battery.
7th Wisconsin Battery.

Cavalry (Mizner).

11th Illinois Cavalry.

3d Michigan Cavalry.

1st West Tennessee Cavalry.

FOURTH DIVISION (LAUMAN).

First Brigade (PUGH).	*Second Brigade* (HALL).	*Third Brigade* (BRYANT).
41st Illinois.	14th Illinois.	28th Illinois.
52d Illinois.	15th Illinois.	32d Illinois.
3d Iowa.	46th Illinois.	53d Indiana.
33d Wisconsin.	76th Illinois.	12th Wisconsin

Artillery.

2d Illinois Artillery, Co's. E and K.   7th Ohio Battery.
5th Ohio Battery.   15th Ohio Battery.

Cavalry.

Detachment 15th Illinois Cavalry.

DISTRICT OF MEMPHIS (VEATCH).

Infantry.

63d Illinois.	120th Illinois.	1st United States.
64th Illinois.	131st Illinois.	15th United States.
66th Illinois.	25th Indiana.	32d Wisconsin.
87th Illinois.	89th Indiana.	Convalescents.
117th Illinois.		

Cavalry.

1st Missouri Cavalry.   3d U. S. Cavalry.
5th Ohio Cavalry.   2d Wisconsin Cavalry.

Artillery.

Hurlbut Battery.

DISTRICT OF COLUMBUS (ASBOTH).

Columbus, Ky.	Clinton, Ky.	Island No. 10.
Detachment 16th U. S.	23d Missouri.	Det. 15th Wisconsin.
21st Wisconsin.	Det. 2d Illinois Cav.	
25th Wisconsin.	Det. 4th Illinois Cav.	**Fort Heiman, Ky.**
34th Wisconsin.		111th Illinois.
Det. 2d Illinois Cavalry.	**Cairo, Ill.**	3d Minnesota.
Det. 15th Kentucky Cav.	128th Illinois.	Det. 15th Kentucky Cav.
Det. 4th Missouri Cav.	35th Iowa.	Det. 9th Indiana Battery.
Det. 3d U. S. Cavalry.		
Det. 9th Indiana Battery.		
	Paducah, Ky.	**Fort Pillow, Tenn.**
Hickman, Ky.	40th Iowa.	Det. 52d Indiana.
Det. 13th Wisconsin.	24th Wisconsin.	Det. 32d Iowa.
Det. 15th Illinois Cav.	Det. 15th Kentucky Cav.	Det. 2d Illinois Cavalry.

FIRST CAVALRY DIVISION (WASHBURNE).

First Brigade (GRIERSON).	*Second Brigade* (McCRILLIS).
6th Illinois Cavalry.	3d Illinois Cavalry.
7th Illinois Cavalry.	4th Illinois Cavalry.
2d Iowa Cavalry.	7th Kansas Cavalry.

Abstract from Return, showing strength of Troops in the Department of the Tennessee, commanded by MAJOR-GENERAL U. S. GRANT, *for the month of April*, 1863.

COMMANDS.	Present for duty. Officers.	Present for duty. Men.	Aggregate present.	Present and absent.	Guns.
THIRTEENTH ARMY CORPS—Major-Gen. J. A. McCLERNAND.........	11	......	11	14	..
9th Div., Brig.-Gen. P. J. Osterhaus.	195	4,024	6,182	8.583	12
10th Div., Brig.-Gen. A. J. Smith ...	225	3,928	6,521	9,558	12
12th Div., Brig.-Gen. A. P. Hovey ...	293	5,565	7,015	8,269	26
14th Div., Brig.-Gen. E. A. Carr.....	209	3,795	4,662	6,224	12
Total Thirteenth Army Corps ...	933	17,312	24,391	32,648	62
FIFTEENTH ARMY CORPS—Major-Gen. W. T. SHERMAN.....	6	......	6	8	..
11th Div., Major-Gen. Fred. Steele...	339	5,787	8,319	11,272	10
5th Div., Maj.-Gen. F. P. Blair, Jr...	315	5,531	6,916	10,001	18
8th Div., Brig.-Gen. J. M. Tuttle....	233	3,764	3,997	6,135	8
Total Fifteenth Army Corps.....	893	15,082	19,238	27,416	36
SEVENTEENTH ARMY CORPS — Major-Gen. J. B. McPHERSON	9	......	9	11	..
3d Div., Major-Gen. J. A. Logan.....	362	6,136	7,076	9,160	24
6th Div., Brig.-Gen. J. McArthur....	244	3,959	4,582	5,829	16
7th Div., Brig.-Gen. J. F. Quinby ...	293	4,845	5,815	8,154	20
Total Seventeenth Army Corps ..	908	14,940	17,482	23,154	60
Aggregate of troops near Vicksburg.	2,734	47,334	61,111	83,218	158
DISTRICT OF EASTERN ARKANSAS—Major-Gen. B. M. PRENTISS..........	......	......	......	......	..
13th Div., Brig.-Gen. L. F. Ross.....	178	3,502	4,731	5,574	6
2d Cavalry Div., Col. Cyrus Bussey..	189	3,094	4,721	5,910	12
Detachments	27	310	400	584	..
Total District Eastern Arkansas .	394	6,906	9,852	12,068	18
SIXTEENTH ARMY CORPS—Major-Gen. S. A. HURLBUT	9	29	38	38	..
1st Div., Brig.-Gen. W. S. Smith	433	7,530	9,427	11,312	7
Dist.of Corinth,Brig.-Gen.G.M.Dodge	679	12,168	15.484	17,970	..
3d Div., Brig.-Gen. N. Kimball... ..	365	6,466	8,227	9,8 .7	18
4th Div., Brig.-Gen. J. G. Lauman ..	320	5,824	7,002	8,350	22
Dist. of Memphis, Bg.-Gen.J.C.Veatch	297	4,939	7,614	8,691	..
Dist. of Columbus, Bg.-Gen. A. Asboth	392	6,990	9,026	10,200	118
1st Cav. Div., Bg.-Gen. C.C. Washburn	153	2,827	3,873	4,628	..
Engineer Detachments..............	52	1,186	1,238	1,543	..
Total Sixteenth Army Corps— (Tennessee and Kentucky)	2,700	47,959	61,929	72,569	

RECAPITULATION.

	For duty.	Present.	Present and absent.
Near Vicksburg	50,068	61,111	83,218
District of Eastern Arkansas............	7,300	9,852	12,068
In Tennessee and Kentucky.............	50,659	61,929	72,569
Aggregate in the Department	**108,027**	**132,892**	**167,855**

NOTE.—The above figures are taken from the monthly return for the month of April, 1863. The tri-monthly return for April 30, 1863, gives substantially the same figures for totals in the Department, but different figures for the three corps near Vicksburg, as follows :

13th Corps.......................................	18,623
15th Corps.......................................	17,210
17th Corps.......................................	18,393
Total...................................	54,236

In the War Records Office the monthly return is generally adopted, in cases of discrepancy, as being the more accurate. I have therefore used the figures of that return in the text.

APPENDIX F.

ORGANIZATION OF TROOPS IN THE DEPARTMENT OF THE MISSISSIPPI AND EAST LOUISIANA,

COMMANDED BY LIEUT.-GENERAL J. C. PEMBERTON, FOR THE MONTH OF APRIL, 1863.

FIRST MILITARY DISTRICT, BRIG.-GEN. D. RUGGLES.

(Headquarters at Columbus, Miss.)

Rice's Tennessee Heavy Artillery.
Thrall's Arkansas Light Artillery.
Owen's Arkansas Light Artillery.
13th Alabama Rangers.
3d Mississippi State Troops.
5th Mississippi State Troops.

Gillelyn's Mississippi Cavalry.
Martin's Cavalry Company.
Johnson's Cavalry Company.
2d Tennessee Cavalry.
Warren's Partisan Rangers.

SECOND MILITARY DISTRICT, MAJ.-GEN. C. L. STEVENSON.

(Headquarters at Vicksburg, Miss.)

STEVENSON'S DIVISION (MAJOR-GEN. C. L. STEVENSON).

First Brigade (BARTON).

40th Georgia.
41st Georgia.
42d Georgia.
43d Georgia.
52d Georgia.

Second Brigade (TRACY).

20th Alabama.
23d Alabama.
30th Alabama.
31st Alabama.
46th Alabama.

Third Brigade (TAYLOR).

34th Georgia.
36th Georgia.
39th Georgia.
56th Georgia.
57th Georgia.
43d Tennessee.

Fourth Brigade (REYNOLDS).

3d Tennessee.
31st Tennessee.
59th Tennessee.

Artillery.

Waddell's Light Battery.
Cherokee Light Battery.
Botetourt Light Battery.
3d Maryland Battery.

Vandyke's Cavalry.

SMITH'S DIVISION (MAJOR-GEN. M. L. SMITH).

First Brigade (BALDWIN). *Second Brigade* (VAUGHN). *Third Brigade* (S. D. LEE).

17th Louisiana.	79th Tennessee.	26th Louisiana.
31st Louisiana.	80th Tennessee.	27th Louisiana.
4th Mississippi.	81st Tennessee.	28th Louisiana.
46th Mississippi.	Co. A, Ward's Artillery.	1st Louisiana Heavy Art.
Co. E, Mississippi Lt. Art.	Co. B, Ward's Artillery.	8th Louisiana Heavy Art.
Smith's Partisan Rangers.	Co. I, Wither's Artillery.	23d Louisiana Heavy Art.
		1st Tennessee Heavy Art.

FORNEY'S DIVISION (MAJOR-GEN. J. H. FORNEY).

First Brigade (HÉBERT). *Second Brigade* (MOORE).

3d Louisiana.	2d Texas.
36th Mississippi.	35th Mississippi.
37th Mississippi.	40th Mississippi.
38th Mississippi.	37th Alabama.
43d Mississippi.	42d Alabama.
Hogg's Battery.	Bledsoe's Battery.
Sengstak's Battery.	Tobin's Battery.
McNally's Battery.	
Adam's Cavalry.	

BOWEN'S DIVISION (BRIG.-GEN. J. S. BOWEN).

First Brigade (COCKRELL). *Second Brigade* (GREEN).

1st Missouri.	1st Missouri Cavalry, dismounted.
2d Missouri.	3d Missouri Cavalry, dismounted.
3d Missouri.	12th Arkansas.
4th Missouri.	15th Arkansas.
5th Missouri.	19th Arkansas.
6th Missouri.	20th Arkansas.
Wade's Battery.	1st Arkansas Cavalry.
Landis's Battery.	Western Rangers.
Guiber's Battery.	Lowe's Battery.
	Dawson's Battery.

LORING'S DIVISION (MAJOR-GEN. W. W. LORING).

First Brigade (TILGHMAN). *Second Brigade* (FEATHERSTON).

20th Mississippi.	Waul's Legion.
23d Mississippi.	Pioneer Company.
26th Mississippi.	Point Coupée Battery.
54th Alabama.	1st Tennessee Cavalry.
8th Kentucky.	
McLendon's Battery.	

THIRD MILITARY DISTRICT, MAJ.-GEN. FRANK GARDNER.

First Brigade (MAXEY). *Second Brigade* (BEALL). *Third Brigade* (GREGG).

42d Tennessee.	11th Arkansas.	3d Tennessee.
46th Tennessee.	12th Arkansas.	10th Tennessee.
48th Tennessee.	14th Arkansas.	30th Tennessee.
49th Tennessee.	15th Arkansas.	41st Tennessee.
53d Tennessee.	16th Arkansas.	50th Tennessee.
55th Tennessee.	17th Arkansas.	51st Tennessee.
4th Louisiana.	18th Arkansas.	7th Texas.
30th Louisiana.	23d Arkansas.	1st Tennessee Battery.
Texas Sharpshooters.	1st Mississippi.	1st Missouri Battery.
Fenner's Battery.	39th Mississippi.	9th Louisiana Battery.
Robert's Battery.	3 Co's. 1st Miss. Art.	Brook Haven Battery.

Fourth Brigade (RUST).	Fifth Brigade (BUFORD).	Unattached.
9th Arkansas.	3d Kentucky.	1st Alabama Artillery.
12th Louisiana.	7th Kentucky.	12th Louisiana Battery.
15th Mississippi.	10th Arkansas.	9th Tennessee Cavalry.
6th Mississippi.	4th Alabama.	9th Louisiana Cavalry.
35th Alabama.	27th Alabama.	Gantt's Cavalry.
1st Conf. Battery.	49th Alabama.	Garland's Cavalry.
Hudson's Battery.	6th Alabama.	Miller's Cavalry.
Point Coupée Artillery.	Watson Battery.	

FOURTH MILITARY DISTRICT, BRIG.-GEN. JOHN ADAMS.

3d Brig. Miss. State Troops.	1st Mississippi State Troops.
14th Mississippi.	Bolen's Cavalry Company.
1st Choctaw Indians.	Terry's Cavalry Company.

FIFTH MILITARY DISTRICT, BRIG.-GEN. J. R. CHALMERS.

1st Mississippi Rangers.	18th Mississippi Rangers.
Blythe's Battalion.	Martin's Battalion.

Six companies State Troops.

Abstract from Return, showing strength of Troops above named, for the month of March, 1863.

COMMANDS.	Present for Duty. Officers.	Men.	Total present.	Present and absent.
First Military District (Ruggles)	152	1,809	2,262	3,031
Second Military District—				
Stevenson's Division	681	9,795	13,268	16,708
Smith's Division	402	4,656	7,112	9,156
Forney's Division	342	3,660	5,254	8,409
Bowen's Division	395	4,169	5,499	6,954
Loring's Division	405	4,783	6,241	8,880
Third Military District (Gardner)	1,366	14,921	20,388	26,728
Fourth Military District (Adams)	53	378	535	980
Fifth Military District (Chalmers)	82	780	936	1,472
Total	3,878	44,951	61,495	82,318

APPENDIX G.

CORRESPONDENCE BETWEEN GENERAL GRANT AND GENERAL BANKS RELATIVE TO THE CO-OPERATION OF THEIR ARMIES.

No. 1.
BANKS TO GRANT.

BATON ROUGE, March 13, 1862.
(Received March 20th.)

Anticipating the success of Admiral Farragut's proposed attempt to run the enemy's batteries at Port Hudson and to open communication with you, I will avail myself of the opportunity to give you a statement of our position, forces, and intentions.

We have at Baton Rouge a force of about 17,000 effective infantry, and one negro regiment; one regiment of heavy artillery with six light batteries, one 20-pounder battery, a dismounted company of artillery, and ten companies of cavalry, of which eight are newly raised and hardly to be counted on. Of this, three regiments of infantry, the heavy artillery manning the siege train, the dismounted artillery, and one company of cavalry, will remain at Baton Rouge. Leaving this force to hold the position of Baton Rouge, we march to-day upon Port Hudson by the Bayou Sara road to make a demonstration upon that work for the purpose of co-operating in the movement of the fleet. The best information we have of the enemy's force places it at 25,000 or 30,000; this and his position precludes the idea of an assault on our part, and accordingly the main object of the present movement is a diversion in favor of the navy, but we shall, of course, avail ourselves of any advantage which occasion may offer.

Should the Admiral succeed in his attempt, I shall try to open communication with him on the other side of the river, and in that event trust I shall hear from you as to your position and movements, and especially as to your views of the most efficient mode of co-operation upon the part of the forces we respectively command.

No. 2.
GRANT TO BANKS.

BEFORE VICKSBURG, MISS., March 23, 1863.
(Received at Opelousas, April 21st.)

Your communication of the 13th instant, per Admiral Farragut, was duly received. The continuous high water and the nature of the country, almost precluding the possibility of landing a force on the east bank of the Mississippi anywhere above Vicksburg has induced the hope that you would be able to take Port Hudson and move up to Black River. By the use of your transports I could send you all the force you would require. . . .

The best aid you can give, if you cannot pass Port Hudson, will be to hold as many of the enemy there as possible. If they could be sent I could well spare one army corps to enable you to get up the river. My effective force, including all arms, will be between 60,000 and 70,000, if I bring all from Memphis that can be spared in an emergency. An attack on Haines' Bluff cannot possibly take place under two weeks, if so soon. My forces are now scattered, and the difficulty of getting transportation is very great.

No. 3.

GRANT TO FARRAGUT.

March 23, 1863.

(Received by Banks April 21st.)

In the various notes I have written, including the despatch for General Banks, I have not mentioned that soon after taking command there in person I collected my surplus troops at Lake Providence, and directed the commanding officer to effect a passage through from the Mississippi River to Bayou Macon. This will give navigable water through by that route to the Red River. This is now reported practicable for ordinary Ohio River steamers. I sent several weeks ago for this class of steamers, and expected them before this. Should they arrive, and Admiral Porter gets his boats out of the Yazoo, so as to accompany the expedition, I can send a force of say, 20,000 effective men, to co-operate with General Banks on Port Hudson.

This force certainly would easily reduce Port Hudson and enable them to come on up the river and maintain' a position on high land near enough to Vicksburg, until they could be reinforced from here sufficiently to operate against the city.

Please inform the General of the contents of this, and much oblige your obedient servant.

No. 4.

BANKS TO GRANT.

CAMP AT BRASHEAR CITY, LA., April 10, 1863.

(Received at Port Gibson, May 2.)

The secretary of Admiral Farragut, Mr. Gabaudan, called upon me at Brashear City this morning and gave me the substance of your despatch. We have 15,000 men that can be moved with facility. The artillery is strong, the cavalry weak, but we hope to strengthen the cavalry without delay, as one of the results of this expedition.

We shall move upon the Bayou Teche to-morrow, probably encounter the enemy at Pattersonville, and hope to move without delay upon Iberia, to destroy the salt-works, and then upon Opelousas. This is the limit proposed. We do not intend to hold any portions of this country, as it weakens our force, but will at once return to Baton Rouge to co-operate with you against Port Hudson. I can be there easily by May 10th.

There are now 4,500 infantry at Baton Rouge, with three regiments of colored troops and two companies of cavalry, three batteries of artillery, with several heavy guns in position, and five gunboats and six mortars. The land force is under command of Major-General Augur; the fleet under Captain Alden, of the Richmond.

We shall endeavor to establish communication with Admiral Farragut near Bayou Sara, but the opening of the levee opposite Port Hudson may make it impossible. If so, we will communicate with you freely, by the way of New York, as to our progress. I shall be very glad if you will communicate with us in the same manner. To avoid delays by mail, I will send my despatches by an officer.

No. 6.

BANKS TO GRANT.

OPELOUSAS, LA., April 23, 1863
(Received about May 10th.)

I have the honor to acknowledge the receipt of your despatches, dated at headquarters, before Vicksburg, March 23, 1863, on the 21st, by the hand of Lieutenant Tenney, of General Augur's division at Baton Rouge. On April 10th, Mr. Gabaudan, private secretary of Admiral Farragut, commanding the Hartford at the mouth of Red River, reported at my headquarters, at Brashear, and gave me verbally the substance of your despatches, which he said he had read, but did not bring with him in the dangerous passage which he was compelled to make of the batteries of Port Hudson.

The information received from Mr. Gabaudan differs somewhat from your despatches. I understand from him that it was your intention to send a force by the way of Lake Providence and the Black River, passing through the intermediate bayous to the mouth of the Black River, on the Red River, and that this force would probably reach the Red River by May 1st, proximo, to co-operate with my command against Port Hudson. . . .

I was disappointed in learning, from the perusal of your despatches, that at their date it was undetermined whether you can send a force to the Red River or not, on account of the deficiency of your transportation. It is a grief on my part that I cannot aid you in this respect. Our transportation is lamentably deficient. I had but one steamer with which to pass two divisions of my corps over Berwick's Bay in this campaign. The route is open, but I can reach Red River only by forced marches. It is six days' march to Alexandria, and four or five to Simsport, at the mouth of the Atchafalaya, but until we can hear from you I shall make Washington, on the Courtableau, my base of operations.

We can co-operate with you in any manner you suggest by a junction on the Red River, or by an attack from Baton Rouge, joining your forces on the Bayou Sara, in the rear of Port Hudson. My belief is that this is the best method, as the passage of the Mississippi from the Red River is very difficult with our short transportation, and will require a landing, and places us between the armies of

Vicksburg and Port Hudson; but we shall not hesitate. I wait anxiously to hear from you upon these points, viz.:

First.—When can you be at the mouth of the Black or Red River?

Second.—In what manner shall my forces co-operate with you?

Third.—Can you furnish transportation for your passage to Port Hudson; or do you rely upon us?

Fourth.—Can you supply your troops; or will you rely upon us?

Fifth.—Is it not practicable for your force to join us by the Atchafalaya?

It is doubtful if we can supply your forces from New Orleans in operating above Port Hudson, on account of our deficient transportation. My belief is that the best junction is by the Atchafalaya. We can reach Baton Rouge by the Grand River and the Plaquemine without transshipment, and our forces united, make the reduction of Port Hudson certain. My own command is insufficient.

Waiting anxiously your response, and with full confidence in your judgment and earnest co-operation, I am, very truly yours.

No. 7.

GRANT TO BANKS.

MILLIKEN'S BEND, April 14, 1863.
(Received at Alexandria May 5th.)

Am concentrating my forces at Grand Gulf. Will send an army corps to Bayou Sara by the 25th to co-operate with you on Port Hudson. Can you aid me and send troops after the reduction of Port Hudson to assist me at Vicksburg?

No. 8.

BANKS TO GRANT.

ALEXANDRIA, May 6, 1863.
(Received about May 10th.)

By the 25th, probably; by the 1st, certainly, I will be there.

No. 9.

GRANT TO BANKS.

ROCKY SPRINGS, MISS., May 10, 1863.
(Received at Alexandria May 12th.)

My advance will occupy to-day Utica, Auburn, and a point equally advanced toward the Mississippi Southern Railroad, between the latter place and the Big Black. It was my intention, on gaining a foothold at Grand Gulf, to have sent a sufficient force to Port Hudson to have ensured the fall of that place with your co-operation, or, rather, to have co-operated with you to secure that end.

Meeting the enemy, however, as I did, south of Port Gibson, I followed him to the Big Black, and could not afford to retrace my steps. I also learned, and believe the information to be reliable, that Port Hudson is almost entirely evacuated. This may not be true, but it is the concurrent testimony of deserters and contrabands.

Many days cannot elapse before the battle will begin which is to decide the fate of Vicksburg, but it is impossible to predict how long it may last. I would urgently request, therefore, that you join me, or send all the force you can spare to co-operate in the great struggle for opening the Mississippi River.

My means of gaining information from Port Hudson are not good, but I shall hope, even before this reaches Baton Rouge, to hear of your forces being on the way here.

Grierson's cavalry would be of immense service to me now, and, if at all practicable for him to join me, I would like to have him do it at once.

For fear of this accidentally falling into the hands of the enemy I will not communicate to you my force.

No. 10.

BANKS TO GRANT.

ALEXANDRIA, LA., May 12, 1863—8 A.M.
(Received about May 15th.)

Your despatch of the 10th instant I received by the hand of Captain Effers, this morning at 6.30. I regret to say that it is impossible for me to join you at Vicksburg in time, or with force to be of service to you in any immediate attack. I have neither water nor land transportation to make the movement by river or by land. The utmost I can accomplish is to cross for the purpose of operating with you against Port Hudson. I could cross my infantry and artillery without transportation, receiving supplies from Baton Rouge, in the rear of Port Hudson. That is the utmost I can accomplish on the other side of the Mississippi, above Port Hudson. Were it within the range of human power I should join you, for I am dying with a kind of vanishing hope to see two armies acting together against the strong places of the enemy. But I must say, without qualifications, that the means at my disposal do not leave me a shadow of a chance to accomplish it. I have been making preparations to join your corps at Bayou Sara, and though this would have laid all my trains and supplies open to the enemy's cavalry, I should have risked it.

We believe that a force of about 7,000 of the enemy has left Arkansas River to join Kirby Smith at Shreveport, leaving the Washita at Pine Bluff, near Monroe; then to come down the Red River to Grand Ecore, above Natchitoches, where they are fortifying in strong position. There is undoubtedly a Texan column on the road to join them. My advance is now sixty miles above Alexandria. The only course for me, failing in co-operation with you, is to regain the Mississippi and attack Port Hudson, or to move against the enemy at Shreveport. Port Hudson is reduced in force, but not as you are informed. It has now 10,000 men and is very strongly fortified. This is the report of Admiral Farragut, whose fleet is above and below the works.

I regret very much my inability to join you. I have written Colonel Grierson that you desire him to join you, and have added my own request to yours. Captain Effers goes to Baton Rouge to communicate with him.

Wishing you all possible success, and feeling that you have all the prayers of our people, I have the honor to be, with sincere respect, your obedient servant.

APPENDIX H.

UNION LOSSES IN THE VICKSBURG CAMPAIGN.

THE statements of losses in the foregoing pages are invariably taken from the official reports made at the time. Since these pages were sent to press the following statement of Union losses in the Vicksburg campaign has been compiled with great care in the Adjutant-General's office. The numbers differ very slightly from those given in the text, but as they form the final official statement in the matter they are here published.

	Killed.	Wounded.	Missing.	Total.
Port Gibson, May 1st	131	719	25	875
Raymond, May 12th	66	339	37	442
Jackson, May 14th	42	251	7	300
Champion's Hill, May 16th.........	410	1,844	187	2,441
Big Black Bridge, May 17th........	39	237	3	279
Skirmishes at Vicksburg, May 18th, 20th, and 21st	45	194	2	241
Assault of Vicksburg, May 19th	157	777	8	942
Assault of Vicksburg, May 22d	501	2,551	147	3,199
Siege of Vicksburg	100	419	7	526
Various skirmishes	20	65	30	115
Total	1,511	7,396	453	9,360

INDEX.

Chalmers, Brig.-Gen. J. R., 120 et seq.

Champion, plantation of, 154 et seq.

Champion's Hill, Miss., 153 et seq., 162, 166, 170, 186, 207

Chancellorsville, Va., 108, 137

Chattanooga, Tenn., 2, 11, 29 et seq., 33 et seq., 66 et seq., 75, 109, 118 et seq., 177, 190, 207 (note), 237

Chewalla, Tenn., 43, 45, 47, 52

Chickamauga, Tenn., 207 (note), 237

Chickasaw Bayou, Miss., 138, 177

Chickasaw Bluffs, Miss., 71 et seq., 76

Churchill, Gen. T. J., 84, 87

Cincinnati, O., 8, 31, 88

Cincinnati, the, 8, 14, 84, 197

Clark, Brig.-Gen. Charles, 27

Clifton, Tenn., 67 et seq.

Clifton, the, 220

Clinton, La., 230

Clinton, Miss., 144, 146, 148 et seq., 171, 196

Cockrell, Col. F. M., brigade of, 128 et seq., 157, 162, 184

College Hill, Miss., 63, 66

Columbia, Tenn., 67, 100

Columbus, Ky., 6 et seq., 10 et seq., 13, 27, 32, 34, 55, 61, 63, 66 et seq., 70, 72, 91

Columbus, Miss., 120, 122, 127

Comstock, Capt. C. B., 186

Conestoga, the, 9, 17

Cooke, Lieut.-Comdr. A. P., 220

Corinth, Miss., 11, 13, 20, 28 et seq., 55 et seq., 61 et seq., 64, 67 et seq., 72, 81, 100, 107

Crocker, Brig.-Gen. M. M., brigade of, 47, 132 et seq., 142 et seq.,

147 et seq., 156, 158 et seq., 167 (note)

Crum's Mill, Miss., 52

Crystal Springs, Miss., 159

Cumberland Gap, Tenn., 30

Cumming, Brig.-Gen. Alfred, brigade of, 156 et seq., 176

Curtis, Fort, Ark., 234

Curtis, Maj.-Gen. S. R., 17 et seq., 30, 35, 56, 61, 64, 88, 235

Davies, Brig.-Gen. T. A., division of, 46 et seq.

Davis, Commodore C. H., 14 et seq. ; Memphis surrenders to, 17 et seq., 23 et seq.

Davis, Jefferson, 4, 53, 66 et seq., 99, 137, 144 et seq., 172 et seq., 206 (note)

Davis' Mills, Miss., 52, 71

Decatur, Ala., 36

De Courcy, Col. J. F., brigade of, 78 et seq., 86 et seq.

De Golyer, Capt. S., battery of, 142

De Kalb, the, 84

Demopolis, Ala., 206

Dennis, Brig.-Gen. E. S., brigade of, 142 et seq.

De Russy, Fort, La., 213

Des Allemands, Bayou, La., 232 et seq.

De Shroon, plantation of, 125

De Soto, La., 95

De Soto, the, 111, 214

Dodge, Brig.-Gen. G. M., 55, 68 et seq.

Donaldsonville, La., 219, 231 et seq.

Donelson, Fort, 10, 13 et seq., 19, 109 et seq.

Dresden, Tenn., 68

Duckport, La., 109, 113, 115

INDEX. 271

Natchez, Miss., 19, 21, 28, 111, 224
New Carthage, La., 106 et seq., 109
et seq.
New Era, the, 111
New Madrid, Mo., 5 et seq., 11 et
seq.
New Orleans, La., 7, 9, 18 et seq.,
21, 24, 27, 44, 59 et seq., 82,
159, 195, 209 et seq., 214, 218
et seq.
Newton Station, Miss, 121 et seq.
New York, N. Y., 82, 209

OGLESBY, Brig.-Gen. R. J., 53
Okolona, Miss., 121 et seq.
Oneida, the, 19
Opelousas, La., 213, 219 et seq.,
222 et seq., 231, 233
Ord, Maj.-Gen. E. O. C., division
of, 38 et seq., 42 et seq., 52;
severely wounded, 194 et seq. ;
supersedes McClernand, 199 et
seq., 204
Osterhaus, Brig.-Gen. P. J., division of, 110, 116, 127 et seq.,
152, 154 et seq., 159 et seq.,
163 et seq., 169, 180 et seq.,
192 et seq.
Owen, Lieut.-Comdr. E. K., 84, 123
Oxford, Miss., 62 et seq., 68, 72

PADUCAH, Ky., 6, 11
Palmer, Capt. J. S., 215
Panola, Miss., 62
Parke, Maj.-Gen. J. G., 188 et seq.,
193 et seq.
Parker's Cross Roads, Tenn., 69
Parsons, Capt. L. B., 73
Pattersonville, La., 219
Pea Ridge, Ark., 17
Pemberton, Fort, 100 et seq., 117,
119, 122, 166

Pemberton, Lt.-Gen. J. C., 53,
61 et seq., 65 et seq., 74, 81, 99
et seq., 117 et seq., 121 et seq.,
126 et seq. ; strength of, 135,
137, 142, 144 et seq., 148 et
seq., 154, 157; rout of, 159 et
seq. ; calls a council of war,
168, 171 et seq., 178, 189 et seq.,
199 et seq. ; sends reinforcements to Gardner, 227, 234
Pensacola, Fla., 13, 19 et seq.
Perkins, plantation of, 115 et seq.,
125, 138, 187
Perryville, Ky., 54
Phifer, Brig.-Gen. C. W., brigade
of, 50
Pierre, Bayou, 125, 129 et seq.
Pillow, Fort, 7, 11 et seq., 20, 44,
237
Pillow, Brig.-Gen. Gideon J., 5 et
seq.
Pittsburg Landing, Tenn., 13
Pittsburg, the, 8, 113, 123
Plaquemine, Bayou, La., 213 et
seq., 231
Pocahontas, Ark., 4 et seq.
Pocahontas, Tenn., 39, 43 et seq.,
52
Polk, Maj.-Gen. L., 5 et seq., 10 et
seq., 13, 27
Pontotoc, Miss., 120
Pope, Maj.-Gen. John, 12 et seq.,
34, 35
Porter, Admiral D. D., 65, 72, 80,
83 et seq., 86, 88, 92 et seq., 98,
103 et seq.; Grant's letter to,
107, 112 et seq., 119; at Grand
Gulf, 123 et seq., 178, 197, 199,
220
Porter, Comdr. D. D., 21, 26
Port Gibson, Miss., 122 et seq.,
137, 138 et seq., 144, 161, 170